Colección Támesis

SERIE A: MONOGRAFÍAS, 149

VOICES, SILENCES
AND ECHOES

MARY LEE BRETZ

VOICES, SILENCES AND ECHOES

A THEORY OF THE ESSAY AND THE CRITICAL RECEPTION OF NATURALISM IN SPAIN

TAMESIS BOOKS LIMITED
LONDON

DISTRIBUTORS

Spain: Editorial Castalia, Zurbano, 39. 28010 Madrid

United States and Canada: Boydell & Brewer Inc., PO Box 41026,
Rochester, NY 14604, USA

Great Britain and rest of the world: Boydell & Brewer Ltd, PO Box 9,
Woodbridge, Suffolk, IP12 3DF, UK

First published 1992 by Tamesis Books Limited, London

ISBN 1-85566-014-8

British Library Cataloguing in Publication Data
A CIP catalogue record for this book is available
from the British Library

The paper used in this publication meets the minimum requirements
of American National Standard for Information Sciences –
Permanence of Paper for Printed Library Materials, ANSI Z39.48-1984

Printed in Great Britain by
St Edmundsbury Press, Bury St Edmunds, Suffolk
for
TAMESIS BOOKS LIMITED

CONTENTS

ACKNOWLEDGEMENTS

I have always been averse to writing dedications, not because I didn't feel grateful or have many people to whom I owed a word of thanks, but because it is so very difficult to sincerely express myself in this format. It isn't any easier now, but having built up a large backlog of indebtedness, I would like to publicly acknowledge those who, in one way or another, have supported me both personally and professionally. My colleagues and friends in the Department of Spanish and Portuguese at Rutgers University have been a constant source of inspiration and encouragement. I would particularly like to thank Carl Kirschner, Chair of the department and friend, who has been an ardent and successful advocate for the department and for me personally. Daria Cohen, Gabriela Mora, Carlos Narvéz, Margo Persin and Phyllis Zatlin have read this manuscript as well as many others and have been extraordinarily generous of their time and expertise. They and other members of the Spanish and Portuguese Department have made working a truly collegial experience and have enriched my life both professionally and personally.

Many friends in Spain have contributed in important ways to my study and enjoyment of Spanish literature and culture. I am particularly indebted to Elvira Alcalá Zamora, Janet DeCesaris, Sonsoles Díaz-Berrio, Tomás and Hilda Domínguez, Amalia Fernández de Ana Magán, Francisco Fernández de Ana Magán, Manolo López López, Josep Llorens, Pedro López, Carmen Portela, Dolores Sacristán Pérez, and Jesús Valverde, each of whom has helped to make Spain a home for me. My friend Linda Metzler has shared Spain, literature, art, and life with me. My sisters Betsy Cole and Juliana Patten have been a source of laughter and strength, born of a shared past and a hard-fought battle for the present. For my husband Norton and my children Lee and Jay, there are no words to express my feelings and my gratitude for your presence in my life.

To all of those named and to many others who have enriched my life and my learning, I am sincerely and deeply grateful.

INTRODUCTION

The essay as a genre has received little recent critical attention. While our understanding of the novel, poetry, drama, and to a lesser extent, the short story, has been considerably enriched through the application of various philosophies and contemporary literary theories such as phenomenology, reception theory, structuralism, semiotics, post-structuralism etc., the essay is still largely defined in formalist and New Critical terms. Notwithstanding the obvious pragmatic aspect of essayistic discourse, critics and theoreticians tend to stress its "literary" nature. In the preface of *Literary Nonfiction* (1989), Chris Anderson describes the essay as "reflective and exploratory and essentially personal. Its purpose is not to convey information, although it may do that as well, but rather to tell the story of the author's thinking and experience" (x). Without denying the literary qualities of many essays, I suggest that our emphasis on this aspect has been excessive and has limited our understanding of individual essays and of the essay as a genre.

Recent literary and cultural theory provide the impetus and the means for broadening our approach. The New Critical insistence on isolating the literary from other areas of human activity has given way to a variety of movements or schools of thought which reinscribe the social and the political in the literary. Reader-response criticism stresses the reception of the text and as Hans Robert Jauss points out, the reader is always inserted in the historical world (38ff). Feminist, Marxist, and New Historicist approaches to literature all insist on opening the literary text to the socio-historical world that lies beyond (and within) its borders. Deconstructive criticism, with its emphasis on undermining hierarchical oppositions (Derrida; Culler) also breaks down divisions between literature and other areas of human activity. Mikhail Bakhtin's theory of language and literature contributes similarly to a broadening of our field of vision. "Literature is an inseparable part of culture and it cannot be understood outside the total context of the entire culture of a given epoch" (*Speech Genres* 2). For Bakhtin, language is "ideologically saturated" (*Dialogical Imagination* 271) and always expresses a world view. In seeking to establish certain fundamental laws of human communication, speech-act theory and pragmatics also argue against a separation of literary and other forms of discourse.

The current emphasis on "text in context" necessitates that studies of essays and of the essay as a form pay particular attention to the cultural milieu of a given text or series of texts as well as to the interrelations of the text(s) and the social, political, historical circumstances in which they are produced. In this study, I will focus on one particular period of modern Spanish history and will analyze a series of essays with the purpose of better understanding the nature of essayistic discourse and the period in question. I have located the study in late nineteenth-century Spain,

1

and in particular, in the polemic surrounding the introduction of naturalism in Spain, for a number of reasons. During these years the essay is cultivated extensively and acquires greater generic identity. Furthermore, as I will attempt to clarify in the course of this study, the polemic surrounding the reception of naturalism functions as a vehicle for the expression of the social and political tensions that mark late nineteenth-century Spain. Previous literary studies of the period have largely silenced any consideration of social and political factors. Influenced by New Critical definitions of literature and of the essay, they have focused primarily on the literary aspect of naturalism and have considered the texts involved in the polemic as mere vehicles for the expression of late nineteenth-century views on literature. This approach not only divorces the literary from other cultural phenomena, but it also fails to consider the complex interplay between ideology and the linguistic forms that express it. Language, discursive modes, and genres are no longer seen simply as vehicles for the expression of ideas. Sapir and Whorf first pointed out how language can and does condition the form and substance that these ideas take and contemporary literary theories continue to investigate how discourse both reflects and produces ideology.

The literary debates that occur in late nineteenth-century Spain are especially fruitful for a study of the interplay between literature and other expressions of culture as well as for an examination of the interrelations of discourse and ideology. The period marks a critical juncture in Spanish cultural evolution and represents the definitive entry of the modern period in Spain. Roland Barthes, Mikhail Bakhtin, and Michel Foucault all write of the transition from the classical age to the modern and link the ideological change with the appearance of new and varied forms of discourse. All three writers identify this moment at approximately the end of the eighteenth century or the beginning of the nineteenth. In *Writing Degree Zero*, Barthes identifies classical writing with "class" writing in that the producers of the texts are members of the group that is closest to those in power. Following the French Revolution, popular and "bohemian" linguistic forms start to intrude on the established "classical" language and by the 1850s, French modes of writing begin to multiply (57–80). Bakhtin defines classical language as monologic, single-voiced, stripped of its association with a speaking person and a historical, cultural context. In contrast, romanticism introduces authorial personality and language as shot-through with a multiplicity of resonances (*Problems of Dostoevsky* 200–01). Foucault's discussion of the shift from the classical to the modern period stresses a dramatic change in the view of humanity and of language. Whereas in the classical period the human subject seeks to elucidate an external order that is created by God, in the modern period, the human subject becomes the object of his/her own examination. This shift accompanies the changing view of language from the classical belief in the correspondence of the word, or "name" as Foucault designates it, and the essence of the thing named (*Order* 120), to a discovery of the very problematic nature of language. "Man now appears limited by his involvement in a language which is no longer a transparent medium but a dense web with its own inscrutable history" (Dreyfus 28).

In Spain, as in other European countries, local historical circumstances intersect with the changing vision of the human subject and of language to accelerate, retard, shape and modify the new discursive practices. Since the Counter Reformation, there had been an attempt to impose a homogeneous character on the nation. With the entry of the Bourbon monarchy in the eighteenth century, Spain moved into the classical period, as defined by Barthes, Bakhtin, and Foucault. During this period, power continued to be concentrated in a few clearly identifiable institutions: the monarch, the Catholic church, and the nobility. In that the clergy were largely drawn from the upper classes, the interests of the church and the landed gentry were often indistinguishable. Most books were still written by nobles and *hidalgos* and were addressed to members of these same groups (Glendinning 11). When Benito Jerónimo Feijoo wrote his *Teatro crítico universal* (1727-1739), he generally addressed his fellow churchmen and the educated elite and when some members of these groups attacked him, it was King Ferdinand VI who intervened to protect him and silence his critics. In the face of a still very centralized power, writers masked any criticism of the existing institutions and sought to create a sense of identity between their word and that of the authorities. Feijoo frequently evoked the authority of the church, alluding to his own ecclesiastical status ("La cuaresma salutífera", "Verdadera y falsa urbanidad – Apéndice") or citing Biblical and other religious texts ("Astrología judiciaria y almanaques", "Honra y provecho de la agricultura") and he prefaced his criticisms of present-day Spain with declarations of patriotism or respect, attempting to minimize his distance from his reading public ("Fábulas gacetales", "Honra y provecho de la agricultura"). The power of the king, of his favorite ("privado") and of the upper classes continued throughout the century, as is evident in the writing of Gaspar Melchor de Jovellanos. His "Memorias" and "Informes" were addressed primarily to the king or to such select bodies as the Supreme Council of Castile. Furthermore, Jovellanos's fortunes and access to speech were largely dependent on royal favor, which was dramatically illustrated when he was banished to Gijón under Carlos IV, returned briefly to power as Minister under Godoy, and subsequently imprisoned in Palma de Mallorca.

The nineteenth century represents a critical moment in the struggle between a hermetic and an open Spain, and the struggle corresponds roughly to the transition from the classical to the modern age described by Barthes, Bakhtin, and Foucault. In all realms of Spanish culture, new ideas and forms took root and challenged the hegemony of established authorities, traditional modes of existence and attitudes toward life. Attempts to resist the emergence of new and diverse voices, notably under Ferdinand VII (1814-1833) and the early years of the Restoration (1874-1881), succeeded only temporarily. Politically, absolutism gave way to representative government in the form of a constitutional monarchy and briefly, a republic (1873-1874). Alongside the traditional Monarchists and reactionary Carlists, other groups such as the Liberals, Republicans, Democrats, Socialists, Marxists and Anarchists made their appearance. Catholic control over Spanish thought progressively lost strength over the course of the century. The abolition of the Inquisition, the disentailment of church lands, the increasing – although still far from total – secularization of education, the growing calls for religious tolerance and separation of church and state, the intellectual prestige of the liberal Krausist movement as well as the religious indifference of the urban working class reflect a

breakdown of religious unity. Traditional Catholic thought persisted in differing
degrees and expression in Jaime Balmes, Juan Donoso Cortés, Juan Manuel Ortí y
Lara, Ramón Nocedal and Marcelino Menéndez Pelayo, but it was actively debated
and lost ground to various forms of German idealism (Krausism, neo-Kantism,
Hegelianism) and later positivism.

Although many of these new currents of thought had their roots in the eighteenth
and early nineteenth century, their full impact was not felt until the second half of
the 1800s. As in other European countries, the romantic movement introduced new
forms of discourse and new voices, but a number of factors impeded or delayed
their development. The absolutist reign of Ferdinand VII, the reimposition of
censorship – the Inquisition was reestablished from 1814 to 1820 –, and the
economic devastation during the war against Napoleon are some of the more
obvious causes. In this and in the following period, significant transformation
occurred. Increasing urbanization, the growth of the bourgeoisie, the greater
importance of journalism, and the gradual entry of the middle class into the political
process – among other factors – signalled a major shift in Spanish social and
cultural structures.

By the second half of the nineteenth century, authority had become notably more
diffuse. The old ideas, attitudes, and voices had not disappeared; however, they
now faced other, increasingly diverse competitors for public space. Large sectors
of the middle and lower classes joined in the call for change, some groups voicing
the need for moderation while others grew increasingly strident. In the 1860s, 70s
and 80s, a variety of parties argued and at times fought for political and ideological
control. In the years following the Revolution of 1868, previously marginal and
oppositional groups moved into positions of authority. The overthrow of Isabel II,
the selection of Amadeo of Savoy as king and his subsequent abdication, the
declaration of the First Spanish Republic, the Carlist revolt in the North and the
cantonalist movement in the East and the South – with the surfacing of Anarchist
challenges in some areas – all represent a clear breakdown of a central authority.
Individuals seeking to introduce new ideas and attitudes no longer limited their
appeal to the king or the elite. In the 1850s and 60s, Julián Sanz del Río formed his
own group of dedicated, middle-class intellectuals who utilized the newspaper, the
Ateneo[1], the university podium, conferences and regular group discussions
("tertulias") in an effort to introduce the Krausist philosophy and thus, challenge
traditional Catholic thought. The founding of the privately funded Institución Libre
de Enseñanza[2] in 1876 further indicated a belief in the ability to change society from
within. Under the direction of Francisco Giner de los Ríos, the ILE worked
assiduously and through a variety of channels to influence public opinion. In
addition to the establishment of a progressive, secular primary and secondary

[1] The Ateneo was a literary and political club established in Madrid in 1835. It organized
frequent lectures on contemporary literary, social, and political topics. A number of debates
on idealism, realism, and naturalism took place in the club in the 1860s, 70s, and 80s.
[2] The Institución Libre de Enseñanza was originally founded in 1875 as a private
University but was soon converted to a private primary and secondary school. It was a major
liberalizing influence in Restoration Spain and pioneered many pedagogical reforms.

school, Giner and his colleagues founded the *Boletín de la Institución Libre de Enseñanza*[3] and organized conferences and public lectures.

Writers of the period were acutely aware of the transformation that Spain was experiencing both in terms of ideological and linguistic change. In 1881, Leopoldo Alas (Clarín) stressed the proliferation of new voices that surfaced in the Revolution of 1868 and the extent to which they penetrated Spanish society:

> Pero la revolución de 1868, preparada con más poderosos elementos que todos los movimientos políticos anteriores, no sólo fué de más trascendencia por la radical trasformación política que produjo, sino que llegó a todas las esferas de la vida social, penetró en los espíritus y planteó por vez primera en España todos los árduos problemas que la libertad de conciencia había ido suscitando en los pueblos libres y cultos de Europa.
>
> La religión y la ciencia, que habían sido aquí ortodoxas en los días de mayor libertad política, veíanse, por vez primera, en tela de juicio y desentrañábanse sus diferencias y sus varios aspectos; disputábanse los títulos de la legitimidad a cuanto hasta entonces había imperado por siglos, sin contradicción digna de tenerse en cuenta; las dudas y las negaciones que habían sido antes alimento de escasos espíritus llegaron al pueblo, y se habló en calles, clubs y Congresos, de teología, de libre examen, con escándalo de no pequeña parte del público, ortodoxo todavía y fanático o, por lo menos, intolerante. (*Solos* 52–53)

The diffusion of authority and the proliferation of competing voices are fundamental features of Spanish culture in the latter half of the nineteenth century and must be taken into account in any study of the period. While political histories routinely trace the complex interplay of the diverse political and social forces[4], literary studies have been slower to recognize the impact of a breakdown in centralized authority on their field of study. The question of naturalism in Spain and the nature of its relation to realism has provoked considerable debate among literary critics, but they have either attempted to define the problem in purely literary terms, they have oversimplified the number of factors involved or they have not considered the discursive forms which shape the debate. Donald Fowler Brown stresses the importance of Catholicism as a primary influence on Emilia Pardo Bazán's modification of Zola's naturalism in his study *The Catholic Naturalism of Pardo Bazán* and Esteban Soler reiterates the same idea with respect to the reception of the movement in general (17). Walter Pattison, José Antonio Gómez Marín, Mariano López-Sanz, and Luis López Jiménez speak of a political division between liberals and conservatives in the nineteenth-century debates regarding idealism, realism, and naturalism but they swerve away from any real consideration of political factors. Pattison incorporates the philosophical and theological dimensions, to the exclusion of the political: "Las causas de la animadversión

---

[3] *The Boletín de la Institución Libre de Enseñanza* (1876–1936) was the official publication of the Institución. It published articles on literature, law, sociology, and philosophy and sought to expose its readers to contemporary European thought.

[4] Raymond Carr and Juan José Gil Cremades are excellent examples of historical studies that incorporate the multiple groups that compete for political, religious, or cultural dominance in late nineteenth-century Spain.

tradicional son varias: las políticas y las personales no nos interesan aquí. Haremos hincapié en el aspecto religioso y filosófico (21)."

In his study of Valera and naturalism, López Jiménez emphasizes artistic criteria, arguing that Valera's primary motivation in writing his *Apuntes sobre el nuevo arte de escribir novelas* was to defend classical aesthetic values, with the defense of Catholicism a secondary factor (44, 342). Similarly, he traces Menéndez Pelayo's opposition to Zola and naturalism to his aesthetic convictions (181). Although López Jiménez recognizes that Valera himself often alludes to political, social, and non-aesthetic issues, the critic views these as unfortunate digressions, with little or no relevance to the discussion of naturalism:

> La afirmación de Valera manifiesta que su crítica se refiere con demasiada frecuencia, como venimos viendo, a aspectos ajenos a la realización literaria. El arte de la novela era el tema fundamental, pero el autor se nos va muchas veces por los cerros de Ubeda, en nombre de la Religión, de la Moral, de la Metafísica, sin centrarse en el hecho literario. (211)

López-Sanz commences his study of naturalism in Pardo Bazán and Galdós with a review of the ideological polarization in the 1870s and 1880s (23) but subsequently moves away from a consideration of non-literary factors and eventually to their exclusion. He argues that Spanish naturalism is a purely literary conception (35) and goes on to state that Spanish novelists only adopted naturalism as a means to renovate the novel (47). Several studies in a recent study of realism and naturalism reiterate this same idea (Asún, Robin in Lissorgues).

Gifford Davis, on the other hand, emphasizes political influences on the critical reception of naturalism and correctly traces the polemic to the earlier debate over realism and idealism (*PMLA* 1649). Unfortunately, Davis collapses the diverse political professions into a simple dichotomy, liberalism versus neo-Catholicism, and, consequently overlooks the breakdown of the left and the right into various competing viewpoints. Furthermore, in stressing the "continuity of nineteenth-century criticism", he excludes the diachronic and fails to note the evolution of the different positions. The curious and puzzling aspect of the reception of naturalism is precisely the movement of the various groups towards positions that in significant aspects stand in opposition to their own formerly held beliefs. Davis refers to the rejection of French literature as a constant in the debates over realism and idealism and later, realism, idealism, and naturalism (1650), but he glosses over the fact that while both the left and the right share a marked Francophobia in the 1860s and 70s, certain groups within the left are strong proponents of French ideas in the 1880s.

A similar transformation can be observed regarding the issue of *arte docente*, the term used during the period to designate art with a didactic or moralizing purpose. Davis remarks on the political basis for the debate, identifying those who defend art for art's sake as liberals and those who argue for moral teaching through art as conservatives   But Luis Vidart, the same liberal cited by Davis as vociferously denouncing the subordination of art to ultramontane theology in 1877 ("El arte por la belleza"), rejects – only five years later – Emilia Pardo Bazán's arguments in favor of art for art's sake and argues that a thesis is not necessarily deleterious to art

("El naturalismo en el arte"). Furthermore, even in the mid-1870s, the identification of liberal with art for art's sake and conservative with *arte docente* is tenuous. Davis identifies José de Navarrete as a strong defender of *arte docente* and a supporter of Pedro de Alarcón's acceptance speech to the Spanish Royal Academy, "Discurso sobre la moral en el arte" (1877). However, Navarrete was a liberal, who participated in and actively supported the Revolution of 1868 (*Enciclopedia universal ilustrada*) and his defense of *arte docente* has its roots in attitudes that are diametrically opposed to those of Alarcón. Writing in 1875, Navarrete voices his faith in science and progress. He calls for a literature which will destroy the "piedras cimentales del edificio del error" (qtd. in "El ideal del arte" 476) and pave the way for a new world. Alarcón, as is well known, used his acceptance speech as a means to publicize his abjuration of his youthful liberalism and his return to conservative, neo-Catholic ideals. In contrast to Navarrete's praise of science, Alarcón rejects it as independent of morality and in opposition to Navarrete's calls for change, Alarcón clings to the past, defining Art as "el gran elemento conservador" ("La moral en el arte" 236). The conflation of these two discourses into a single text reveals a simplification of the political and historical forces that are operative in the 1860s, 70s, and 80s and inhibits an understanding of the various debates that take place during the period.

If a discussion of the political, social, and other non-literary factors is to be at all useful to an understanding of the literary debates of the 1800s, it must enable us to further discriminate among the various groups that intervene in the discussion and to understand the complex nature of their interaction. Movements, texts, and genres are not closed and stable but dynamic and open. The diverse discourses that surface between 1860 and 1890 interact with each other and with the social, political, and other cultural phenomena that come together in late nineteenth-century Spanish writing. Furthermore, the discursive forms available for the expression of the various viewpoints also condition their form and substance. The controversy unfolds largely in the Ateneo, in oral debate, and in essays published in newspapers and journals, which are often reprinted later in book form. Both the debate and the essay have their own structures and their own conventions. As I indicated earlier, contemporary cultural studies and literary theory have increased our awareness of the complex interplay of ideology and discourse but a better understanding of the nature of the essay is necessary in order to examine its impact on the expression of ideas. All too frequently scholars interpret essays as the unmediated expression of the author's thought. Studies on the naturalistic movement in Spain routinely quote essays written by Pardo Bazán, Alas, Valera as if language were a transparent medium and their words existed in a vacuum. As Bakhtin has shown us, the word is inherently dialogic and as Foucault observes, language carries history within it. Feminist literary theory has shown that women writing in patriarchal cultures typically rely on indirect language and hidden communication to express their ideas. This has important consequences for studies of Emilia Pardo Bazán's writing and her essays, in particular. Drawing on contemporary literary and cultural theory, I intend to study the essay as a discursive form and to analyze the various texts, discourses[5] and voices[6] that come together in the critical reception of naturalism so as to better understand the movement and literary, social, political movements in general.

No literary, social, or political phenomenon can be reduced to a list of characteristics or a single discourse, divorced from the other discourses that compete with it in a given historical time and place. Naturalism is not a purely "aesthetic" question nor is it a largely "literary" matter with secondary "religious" or "aesthetic-philosophical" considerations. It incorporates all of these discourses, as well as many others. The very nature of the period requires the inclusion of extra-literary phenomena. The individuals who intervene in the various literary debates are generally active in politics and can almost never be defined solely as "literary writers". In a period where specialization is the exception rather than the norm, the leading intellectual figures are simultaneously involved in politics, the practice of a profession (generally law), university teaching, lecturing at the Ateneo, the study and dissemination of philosophy, and the publication of both literary and non-literary works. These diverse activities clearly overlap in their lives and in their writings.

A number of the discourses and voices that are active in the discussion of naturalism have been identified in previous studies, others have been under-estimated, and still others have not been adequately specified. Among the latter are specific voices that are significant in their partial or total absence from the debates. The omissions are extremely meaningful and have not been adequately addressed by earlier studies, which curiously duplicate the silences displayed in the texts being examined. The silences are, however, very audible and can be perceived in certain resonances within the discussion. Furthermore, they contribute significantly to the unfolding of the debate. Of particular interest is the deliberate sidestepping of explicit commentary on political events and attitudes. Given the radical political stance adopted by Zola and the political upheaval that occurred in Spain immediately prior to the period in which the debate regarding naturalism takes place, this is an extremely curious omission. Even more intriguing is the avoidance of an open discussion of the implications of the female voice and its appearance in the polemic. Emilia Pardo Bazán's *La cuestión palpitante* is a pivotal text in the critical reception of naturalism and her presence dramatically affects the subsequent development of the polemic. In this study, I will examine the silencing of these factors and analyze their dynamic interrelations with other elements of the debate. I will study the essay as argumentative discourse and explore the consequences of the use of essayistic discourse for the expression and production of ideology. It is my

---

[5] I am using the term "discourse" as defined by Michael Hoey: "Any stretch of spoken or written language that is complete within itself" (15). In this study, it could refer to a specialized discourse, such as theological, philosophical, aesthetic, or political as well as to the entire debate regarding naturalism or to specific exchanges between writers or to individual texts within that larger discussion.

[6] I am using the term "voice" in a Bakhtinian sense to designate the utterances produced by a speaking personality, which are essentially multi-voiced in that they echo the words and the voices of other speakers.

hope that this approach will not only enrich our understanding of naturalism and of late nineteenth-century Spain, but may also serve as a model for other studies on the essay, on literary polemics, and on the relationship between literature and culture in general.

In chapter 1, I will explain more fully the theoretical basis for my study, with emphasis on the implications of contemporary literary theory for an understanding of the essay and of argumentative discourse. The lack of transcripts of Ateneo proceedings precludes a consideration of the oral debate *per se*, although the discussion of argumentative discourse necessarily deals with structures and strategies that are common to both the essay and the debate. In chapter 2, I will review the principal philosophical and literary movements and discourses that compete for public attention in the period leading up to the debate on naturalism. Chapter 3 will be concerned with a discussion of key political and social events that play a fundamental role in the polemic but have been largely silenced both by the writers of the time and by critics studying the reception of naturalism. They include both a middle-class fear of the radical left and of the movement for women's emancipation. In chapters 4 and 5, I will study the interaction of these various spheres of activity in specific texts and will analyze the impact of the interaction of the diverse discourses and voices on the content and expression of their point of view. I will conclude with a review of the principal issues elaborated in the study and a discussion of their implications. By means of an interdisciplinary approach, the multiple voices and discourses that come together in late nineteenth-century Spain are examined as they unfold and transform in dialogic relation with each other. Through the study of this diversity of voices and discourses, literary history, the history of ideas, and discourse analysis join to explore the inextricable relations of literature, society, and ideology.

I

A THEORY OF THE ESSAY

The essay, like the novel, is a relatively modern genre, but while narratology has experienced a tremendous growth during recent years, studies on the essay have not kept pace[1]. This lack of interest is due in part to the decline in genre studies, on the heels of Benedetto Croce's rejection of genre and other classifications (*Aesthetic*). It is abetted by the very malleability of the essay, which many critics have observed. Joseph Epstein is representative when he defines the essay as "a pair of baggy pants into which nearly anyone and anything can fit" (27). The definition invites comparison with Pío Baroja's description of the novel as "un saco donde cabe todo" and raises the question as to why elasticity has not been an impediment to the development of narratology while it has deterred the study of the essay. An answer may lie in the relative position of the two genres with respect to non-literary phenomena. Although the novel incorporates historical or biographical informa-tion, traditionally it has been seen as a "fictional" structure, clearly situated within the borders of the "literary". The essay, in contrast, is generally defined as a hybrid construction (Lukacs 13; Foster 1; Scholes 4–6; Anderson x, 325). It straddles the boundaries of the "literary" and the "real"; it is neither pure observation nor pure invention, neither totally objective nor totally subjective, neither a scholarly treatise nor a literary creation. Derrida has studied the interdependence of speech and writing in all texts (*Of Grammatology*), and this is particularly evident in the essay. It has been related to rhetoric (Adorno 168), to lyric poetry (Bleznick 6), to dramatic monologue (Champigny 108), and to the sermon (Léturneau in *Etudes littéraires* 53), forms which frequently or exclusively achieve expression through speech. Other critics place the essay in close relation to the personal letter (Concejo 163), narrative and scientific discourse (Foster 1), the article or treatise (Martínez 11–12), all of which communicate primarily or exclusively through writing. Although the essay is a written text, it consistently

[1] This lack of attention may be changing. Several recent publications on the essay suggest the need to reexamine the genre. See *Essays on the Essay*, ed. Alexander J. Butrym and *Literary Non-Fiction*, ed. Chris Anderson. Both contain important studies that seek to remedy traditional and confining definitions of the essay. However, of the five articles in Anderson's volume devoted to theory and generic classification, two address the presence of narrative in the essay while Carl Klaus's "Essayists on the Essay" is primarily an overview of traditional definitions. Butrym's collection consists primarily of comments by essayists or studies of specific essayists and essays, although it does contain several interesting studies that examine theoretical and pedagogical issues.

draws on spoken speech and foregrounds the complex interplay of speech and writing.

The hybrid nature of the essay confounded formalist, New Critical and neo-Aristotelian theory, which sought to clearly demarcate the literary from the non-literary (Wimsatt and Beardsley, "The Intentional Fallacy" and "The Affective Fallacy" in *The Verbal Icon*; Cleanth Brooks, *The Well Wrought Urn*) and similarly strove to identify genres and subgenres as largely stable and independent structures (Crane, *The Languages of Criticism and the Structure of Poetry*; Frye, *Anatomy of Criticism*). Recent literary theory emphasizes change over permanence and offers a view of genre that proves much more fruitful to the study of the essay. Furthermore, contemporary theorists reject the formalist separation of the literary and the non-literary as artificial and sterile.

Early in his writings, Mikhail Bakhtin observes the simultaneous continuity and discontinuity of genres; they are "always the same and yet not the same", "reborn and renewed at every new stage" (*Problems of Dostoevsky's Poetics* 106). Jacques Derrida affirms the existence of genre but stresses that there is no pure generic form: "A text cannot belong to no genre, it cannot be without or less a genre. Every text participates in one or several genres, there is no genreless text; there is always a genre and genres, yet such participation never amounts to belonging" ("The Law of Genre" 212). In a similar vein, Gustavo Pérez-Firmat writes that "a work does not belong to a genre as a part belongs to a whole . . . since not every feature of a work is genre bound" (278). Robert Elbanz contrasts this open, or as he calls it "dynamic" approach to genre with the traditional "topological" approach. The latter ignores historical development and seeks to establish specific dates and authors as the initiators of a generic form, such as the autobiography. In order to do so, however, a topological approach inevitably falls into the "hermeneutic circle"[2]:

> . . . for dating the beginning of a genre at a specific point in time is dependent on a prior process of synthetization. First, one establishes a series of formal conditions through the apprehension of a multiplicity of autobiographies. Then these formal conditions are solidified into one specific text (Rousseau, for example) which hypostasizes them all. Each particular autobiography is, in turn, perceived in terms of the model which it has helped establish in the first place. (187–88)

In contrast, the "dynamic" approach incorporates history and consequently, change. Genre is a "transcendental structure moving with historical fluctuations",

---

[2] Martin Heidegger describes the hermeneutic circle in *Being and Time*:
Any interpretation which is to contribute understanding, must already have understood what is to be interpreted. This is a fact that has always been remarked, even if only in the area of derivative ways of understanding and interpretation, such as philological Interpretation. The latter belongs within the range of scientific knowledge. Such knowledge demands the rigor of a demonstration to provide grounds for it. In a scientific proof, we may not presuppose what it is our task to provide grounds for. But if interpretation must in any case already operate in that which is understood, and if it must draw its nurture from this, how is it to bring any scientific results to maturity without moving in a circle, especially if, moreover, the understanding which is presupposed still operates within our common information about man and the world? Yet according to the most elementary rules of logic, this *circle* is a *circulus vitiosus*. (Qtd. in Hoy, 2)

and each text reflects a balance between similarity and difference (Elbanz 190). In Elbanz's view, generic change is grounded in what Hans Robert Jauss calls the "horizon of expectations". Each text awakens in the reader a series of expectations based on a shared cultural and literary heritage and then proceeds to alter or confirm those expectations (Jauss 23). Generic attributes form part of the horizon of expectations but they too are continually varied, reorganized, restructured (Jauss 106). Adena Rosmarin points out the essentially pragmatic nature of Jauss's approach and argues that genres are tools rather than inherent categories. More descriptive than prescriptive, they involve value judgments and limit interpretation but they also enable the reader/critic to extract meaning from the text. Their value lies precisely in their explanatory ability; thus, a generic definition is valid if it provides a framework for understanding the texts under consideration. "What makes a genre 'good', in other words, is its power to make the literary text 'good' – however that 'good' be presently defined by our audience" (49).

New Critical or formalist studies struggled to say "good" or positive things about the essay. In the context of the Formalist and New Critical definition and evaluation of a literary work as "self-sufficient", "complete", "organic"[3], the adjectives used to describe the essay convey a certain inadequacy: "digressive" (Martínez 9; Gómez-Martínez 68), "unfinished" (Bioy Casares ix), "fragmentary" (Gómez-Martínez 33) "open, loose" (Klaus in Anderson 156), "slovenly" (Hardison in Butrym 14). In contrast to the view of the poem as a well wrought urn, the essay was described as a "spontaneous" structure. To distinguish the "literary" quality of the essay from science and other non-literary forms of discourse and to imbue it with "literary" value, great emphasis has been placed on its "imaginative" or "intuitive" character (Carpenter vii; Varela in *El ensayo*: *Reunión de Málaga* 50). In the same vein, the essayist has been said to speak only for him- or herself (Paquette in *Etudes littéraires* 87) in a sort of "thinking in public" (Gerould 412; Hall 438) with no real attempt to convince the reader (O'Leary 23, 57; Zeiger in Anderson 237–38). This emphasis on the essay as monologic, in that it was perceived to be largely bound to the authorial voice and is purely "literary", pervades the bulk of the writing that has appeared on the genre. Even studies that show the influence of structuralist, poststructuralist, and reader-response literary theories have not been able to totally throw off this formalist/New Critical heritage. In the special issue of *Etudes littéraires* dedicated to the essay, articles that are informed by Barthes and other contemporary theorists strive to demonstrate the literary and imaginative qualities of the genre (Roy 28; Brouillette 45). Although several critics have mentioned persuasion as an essential essayistic characteristic, the emphasis on authorial meditation, on subjectivity and on imaginativeness has largely supplanted this rather "non-literary" trait. In his brief but much cited study on the essay, Robert Scholes recognizes that "its essential quality is persuasion" (5) and that "Persuasion . . . is at the heart of all essays" (6) but then proceeds to a four part classification which undermines his own definition and foregrounds other, primarily literary elements. The titles given to the four

---

[3] Cleanth Brook's metaphorical use of "the well wrought urn" to describe a poem reflects this view of the literary work.

types are revealing in this respect, in that three relate the essay to "literary" genres: the argumentative essay, the narrative essay, the dramatic essay, and the poetic essay. It is not surprising that subsequent critics have passed over Schole's insistence on the persuasive character of the genre, given the emphasis of his classificatory system and the general tenor of New Critical approaches to language and literature.

Structuralist and post-structuralist literary theory, speech act and discourse theory reject the formalist insistence on literary language as distinct from every-day language. One of the few critics to have approached the essay from this perspective is Walter Mignolo, who coincides with Bakhtin, Derrida, Rosmarin and others in arguing for a flexible view of genre and of "literature" in general (210–13). With specific reference to the essay, Mignolo seeks to identify the discursive frames that characterize essayistic writing and concludes that it is marked by expository and argumentative structures (216). The focus on the argumentative element marks an important turn in studies of the essay. It explodes the myth of the "autonomy" of the essayist, reinserting him/her into the non-literary world and opens the way for a consideration of previously unexplored aspects of essayistic discourse[4]. Building on Mignolo's comments, I propose to further examine the consequences of the argumentative character for the representation of the essayist in the text, for the relationship of the reader(s) with this representation of the essayist, and for the various discursive practices that emerge and interweave in essayistic writing. I am not suggesting that description, narration, and personal exploration are absent from the essay, but in some sense, all essays seek to move the reader toward the acceptance or appreciation of an emotion, a perception, or a point of view which he/she did not initially share. Many essays conceal their persuasive character so as not to provoke an oppositional stance in their public, but this is simply one of many textual strategies geared to maximize the effect of their stated or silenced argument. In emphasizing the persuasive nature of the essay, I am not denying its "literary" qualities; rather, I am following other theorists who argue that the term itself is much more elastic than we had previously thought (Eagleton 204–05; Anderson xx). Furthermore, I hope to demonstrate that privileging the imaginative and subjective aspects of essayistic discourse has limited our understanding of the genre and of individual texts.

In *Argumentative Text Structure and Translation*, Sonja Tirkkonen-Condit writes that the illocutionary point of an argumentative text is to convince, while that of the expository text is to inform (15). In some sense, the distinction between these two modes collapses, in that new knowledge or a different way of viewing a concept or a segment of reality necessarily alters our response to it. To inform is to transform. A brief look at the history of essayistic discourse will help to illustrate its

---

[4] Essay writers have also generally avoided, denied, or sidestepped the "persuasive" character of the essay, preferring to emphasize the autonomy of the essay writer and the creation of a "literary" text. Contemporary literary theory's insistence on the undecidability of the categories of fiction/non-fiction may effect a change in the essayists' view of their craft. Joan Didion, in both theory and practice, combines the literary and the persuasive. In defining her writing, she states that it is "the act of saying I, of imposing oneself upon other people, of saying *listen to me*, see it *my way*, change your mind" (2).

expository/argumentative qualities. The essay emerged precisely at a time of social, ideological, and philosophical motility. Although it clearly existed as a discursive mode within other texts, it is widely considered to have achieved what Claudio Guillén refers to as "official form"[5] (123) well after Michel de Montaigne (1533– 92) published his *Essays*. Many critics have pointed out Montaigne's skepticism, which led him to question the validity of institutionalized thought and to explore other modes of viewing human experience (Hallie; Frame). The choice of the term "essais", derived from "essayer" / "to test, try out", reflects the breakdown of a single authoritative world view and the desirability of probing, experimenting, questioning. The passage from the Medieval period to the Renaissance and then to the Modern Age accompanies a shift away from centralized authority (whether of the church, the king, the nobility) and the rise of new and varied social structures. New social classes, new professions and increased geographic mobility, among many other factors, bring new forms of discourse into play, which compete with traditional authoritative discourse.

Bakhtin has written extensively on authoritative discourse, which he characterizes as closed, monologic, and stable:

> . . . it remains sharply demarcated, compact and inert: it demands, so to speak, not only quotation marks but a demarcation even more magisterial, a special script, for instance. It is considerably more difficult to incorporate semantic changes into such a discourse, even with the help of a framing context: its semantic structure is static and dead, for it is fully complete, it has but a single meaning, the letter is fully sufficient to the sense and calcifies it. . . . It is not a free appropriation and assimilation of the word itself that authoritative discourse seeks to elicit from us; rather, it demands our unconditional allegiance. (*Dialogic Imagination* 343)

In most of Europe the "special script" reserved for authoritative language was Latin, which was closed and stable precisely because it was no longer a living language. The use of the vernacular represented a challenge to the centralized control exerted through Latin and accompanied the Renaissance exaltation of the individual and of spontaneous human activity. Essayistic discourse surfaced during this period and was marked by opposition to the authoritative word. Montaigne advocated a humanistic ethics that stood in opposition to rigid scholasticism. Francis Bacon, considered one of the founders of the genre, also proposed new modes of inquiry and contributed to the breakdown of Medieval thought. Other writers followed suit.

With the breakdown of a commonly accepted authoritative discourse, the essayist sought to establish a new, personal authority, to stake out a claim in the confusion of multiple and clashing discourses. In Spain and in other countries, the eighteenth and nineteenth centuries witnessed a dramatic increase in the cultivation of the essay. As I mentioned in the introduction, during these same centuries, the established central authorities were continually challenged, broken down, and

---

[5] Claudio Guillén describes how a genre achieves "official form" when it has been accepted by the poetics of the period. Critics approve of the genre and determine that it exists as a viable model (125).

displaced. Although every period has its own voices of authority (Bakhtin, *Speech Genres* 88), it became more and more difficult for any one voice to claim exclusive control of discourse. Some early Spanish essayists wrote precisely out of a need to decry the breakdown of the authoritative word. Juan Pablo Forner in the eighteenth century and Jaime Balmes and Juan Donoso Cortés in the nineteenth called repeatedly for the reestablishment of discursive modes that were previously dominant. More commonly, the essayist advocated a break with formerly accepted authoritative discourse, suggesting with more or less caution the acceptance of new forms of thought and of expression. Prominent examples in Spanish literature are Feijoo, Jovellanos, Mariano José de Larra, Francisco Giner de los Ríos, Miguel de Unamuno, and José Ortega y Gasset.

It is difficult to think of any of these writers as merely exploring or talking out loud with no desire to persuade and transform their reader. Feijoo's texts clearly strive to refute erroneous beliefs and to move the reader to accept a new basis of thought and action. The following passage, taken from "La ociosidad desterrada y la milicia socorrida" is only one example of a stated desire to inspire the reader to action:

> Yo no sé qué esperanza me puedo formar de que esta representación mía produzca el efecto que deseo. Si los que pueden influir en la ejecución no atienden más que a la autoridad del que la hace, nada puedo esperar. Si considera, como es creíble de su celo y capacidad, la utilidad de la propuesta, separada o abstraída de la pequeñez del autor, debo esperar mucho. (*BAE* 56:469)

Larra's articles sometimes insist that their only goal is to entertain but this is clearly a textual strategy, designed to mask other purposes. In "Dos palabras", the initial paragraphs deny any attempt to "instruct" and stress the desire to "entertain". For this reason, the text speaker promises not to offend any of his readers. He adds, however, that if any readers note a similarity between themselves and the textual portrait, they should change their ways (*BAE* 127: 71). Many of Larra's articles play with this entertain-instruct polarity and the rapid alternation of the serious and the jocose contributes in no small degree to their effectiveness. A significant number of Larra's texts abandon any pretext of "pure entertainment" in the concluding paragraphs and lay bare their argumentative character. This occurs in the original versions of "El casarse pronto y mal" (*BAE* 127: 112–13), in "En este país" (*BAE* 127: 219) and in "Jardines públicos":

> En nuestro entender, cada uno de estos jardines merece una concurrencia sostenida; las reflexiones con que hemos encabezado este artículo deben probar a sus respectivos empresarios que si hay algún medio de hacer prosperar sus establecimientos en Madrid es recurrir a todos los alicientes imaginables, a todas las mejoras posibles. De esta manera nos lisonjeamos de que el público tomará afición a los jardines públicos, que tanta influencia pueden tener en la mayor civilización y sociabilidad del país y cuya conservación y multiplicidad exige incontestablemente una capital culta como la nuestra. (*BAE* 127:413)

Unamuno's frequent statements of the need to "awaken his readers" follow in the same tradition. The closing paragraphs of *En torno al casticismo* (3: (1958) 303) and *Del sentimiento trágico de la vida* (7:(1967) 302) exhort the reader to take action. Even in essays produced in what Blanco Aguinaga refers to as Unamuno's "contemplative" mode[6], the persuasive element is never far from the surface. The final paragraph of "Guadalupe", a text written in the contemplative mode and appearing in *Por tierras de Portugal y España* reveals the underlying desire to change his Spanish reader through the description of Spanish towns and landscape:

> Es una lástima que la ramplonería de la rutina española lleve a tanta gente a pueblecillos triviales, de una lindeza de cromo que encanta a los merceros enriquecidos, y haga les asuste pasar incomodidades para ir a gozar de visiones que están fuera de tiempo. (1:(1958) 409)

Whatever form the essay takes, it is always a response to another's discourse and always seeks to present its own voice as worthy of recognition. In this respect, it often overlaps and borrows from oral debate, incorporating many traits of spoken discourse: specific recognition of the previous speaker, a justification of one's own right to speak, general or specific analysis and then refutation of the previous speaker's assertions. The so-called descriptive essay often strives to mask its persuasive character but in the end, the discourse reveals ideology and the desire to control. Mesonero Romanos constantly describes himself as an "observer" ("El observatorio de la Puerta del sol" vol. 2) and as only describing what he himself has seen ("La romería de San Isidro" vol. 1). In one of his prologues he refers to his "pintura sencilla e imparcial . . . sin exageraciones y sin acrimonia" but breaks immediately with his expressed objectivity in stating his desire to exalt the virtues of his countrymen, to castigate their vices and to softly satirize their foibles (1: 11–12). Time and again he expresses nostalgia for what he calls "una socieded apacible y normal" ("Advertencia" 1: 343; "Advertencia del autor para esta segunda serie" 2: 17). The rather evident subtext of Mesonero's *artículos de costumbres*[7] decries the loss of the old Spain and argues against French influence and the modernization of the country.

In the *artículo de costumbre*, as in all essayistic writing, there is a debate or dialogue between at least two modes of discourse, that suggested by the essayist and that which he/she attempts to displace. In some cases, the displaced discourse is a veiled subtext, which the reader perceives only dimly as a backdrop but causal force for the text at hand. In others, the essay actively incorporates the refuted discourse; it adopts alien terminology and then proceeds to appropriate this terminology for its own ends. In seeking to persuade the reader of a particular point, the text adopts the language of the opposition, and this alien language is brought into dynamic interplay with the language and ideology argued for in the essay. This practice is related to what Bakhtin refers to as "internally persuasive discourse", or language that is "tightly interwoven with 'one's own

---

[6] Blanco Aguinaga contrasts the "agonic" Unamuno, characterized by a will to struggle for the persistence of his individuality beyond death, and the "contemplative" Unamuno, who lets himself be drawn towards unconsciousness and quietude (34–35).

[7] Many critics see the *artículo de costumbre* as the origins of the modern Spanish realist novel, but it is generally classified as essayistic discourse.

word' "(*Dialogic Imagination* 345). As the individual develops ideologically, he/she is the site of a struggle between various discourses (*Dialogic Imagination* 346). A language that is totally foreign can neither communicate meaning nor move us to action. On the other hand, a language that merely duplicates our own communicates meaning but fails to persuade us; it simply validates and reinforces our initial position. Argumentative texts use a language that is familiar but also different: "In the everyday rounds of our consciousness, the internally persuasive word is half-ours and half-someone else's" (*Dialogic Imagination* 345). In this sense, essayistic discourse is always characterized by what Bakhtin has termed "heteroglossia" or a plurality of voices (*Dialogic Imagination* 426–28). It always incorporates at least two voices and two ideologies, and usually more, for within the two voices, there are generally a variety of voices taken from other discourses:

> . . . any utterance, when it is studied in greater depth under the concrete conditions of speech communication, reveals to us many half-concealed or completely concealed words of others with varying degrees of foreignness. Therefore, the utterance appears to be furrowed with distant and barely audible echoes of changes of speech subjects and dialogic overtones . . . (Bakhtin *Speech Genres* 93).

Furthermore, the relationship between these two voices is dynamic, or "dialogic". Bakhtin observes that all speakers respond to some prior speaker and enter into a dynamic interaction with their predecessors' language:

> . . . any speaker is himself a respondent to a greater or lesser degree. He is not, after all, the first speaker, the one who disturbs the eternal silence of the universe. And he presupposes not only the existence of preceding utterances – his own and others' – with which his given utterance enters into one kind of relation or another (builds on them, polemicizes with them, or simply presumes that they are already known to the listener). Any utterance is a link in a very complexly organized chain of other utterances. (*Speech Genres* 69)

Many essays are a response to specific texts, written or oral, and all essays respond to existing discourses. Whether explicit or implicit, the coming together of the texts and the discourses is dynamic; in the process, the two discourses may clash or merge but they always influence each other.

The dialogic character of the essay signals once more the presence of the spoken word in the written text. Dialogue evokes the image of two speakers in active communication and the essay, more than any other genre, organizes itself around the response to a previous text or speaker. The peculiar nature of the relationship between essayistic text speaker and reader further underscores the dialogic nature of the essay and may help to clarify why the essay, more insistently than any other genre, plays with the uneasy alliance of speech and writing. Wolfgang Iser, Stanley Fish, Umberto Eco and others have analyzed and identified the various categories of the reader. Although no specific study has been made of the essay reader, Robert Spires in *Beyond the Metafictional Mode* has developed a three-part classification of the reader of narrative that can be usefully applied to the essay: text-reader, text-act reader, and real reader (11–12). The "text-reader" is addressed within the text, although in the essay he/she is rarely identified or named. Rather, generic terms are used, such as "queridos amigos" (Bécquer, *Desde mi celda* in *Obras* 149, 169, 181), "Señor Público" (Clavijo y Fajardo, *El Pensador* 14) and "vosotros" or "Ustedes" (Ortega y Gasset, *España invertebrada* in *OC* 83, 92). Spires defines the "text-act reader" as the implicit or explicit recipient of all of the voices within the text.[8] In contrast to the "text reader", whose context is limited to the information provided directly to him/her by the text itself, "the context of the text-act reader is the socio-historical world in which the work is created" (12).

In the case of the essay, there is often a play of levels between the text reader and the text-act reader. An obvious example is Cadalso's *Cartas marruecas*, in which the text-act reader is presented with a series of letters addressed to a variety of text readers (Ben-Beley – the Moorish mentor of the young Gazel, Gazel himself, and Nuño – his Spanish guide and advisor). The various text readers are privy only to the information that is addressed to them in the letters they receive, whereas the text-act reader has access to the entire manuscript and to the socio-historical context which opens up the text to interpretation. In other essays, the distinction between the text and the text-act reader is less obvious but still pertinent. Ortega's "you" is a text-reader, who surfaces at certain strategic moments in the text. The text-act reader internalizes not only the information provided in these passages but all of the information contained in the text and that provided by contextual clues. The "real reader" is the flesh-and-blood human being who "projects him or herself into the role of the text-act reader so as to apprehend as accurately as possible the text's message" (Spires 12).

Notwithstanding the applicability of terms drawn from narratology to characterize the essay reader, the relationship between the text-act and real reader, the text-speaker, the textual world and the context differs significantly in the novel and the essay. The novel and the short story invite the reader to enter a fictional construct, to undergo a "willing suspension of disbelief". As Norman Holland has pointed out, this involves a separation of the inner world of fantasy and the external world of lived experience. In entering the fictional world, we accept that "it will not require us to act on the external world" (Holland 79) and we partially relinquish our attachment to our own self and our reality. A successful work of fiction requires that we give ourselves over at least in part to the world that has been created.

In the essay an entirely different process occurs. Although invention can and often does occur within essayistic discourse, the essay does not invent a fictional world; it speaks of a world that already exists (Aullón de Haro 12; Lukacs 10; Filloy in Anderson 68) and this has important consequences for the relationship of the text and the reader. The text always retains a direct and immediate connection with the author and the reader's world. The reader is actively reminded of this connection through the use of references to historical or contemporary events, places, and individuals, through quotations taken from familiar non-fictional sources or living or historical figures and through allusions to a shared, external experience. The presence of internally persuasive discourse also serves to reinforce

---

[8] Spires chooses the term "text act reader" over Iser's "implicit reader" because both the text reader (the reader embedded within the text) and the text-act reader (the reader who is located outside of the text) may be implied.

the sense of the "real". The use of a language that is at least in part that of the readers and saturated with their ideology and that of their experienced world precludes the escape into a fictional world. Narratives may and do occur within essayistic writing, but they are subordinated to the reconstruction of a shared, external world. The reader is thus constantly discouraged from suspending disbelief and is led to perceive the textual world as at least partially at one with his/her lived world. Consequently, the reader can no longer rest sure in the belief that he/she will not have to act. In conjunction with the argumentative character of the essay, this implies a number of discursive strategies and textual peculiarities. Before further discussion of these topics, however, it is necessary to differentiate between the essay and the treatise or learned article.

The treatise is written by a specialist in a field to an audience that is familiar with the material under discussion. The format of the specialized "journal" – subdued tones on the cover, no glossy pictures, high density of print and of content – marks the publication off from the more general and popular "magazine". As George Dillon points out, the learned article assumes large amounts of shared information and a common outlook (24). The use of specialized jargon serves to establish and reinforce a closed readership. Furthermore, the mastery of jargon attests to the authority of the writer and his/her credentials as a member of the discipline. The mention of academic or professional affiliation and the listing of titles after the author's name serve the same end. The reader may or may not agree with the information presented in the treatise but he/she accepts, at least initially, the author's authority to speak. In sum, the topic, the discourse, and the readership of the learned article are substantially fixed and the author can assume a significant amount of shared knowledge as well as a tacit recognition of his/her expertise.

The essay writer, by comparison, is a generalist – an individual with a broad cultural knowledge who addresses a non-specialized readership on any variety of topics (Lukacs 16; O'Leary 53). Both William Gass (25) and T. W. Adorno (164) characterize the essay as anti-methodical. Lacking a specific method as defined by an established discipline, the essayist can assume much less shared information and no common outlook. He/she must work to establish a shared language and a community of beliefs even before addressing the specific issue under discussion and must continue to do so throughout the essay. Geoffrey Leech argues that in order to get an addressee to do something, the speaker relies either on the power factor or the solidarity factor. The power factor operates on the recognized superiority of the speaker and functions, as previously mentioned, in the treatise and more directly, in authoritative discourse such as the religious sermon or the military command. A speaker depends on the solidarity factor when there is a mutual bond with the audience, a shared commitment or a common set of beliefs. The solidarity factor operates in political diatribe and shades into demagoguery. If neither the power nor the solidarity factor is operable, the speaker must rely on the tact principle in order to minimize conflict with the public (Leech 108).

The tact principle governs not only the discursive practices that come into play within the essayistic text but the very right of the essayist to the control of discourse. Mary Louise Pratt and others have studied the subtle mechanisms that allow for turn-taking in conversations. Participants are generally reluctant to cede the floor and will do so only under certain conditions. Pratt observes that in the narrative, the listener/readers generally surrender their right to speak until the conclusion. She suggests that "more than any other speech act . . . narratives, once begun, are immune to control by other participants in a conversation" (104). The fact that the narrative world is invented and that the listener/reader is not expected to act on the external world clearly contributes to this willingness to cede the floor. In the learned article, the listening or reading public surrenders its right temporarily, due to the recognition of the specialist's credentials and the existence of a shared language and a community of beliefs. However, the public quickly reclaims the floor, either in the question-answer session following a lecture or in written debates in the form of letters to journals or in subsequent articles. Evaluative comments to colleagues or students also represent a retaking of the floor. The fact that these appraisals are often negative reflects our disinclination to cede our turn. As Pratt observes, "in compensation for the asymmetrical distribution of turn-taking rights that prevails in speaker/Audience situations, the Audience is entitled to expect more of the speaker than they would if they were playing a participant role" (109).

These heightened expectations are particularly evident in the essay. In contrast to the narrative, the essayistic text world is primarily a recreation of the contemporary reader's world, with the ideological traces more clearly exposed. Although there may be invention within the essay, the text does not create a coherent fiction. There is no pretense of another world. The reader lives and acts in a world that is mirrored in the text. While it is true that readers from another place or time may not perceive the ideology nor experience the world reflected in the text, their choice is to reconstruct the essayistic text world and project themselves into the role of the text-act reader or to redefine the essay, cut it free from its context, and treat it as fictive discourse[9]. The essayistic text implicitly calls for the reader to take a stance, to act on the external world. But the text-speaker cannot depend on the power factor, both because the essay exists in a world in which competing discourses vie for authoritative stature and because the essayist has no claim to expertise. Nor can the essayist rely on the solidarity factor, since the essay, as an argumentative-expository discourse, is addressed to a public that is not initially in agreement with the point of view expressed in the text. As a consequence, essayistic discourse invests a tremendous amount of energy into constructing its own authority. At the same time, since excessive emphasis on authority threatens the equilibrium between speaker and audience, the discourse plays down any claim to control. There is a constant movement of assertion and then denial of authority, of deference to the reader followed by the affirmation of authorial identity and will. The traces of speech and oral discourse serve to recreate an illusion of equality between the reader and the text speaker, a partial recreation of the spoken conversation in which the speakers are co-participants. Even when one speaker cedes the floor to the other, he/she always retains the power to retake it. Given the peculiar relation between the essayistic text speaker and essay reader, the privileging of speech,

---

[9] See Barbara Herrnstein Smith for a more complete consideration of this distinction (80–85).

which Derrida has identified as characteristic of Western thought (*On Grammatology*), takes on a very specific and pragmatic function within the essay. However, the power and prestige attributed to the spoken word breaks down in the face of the written character of the essay. Speech or rather the illusion of speech in essayistic discourse is a continual presence in the essay but it must always contend with the glaring evidence of writing.

The tension between speech and writing and between the quest for authority and the denial of any such pretensions structures much of essayistic discourse. It is useful to consider this tension, and others within the essay, as "aporias" rather than contradictions, or mere oppositions. In other words, the conflicting elements are dynamically opposed and cannot be reduced to a synthesis, nor can one simply replace the other (Culler, *On Deconstruction* 96). The essay is neither aligned with speech nor writing, but plays them against each other in a never ending but fruitful struggle. Essayistic expression is not equidistant between artistic and scientific language (Aullón de Haro 107); rather, it is located in the dynamic interplay of these two discourses. It moves back and forth, confronting the imaginative and the logical, and deconstructs the two categories through a dialogic engagement. The essay does not always introduce and stress the "I" of the artist (Paquette in *Etudes*, 87) nor does the essayist spontaneously and directly project his own personality (Gómez-Martínez 50). The textual "I" appears and disappears in a continual play with other "I's" and with the "you" of the text-reader and of the text-act reader.

The tendency to collapse author and text speaker into one entity is wide-spread in discussions of the essay. Critics and students who routinely distinguish between author, implied author, and narrator in narrative texts, revert to a confusion of author and text speaker in dealing with the essay. Writers who seek to separate the two entities do so with a certain reluctance. Northrop Frye's comments are filled with qualifiers and tie the distinction to the "literary" character of the text: ". . . even in lyrics and essays the writer is to some extent a fictional hero with a fictional audience, for if the element of fictional projection disappeared completely, the writing would become direct address, or straight discursive writing, and cease to be literature" (*Anatomy* 53). Robert Scholes is somewhat more forceful but still quite tentative in his discussion of the essayist as a "fiction":

> When reading an essay we often feel as though the author is speaking directly to us. . . . But if you think about the matter a bit, you will see that essayists are not exactly the same in their essays as they are in real life. They cannot be, since in essays they are made up of words, rather than of flesh and blood. Thus the particular personality conveyed in an essay is always in some sense a *fiction*, and we call it a "fiction" because we want to emphasize its imaginative nature. It is something created out of words. (6)

Scholes and other more recent critics who speak of voice (Rygiel in Anderson 38), character or *persona* (Filloy in Anderson 33, 65) or implied personality (Klaus in Anderson 170) seek to distinguish the author from some created "I" but they continue to depict a stable, univocal textually represented personality. Poststructuralist approaches to language disallow such an identification. The view of language as an endless chain of signifiers and the belief that meaning can never be identical with itself undermines the faith in a stable human identity. As Eagleton states, since I come to know myself through language and express my knowledge of myself in language, "I can never be fully present to myself . . . It is not that I can have a pure, unblemished meaning, intention or experience which then gets distorted and refracted by the flawed medium of language: because language is the very air I breathe, I can never have a pure, unblemished meaning or experience at all" (Eagleton 130). Foucault undertakes the application of this concept to the role of the author in "What is author":

> . . . all discourses endowed with the author-function do possess this plurality of self. The self that speaks in the preface to a treatise on mathematics – and that indicates the circumstances of the treatise's composition – is identical neither in its position nor in its functioning to the self that speaks in the course of a demonstration, and that appears in the form of "I conclude" or "I suppose". In the first case, the "I" refers to an individual without an equivalent who, in a determined place and time, completed a certain task; in the second, the "I" indicates an instance and a level of demonstration which any individual could perform provided that he accept the same system of symbols, play of axioms, and set of previous demonstrations. We could also, in the same treatise, locate a third self, one that speaks to tell the work's meaning, the obstacles encountered, the results obtained, and the remaining problems; this self is situated in the field of already existing or yet-to-appear mathematical discourses. (in Harari 152)

All essays exhibit this plurality of self, sometimes through the creation of fictional speakers, sometimes through the interweaving of different discourses which reflect a plurality of speaking subjects. In the creation of fictional identities, some texts foreground the creation of the fictional speaker(s) more than others. Cadalso's use of multiple letter writers in *Cartas marruecas* and Larra's adoption of diverse pen names and personalities represent a clear separation of author and fictional representation. As the essay has evolved, the creation of an easily identifiable fictional speaker has become less and less frequent. Larra's own evolution is representative of the genre as a whole. In his early articles, the non-human figure of the ghost or elf ("El Duende") speaks to us. Subsequently it is "El pobrecito hablador", a more human *persona* but still clearly distanced from the author through the condescension connoted by the diminutive and the comic tone. With the adoption of the pen-name "Fígaro" and the very human and often autobiographical depiction he receives in articles such as "La nochebuena de 1836", the separation between author and fictional speaker becomes less obvious. Nevertheless, it continues to operate. In "La nochebuena de 1836", Fígaro transcribes a conversation with his servant and much of the "autobiographical" material is presented in the words and through the perspective of the servant (*BAE* 128: 313–17). The use of multiple speakers is typical of much of Larra's writing and disallows the confusion of author and his fictional representations, as well as the identification of a single, stable speaker. Other writers are less obvious in their creation of fictional representatives. Mesonero Romanos uses a pseudonym ("El curioso parlante") but does not textually underscore the distance between author and text speaker by the use of multiple speakers or other devices. Only readers personally acquainted with the author would realize that the old man who narrates "El retrato" (1: 32) in 1832 could not possibly be confused with the author, who was 29 or 30 at the time. Mesonero himself later expresses his amusement at this fiction (Footnote 1:32) and in subsequent articles, the distance between the author and the speaking subject is minimized. The same holds true for the vast majority of essays written in the nineteenth and twentieth centuries, but the authorial "I" is never identical with the "I" of the essays, or more precisely, with the plurality of "I's" that speak in the essay. Rather than viewing the "I" as a stable creation that stands in for the author in a given text or series of texts, it is useful to think of it as shifting in response to textual needs, as a changing identity resulting from multiple and competing textual strategies.

Because the tendency to conflate the identities of author and textual "I's" is so deeply entrenched in thinking about the essay, I have chosen the term "text speaker(s)" to designate the subjects presenting the material in the essay. "Narrator" is adequate only with reference to some *artículos de costumbre* which adopt a narrative structure but is inappropriate for most essayistic discourse. I have rejected Wayne Booth's "implied author" (71–76) because the very mention of the word "author" conjures up images of the "real author", particularly in the context of the traditional confusion of essayist and text speaker. Furthermore, "implied author" suggests a single, stable entity that can be reconstructed on the basis of the text. In the light of poststructuralist thinking and in view of the previous discussion of the essay as a dialogic response to previous texts and a dynamic interaction with text-act and real potential readers, it is more fruitful to follow Foucault's suggestion that we abandon the search for the subject as originator of meaning and analyze it as a variable and complex function of discourse (in Harari 157–58). The term "text speaker" is sufficiently flexible and depersonalized to achieve this end.

As I mentioned earlier, this text speaker alternately affirms and denies control of the discourse. Through a number of textual strategies, some openly signalled and others subversive, the speaker strives continually to establish and justify his/her authority to speak. A primary means of self-accreditation is the effacement of the "I" in deference to other authorities. This can be effected in a number of ways. Classical authors can be cited in epigraphs or within the essay to create an intertext which ties the text to the literary and cultural tradition of the country. Various critics have noted the presence of quotations within the essay and have commented on the lack of documentation (Gómez-Martínez 40–41; O'Leary 186). In contrast to the learned article, which scrupulously notes the source, date, publishing house etc. for every citation, the essay generally focuses solely on the author or the title. Who spoke is considerably more important than where it appeared and even what was said. Within a given period, the same texts and authors are cited, according to the perception of who are the authoritative figures of the day. Not surprisingly, the neo-classic Feijoo often cites Latin writers, such as Aristotle or Plato, and St. Thomas and other church fathers ("Racionalidad de los brutos" *BAE* 56: 130; "Verdadera y falsa urbanidad" *BAE* 56: 388–402). Balmes prefers church authorities in his attack on Protestantism but also pulls in classical pagan writers to broaden his appeal (4:129–40). Romanticism brings a shift in focus, with greater emphasis on the national past and on popular culture. Larra often incorporates epigraphs by neoclassical Spanish writers such as Moratín ("El mundo todo es máscaras'' *BAE* 127: 140) or Jovellanos (''Empeños y desempeños'' *BAE* 127: 86) while Bécquer quotes from the *Quijote*. Both incorporate popular adages and colloquialisms, such as ''A Dios rogando y con el mazo dando'' in Bécquer's ''La pereza'' (819) and ''¡En este país!'' or ''Cosas de España'', both objects of Larra's commentary in the essay ''En este país'' (*BAE* 127: 216, 218). Moderate and progressive Spanish writers in the latter part of the nineteenth century tend to cite European authorities, such as Taine (Pardo Bazán, *La mujer española* 38), Spencer (Pardo Bazán, *La mujer española* 157), Malthus (Valera, 2: 2092) and Carlyle (Valera, 2: 2156). In general, the use of frequent or extensive quotations varies according to the social status and the power of the essayist. It was still quite frequent in the eighteenth century and decreases steadily throughout the nineteenth. Ortega y Gasset rarely inserts quotations while Emilia Pardo Bazán, writing as a woman in a patriarchal society, frequently transcribes the words of others[10]. Not surprisingly, her sources are uniformly male.

Even when the quotation serves to efface the presence of the text speaker, the contrasting push to assert the textual I is present. Rather than cede to the other's words, essayists often paraphrase, overlaying their own voice on that of the authority. The textual I is sometimes gratuitously underscored, as in common essayistic expressions such as ''I believe it was Unamuno who said'' or ''I don't remember exactly where, but Kant once wrote that . . .'').

An additional strategy utilized to accredit the text speaker is the incorporation of what Roger Fowler, among others, calls ''sociolects'' or the linguistic expression of world views (35). Bakhtin also comments on the presence of these ideologically charged terms, which he refers to as ''masters of thought'':

> In each epoch, in each social circle, in each small world of family, friends, acquaintances, and comrades in which a human being grows and lives, there are always authoritative utterances that set the tone – artistic, scientific, and journalistic works on which one relies, to which one refers, which are cited, imitated, and followed. In each epoch, in all areas of life and activity, there are particular traditions that are expressed and retained in verbal vestments: in written works, in utterances, in sayings, and so forth. (*Speech Genres* 88–89)

Essayistic discourse is replete with ''catch words'' drawn from the sociolect. This practice is obviously related to ''internally persuasive discourse''. Speakers seek to invest themselves with authority and to create a community of belief through allusions drawn from a common language, but at the same time, the sociolect, another's language, comes into dialogic interaction with the speaker's idiolect, one's own language, and both undergo transformation. It is perhaps not surprising to find that progressive writers evoke an established sociolect in an effort to accredit themselves, but even writers who are closely tied to a traditional authoritative discourse seek to make their argument persuasive by utilizing terms and expressions drawn from non-traditional but increasingly powerful sectors of

[10] For an unusual use of quotations in Pardo Bazán, see my article ''Emilia Pardo Bazán on John Stuart Mill: Towards a Redefinition of the Essay''.

society. Consequently, in the defense of Catholicism, Balmes appropriates liberal catch words, which then enter into his own discourse and modify it:

> En la actualidad se proclama como un principio la tolerancia universal y se condena sin restricción todo linaje de intolerancia. ¿Quién cuida de examinar el verdadero sentido de esas palabras? ¿Quién analiza a la luz de la razón las ideas que encierran? ¿Quién para aclararlas echa mano de la historia y de la experiencia? (4: 341)

Not only does the text incorporate the term "tolerance" but the textual practice reveals the assimilation of the mid-nineteenth-century shibboleths of reason ("¿Quién analiza a la luz de la razón las ideas que encierran?"), history and experience ("¿Quién para aclararlas echa mano de la historia y de la experiencia?") to draw in the reader. Although he is presumably incorporating these ideas only to refute them, their presence brings echoes and ideological traces that pervade the text and cannot be effaced by mere verbal refutation. The text speaker in Balmes's essays seeks to reaccentuate the word, to give the sign a univocal meaning, to impose the ideology and the discourse of the speaking "I", but both the nature of language and of the reader's relationship to the text open up the sign to a plurality of meanings. This is not to say that Balmes does not leave a mark. His reaccentuation enters into the play of meanings and it changes the configuration; his voice becomes another link in the chain of signifiers.

Text speakers frequently seek to establish their authority through references to their own moral character – the ancient rhetorical device of *ethos*[11]. These include disclaimers of any ambition to power, as in the case of Clavijo y Fajardo ("Pensamiento I" 1: 16), and Feijoo's occasional references to his clerical status as proof of his veracity. Many essayists suggest moral superiority and devotion to "truth" by describing how they have risked attack in seeking the truth (Feijoo, "Prólogo al lector" 56: 205; Pardo Bazán, *OC* 3: 577). Pérez de Ayala opens his discussion of patriotism with allusions to the theme as both delicate and painful and consequently draws attention to his own bravery and commitment: "Tema doloroso y delicado. No por eso se ha de evitar cobardemente, antes bien, se debe tratar; pero con delicadeza, con tiento" (3: 674).

Claims to sincerity abound in essayistic discourse (Feijoo, "Prólogo al lector" 56: 204; Clavijo y Fajardo, "Pensamiento I 1: 5) and serve to accredit the speaker by underplaying the use of rhetoric and conventional argumentative strategies:

> . . . explicit formulations of the sincerity of the speaker serve the purpose of creating in the hearer the impression that the speaker does not have the intention of imposing his/her opinion on him/her in an incontestable way, since he/she confines himself to expressing a personal belief. (Haverkate 26)

Again, the tension between the imposition of the "I" and deference to the reader surfaces. In the text speaker's act of expressing sincerity, and thus textually foregrounding his/her intentionality and presence, the reader's power to reject the

---

[11] For a more extensive treatment of *ethos* and of rhetorical devices in general, see Dixon, 24 ss.

word and the text is implicitly underscored. The text speaker's sincerity is a precondition to the reader's tolerance and willingness to continue listening/reading. A similar play of speaker-reader power occurs in the use of mitigating devices, such as the expressions "I believe", "It seems to me", which soften the speaker's assertions at the same time that they bring the speaker's "I" to the foreground. Simultaneously, the iteration of opinion on the part of the speaker reminds the reader of his/her own power to form a judgment and thus reject that expressed in the text. In an effort to downplay the ever-present antagonism of speaker-reader, essayistic discourse often seeks to efface the "I" of the text speaker by the use of the first person plural, which similarly serves to involve the reader in a collective "we" (Haverkate 26–27). Passivization and agent deletion are commonly found in essayistic discourse and further aid in maintaining the delicate equilibrium between speaker and audience. The use of "nosotros" and of the Spanish "se" construction, which allows for the effacement of the active agent, are both prevalent in the Spanish essay from its inception and continue until the present time. An example from Carmen Martín Gaite's *Usos amorosos de la posguerra española* combines first person plural, passivization and agent deletion, first by means of "se" and then "uno":

> Ya tendremos ocasión de ver más adelante la importancia que se daba a la apariencia exterior, y hasta qué punto la decencia en el vestir se interpretaba como síntoma de españolidad. Pero, aunque la frase citada no pase de ser una metáfora, mirando las revistas de la época saca uno la consecuencia de que aquel traje castizo que devolvía a España su verdadero ser era una mezcla de bata de lunares y sotana de cura. (20)

Most discursive practices operate on various levels of the text and have multiple functions. A primary example of a polysemic device in essayistic discourse is the use of metaliterary commentaries. Self-referentiality is a fundamental trait of essayistic discourse but it has failed to attract the attention given to self-referential narrative, poetry, or drama precisely because the essay does not create a world that is separate from that of the text speaker and the reader. Metafiction attracts our attention because fiction constructs what we perceive to be a self-contained world and then metafictional practices intrude to break down the frontiers between the fictional world of the characters and the nonfictional world of the reader (Waugh 2). Most essays comment on their genesis and make more or less frequent allusions to their structure, and to the manner in which the contents are presented. One effect of remarks of this nature is to underscore the control of the text speaker by highlighting his/her awareness of the textual practices in operation. They also accredit the speaker by clarifying how he/she has come to the knowledge assumed in the text. It may be that the essay is prompted by the reading of a book (Unamuno 4:(1958) 521) or an article (Pérez de Ayala 2: 1061). Often the genesis of the essay can be found in an event or experience in which the text speaker participated. Thus, Azorín's "La feria de los libros" (35) opens with a description of a visit to the book exhibit, which serves as the point of departure for an essay on books, book exhibits, trains, and other matters.

Self-referential comments in the essay also respond to what Haverkate calls the obviousness precondition (34). In any verbal interchange, the addressee has different expectations according to the illocutionary point of the message. In a narrative, the addressee expects the material to be tellable (Pratt 132–51) and generally asks the question "What happened next?" (Tirkonnen 50), whereas in argumentative-expository discourse, the addressee expects the information to be relevant and non-obvious and asks the question "why are you telling this to me?". While the story teller does not have to justify what is said, the argumentative text speaker is in a different situation (Tirkonnen 50). Many essays open with comments designed to highlight the relevancy of the matter to be discussed and to point out the need to reevaluate the authoritative discourse, either with an eye to refortifying or to modifying it. The initial paragraph of Urbano González Serrano's "Estudio sobre el positivismo" stresses the urgency of the task and thus justifies his treatment of the topic:

> Hoy que la humanidad vive en momentos decisivos para su destino ulterior, hoy que todos los pueblos cultos han perdido las antiguas bases de su organización política, social y aún religiosa; hoy, que nos encontramos entre un pasado repudiado enteramente y un porvenir oscurecido por la polvareda de tanta ruina amontonada alrededor; hoy, que los individuos dudan, los pueblos titubean y las sociedades oscilan entre la libertad y el despotismo, entre el ayer y el mañana, importa más que nunca examinar con ánimo sereno el estado de la conciencia culta, e interesa considerar con mirada imparcial la tendencia que predomina en el criterio habitual y común de los tiempos que alcanzamos. (216)

Essayistic metacommentary also contributes to the creation of textual cohesion, or the sense that the reader is dealing with a meaningful text and not some arbitrary linking of words (Fowler 64). Whereas narratives appear to naturally hang together according to the logic of chronology and sequence, the essay must rely on other factors to create a sense of unity. Explicit discussion of the genesis of the essay and the plan to be followed serve this function. The tendency to utilize a single focalization also contributes to textual cohesion. Not surprisingly, essays in which there is more than one text speaker incorporate many features of narrative discourse, thus supplanting the unity of the "I" with the unifying feature of narrative sequence. Alain Bony has observed the emphasis on space over time in essayistic discourse and the frequency with which essayists draw attention to the specificity of their discourse through references to the quality of paper or their spatial limitations ("L'espace" 19). These features also contribute to the sense of a cohesive creation which is spatially defined and "authorially" controlled.

Along the same lines, much self-referential commentary functions as what Dillon calls "traffic signals"(60), referring back to previous information and announcing what will follow or pointing out the relationship between two areas of the text. While this serves to foreground the presence of the text speaker and his/her control of the discourse, it also suggests the speaker's subservience to external organizing structures. A certain logic prevails and orders the text; the speaker is not arbitrarily imposing a subjective point of view. This function of metaessayistic commentary is related to Todorov's concept of *vraisemblance*, in the sense that it seeks to persuade the reader that the text operates in accordance with external reality and does not simply follow its own rules (Culler, *Structuralist Poetics* 139).

All allusions to the ordering of information, to the planned presentation of details, and to the sources of data tie the essay to the logical, scientific pole of its bipolar logic-emotion, science-art, objective-subjective identity and consequently, to discursive practices that are perceived as "factual" and free from manipulation by the text speaker.

On the other hand, the dialogic, aporetic character of the essay prevents the logical from imposing a univocal discourse, and the announced plan is constantly inhibited by digressions that surface and then subsequently are displaced by the ordered presentation. Many studies on the essay have commented on the use of digressions as a fundamental characteristic of the genre but in New Critical terms, a digression is somehow alien to the unity and the central structure of the text. From a post-structuralist and Bakhtinian perspective, the digression must be seen as an integral piece of the essay and in constant dialogic interaction with the "core". Through the digression, the subjectivity of the textual speaker intrudes on the objective perspective presented in the ordered presentation and maintains the tension between the various components that come into play in essayistic discourse. It is not that the digression is solely constituted by emotion, subjectivity, literariness. Within the digression, as within the nondigressive area of the text, the two modalities surge and withdraw in overlapping and interpenetrating flux. The same rhythm appears in the use of examples designed to corroborate the text speaker's assertion. A consideration of the essay "Paisaje" by Giner de los Ríos will help to illustrate the interweaving of the objective/subjective modality. Giner writes during the period when literary realism dominates, which partially explains his efforts to efface the textual "I" and to avoid any display of subjective emotion. He frequently employs scientific terminology and a distanced, impersonal tone, but the bipolar, dialogical character of essayistic writing is still observable in his texts. In "Paisaje", Giner wishes to better define the term "landscape" and points out that most writers overlook the importance of the soil in their discussion, preferring to concentrate on water, vegetation, and animal life. He begins his commentary with scientific terms, insisting that the soil offers sufficient data to constitute an aesthetics of geology. He then proceeds to classify the soil along geological lines: granitic, basaltic, alluvial. Emotive language surfaces, however, when he introduces examples:

> Todo el mundo, v.gr., distingue el pintoresco dentellado con que se recortan sobre el azul del cielo las Pedrizas del Manzanares en la vecina sierra Carpetana, y el suave modelado de los cerros que rodean a Madrid. (*Ensayos y cartas* 40)

The use of local geography personalizes the description and interjects a subjective mood that is underscored by the use of the adjectives picturesque, blue, and soft. The subsequent presentation maintains a balance, with the unadorned description of the effects of water and temperature change on the granite punctuated by emotionally charged adjectives such as "enormous", "gigantic", "great" and "soft". Towards the end of the description, the subjective note prevails, with only a trace of the geological, scientific perspective retained to structure the description of the beloved local landscape:

En la montaña, severa hasta la majestad, todo es mate y adusto: los líquenes que tiñen el verdoso granito; el monte bajo, cuyo tono apenas templan, allá en la primavera, el morado cantueso, la amarilla flor de la retama, el rojo de tal cual amapola o de las opulentas peonías; el sombrío verdor de los pinos, que se alzan sobre ellos, ora esbeltos y erguidos, ora corpulentos y nudosos, o muertos con el gris de plata de sus ramas desnudas, retorcidas y secas. (*Ensayos y cartas* 56)

The need to maintain a balance of the authority of the text speaker and that of the reader in essayistic discourse militates against the early introduction of the subjective. The initial paragraphs work towards the creation of a community of belief through a variety of strategies, such as evoking authoritative discourse through quotations, "catch words", allusions to cultural codes, or a justification of the relevancy of the materials to be discussed. The expression of a personal opinion and of an emotional commitment to the topic of discussion is normally delayed until the text speaker has accredited him or herself. Typically, the text speaker grows more assertive and the subjective-emotional pole becomes more evident as the text advances. However, deferential treatment of the reader and the logical-objective features continue in a dialogical relationship throughout the text. This constant rhythm of assertion and denial contributes to the non-linear structure of most essays. Tirkonnen-Condit refers to a wave-like process by which many argumentative texts organize their information (37). In contrast to the ideal of the tightly organized and linear structure, essayistic discourse is often repetitive, circling back on itself in a neverending effort to redress imbalances that constantly surface in the text and must continually be rectified.

The peculiar relationship between the reader(s) and the text speaker that constitutes the essay as an argumentative-expository discourse has many ramifications for the study of essayistic discourse. The tendency to associate the essay with the sincere and unmediated expression of the author's literary intention ignores recent theories of language and of the relationship between literature and language. In contrast to a thematic approach to the essay or the descriptive listing of an author's opinions regarding specific topics, we need to view the authorial "I" as an unstable construct, that shifts according to the textual strategies required to enter into dialogic interaction with preceding and contemporary texts and voices. In this chapter I have explored some of the implications of recent theory for a study of the essay. Without any claim to having exhausted the subject and with the belief that future studies will rectify, modify, and expand many of the ideas suggested here, I hope to have provided a step toward a better understanding of essayistic discourse. In the remaining chapters, I will examine the critical reception of naturalism in Spain in the light of the theory presented here, of the changing socio-historical situation that was discussed in the Introduction, and the various voices and discourses that characterize late nineteenth-century Spain. Chapter 2 will trace the development of philosophical and aesthetic discourses during the 1860s and subsequent decades and Chapter 3 will do the same with respect to the expression of political and social ideology.

II

VOICES AND ECHOES

All discourse is composed of many interwoven voices and echoes of other discourses. Any attempt to isolate one or more of these for examination unavoidably suggests a hierarchy of voices, by focusing on one prior to the others. Furthermore, studying one voice in isolation of necessity simplifies the complex interrelations that characterize its connection to other voices. On the other hand, the complexity of a given discourse is difficult to comprehend without extracting and examining its various components. In this chapter I will identify and analyze some of the various strands that come together in dynamic interaction in the critical reception of naturalism, but it must be kept in mind that the focus on a single voice in no way privileges it over others. Furthermore, the significance and tone of a single voice can be comprehended fully only in its relations with the chorus of voices that make up the text. As I proceed in this chapter and the next with the identification of the various strands that come together in the critical reception of naturalism, I will reinsert the isolated voices in the overall pattern and seek to show how they transfigure each other. My analysis of the interaction and mutual transformation will emphasize the diachronic nature of discourse. Between 1850 and 1890, different voices and discourses interact with each other and are affected by historical events in such a way that they undergo fundamental changes in choice of terminology and in the meaning of the terms utilized. I will focus first on the use of patriotic discourse, both because it is in many ways the easiest to disentangle and analyze and because it serves as a cover for many of the others.

Towards the end of the eighteenth century, nationalism took root as a primary force in the formation of European public sentiment. Spain's isolation from the rest of Europe during the earlier period of the Counter Reformation undoubtedly contributed to the creation of a sense of difference, of a peculiar national identity. The Spanish War of Independence (1808–1814) fostered an exalted sense of a Spanish nation which was intensified by the Romantic rejection of Neoclassic emphasis on universality in favor of local color and the particular. Concomitant with the sense of Spanish identity was a rejection of non-Hispanic cultures and in particular a strident Gallophobia. The traditional subordination of Spanish interests to French ambitions under the eighteenth-century Family Pacts, Napoleon's attempt to install his brother as the king of Spain, the French invasion of the Hundred Thousand Sons of St. Louis in 1823 and a traditional distrust of this close European neighbor fed into a rejection of French values and culture in Spanish writers. Gifford Davis identifies a rejection of French literature as one of the components of the debate over idealism and realism and associates the anti-French sentiment with the political right. However, a Gallophobic attitude is shared by the right and the left during the greater part of the nineteenth century and includes a rejection of philosophy and political trends, as well as literature.

Early conservative writers, such as Balmes or Donoso Cortés, stress the unity of Catholic Europe and condemn eighteenth-century French "philosophes" and French revolutionary extremism as forces that contributed to the breakdown of Catholic authority. Balmes's *El protestantismo comparado con el catolicismo* refutes the "heretical" writings of François Guizot and constantly alludes to Voltaire, Rousseau, Robespierre, and other French figures as the incarnation of evil. His essay "Un cristianismo extraño" decries the nefarious influence of Voltaire and exemplifies its consequences by alluding to moral decay in Paris, where he alleges that a third of all children are born out of wedlock (5: 150). Gallophobic rhetoric is even more frequent in liberal writers. Raymond Carr (302) and Juan López-Morillas (24) have commented on Julián Sanz del Río's disdain for French culture and the consequent acceptance of German thought that characterizes certain Spanish moderate and leftist thinkers. In a letter written by Sanz in 1844, he expresses strong criticism of Victor Cousin – the proponent of French eclecticism – and of French influence on Spanish culture:

> Lamento cada día más la influencia que la filosofía y la ciencia francesa – ciencia de embrollo y de pura apariencia – ejerce entre nosotros hace más de medio siglo. ¿Qué nos ha traído sino pereza para trabajar por nosotros mismos, falso saber, y sobre todo, inmoralidad y petulante egoísmo?" ("Cartas inéditas" 66)

Similar views appear in the writings of Francisco de Paula Canalejas, a disciple of Sanz who refers in 1860 to French eclectics as mere rhetoricians, given to stylistic elegance and declamation (*Estudios críticos de filosofía* 286). Francisco Giner de los Ríos broadens the attack, rejecting French literature as affected, frivolous, and lacking in depth and then characterizes French scientific writing as unsubstantial, vague, false, repetitious, lacking technical precision and any systematic organization (*Estudios de literatura y arte* 170).

During the middle of the nineteenth century, Gallophobic discourse constitutes a localized voice of authority which is shared by Spanish writers of the right and of the left and functions as internally persuasive discourse, establishing a relationship of solidarity with the reader. When Giner writes that France reigned despotically in Spanish letters, "sobreponiendo su cosmopolitanismo a la índole nacional de nuestro genio" (*Estudios de literatura y arte* 170), Spanish readers of diverse ideological persuasions hear a language that is half theirs. It is, however, only one of the threads of discourse that weave through the text and as it combines with others, it creates different strands and ultimately different patterns. The liberal rejection of French culture is accompanied by a gradual acceptance of other non-Hispanic cultures and an increasing call for openness to outside influences. At some point, it does a rather abrupt about face and embraces French positivism and naturalism. This turnabout has not been noted in previous studies and I will examine it in further detail in subsequent sections. In comparison with the liberal openness to other cultures and eventual retroversion to French influences, the conservative stance becomes increasingly hermetic and xenophobic (López-Morillas 110). These two discourses, in combination with others that will be studied in other sections of this chapter and in later chapters, come into dynamic interaction and mutually influence their respective subsequent developments.

Early liberal expression of admiration for non-Spanish cultures retains a balanced, guarded tone. Sanz del Río expresses his openness to German influence in the same letter in which he strongly rejects Cousin and the French philosophical tradition, but he couches his statement in cautious, tentative language, stressing the need to avoid the German proclivity for useless abstraction ("Cartas inéditas" 66). Giner de los Ríos's praise of German scientific achievement is balanced by his declaration of the superiority of Spanish and Italian literature and of English political thought and industrial advancement (*Estudios literarios* 103). It is well known that the introduction of German philosophy through Sanz del Río provokes a strong reaction among Spanish traditionalists, who condemn it as pantheistic, heretical, and anti-Spanish. Marcelino Menéndez Pelayo continues the defense of traditional Catholic thought begun by Balmes and Donoso Cortés, but whereas they emphasize the rift between a Catholic and a non-Catholic Europe, Menéndez Pelayo – writing in the post-Krausist period – equates Catholicism exclusively with Spain. In the *Revista Europea*, a weekly publication open to writers of all political persuasions, he launches a strong attack on the *Revista Contemporánea*, a journal founded by José del Perojo with the explicit purpose of publicizing recent German philosophical and cultural developments (Cacho Viu 320–36). In Menéndez Pelayo's view, the journal and all those who support Krausism hate Spain and Spanish culture. In opposition to their wish to open Spain up to non-Spanish intellectual movements, Menéndez Pelayo declares his intention to revive Spanish thought and in the following issue, he publishes his plan for a book on Spanish heterodox thinkers as a means to this end ("Noticias de algunos trabajos" 459–66). In his *Historia de los heterodoxos españoles*, he focuses on the Spanish language as the primary unifying force of the nation and underscores the connection with Latin and with Rome (832). Those who seek to intrude on this great tradition are the Germanic barbarians, and Menéndez Pelayo uses this last word frequently in his discussion of modern heterodox thought. He and other traditionalists specifically attack what they perceive as a barbarous linguistic corruption of Spanish. He comments with sarcasm:

> Y ante todo [el filósofo español contemporáneo] debe olvidar la lengua de su país, y todas las demás lenguas, y hablar otra peregrina y estrafalaria, en que sea bárbaro todo, las palabras, el estilo, la construcción. (732)

In a speech at his induction into the Royal Academy, Vicente Barrantes defends the clarity of traditional scholasticism and the richness of the Castilian language, which he seeks to protect from the jargon of Sanz and his followers, the "Góngoras del filosofismo" ("Las deformidades literarias" 193–94). For Barrantes, the philosophical language of the Spanish Krausists is indicative of their "desprecio hacia todo elemento nacional" (196). Campoamor's debate with Francisco

Canalejas contains similar charges and ties the Krausist corruption of the language to the destruction of the nation ("A la lenteja" 442). Núñez de Arce's dismissal of Gustavo Adolfo Bécquer's poetry as "suspirillos de corte y sabor germánicos" (Prólogo, *Gritos de combate*) exploits the anti-Germanic discourse of the traditionalists.

The Neo-Catholic and conservative appropriation of a patriotic defense of Spain and the Spanish language and their attacks on the barbarous Gongorism of German philosophic language has a number of consequences. Liberal and moderate writers continue to speak out in defense of change and a receptivity to foreign ideas. However, their writing reveals an increasing emphasis on clarity and a well structured argument. Second generation followers of Sanz del Río such as Gumersindo de Azcárate and Giner de los Ríos adopt a clear and succinct style and continually remind the reader of the organizational structure they are following. With the growing emphasis on science during the years preceding and accompanying the arrival of naturalism, the shift away from abstraction and the espousal of a plain, direct style continues. Writing in *La cuestión palpitante* in 1881 Emilia Pardo Bazán states that she will write in a simple and unadorned style, with neither irritating quotes from authorities nor deep philosophy (3: 35). The need to deemphasize any link with heterodox Germanic discourse is further complicated by Pardo Bazán's interest in the equally heterodox French naturalism. I have already pointed out that Spanish liberals and moderates gradually move during the 1860s and 70s from a dependence on Germanic philosophy and a rejection of French culture to an acceptance of French literary and cultural influence. In the process, however, they generally echo in some form the patriotic discourse of the traditionalists. Juan Valera agrees that there is an overwhelming foreign influence on contemporary Spanish thought but he insists that the public debates in the press and in other forums serve to sharpen and make more flexible the Spanish language at the same time that they nationalize the foreign ideas by bringing them into contact with middle and lower class Spaniards (2: 427).

Significantly, Valera's defense of non-Spanish influence appears in an essay entitled "De lo castizo de nuestra cultura en el siglo XVIII y en el presente". A nationalistic voice predominates in the title and serves as a counterbalance to the defense of openness to foreign currents of thought.

The liberal discussion of naturalism abounds with similar juxtapositions of disparate voices. In an early call for a novel that is a faithful mirror of society, Benito Pérez Galdós insists that the Spanish novel has always been a novel of observation and blames the decadence of Spanish narrative on what he calls the novel of impressions and movement, a "peste nacida en Francia" ("Observaciones sobre la novela contemporánea" 164). Writing in 1870, before French naturalism was loudly debated in Spain and before he himself adopted (and adapted) it as a means to renovate the Spanish narrative, Galdós could call for change and frame it in terms of a return to the past and a repudiation of modern French influence. In later writers, the interweaving of a patriotic discourse that echoes the xenophobic nationalism of the right and a progressive discourse that is open to non-Spanish influences grows considerably more complex. Urbano González Serrano, an active collaborator in the Institución Libre de Enseñanza who evolves towards

neopositivism, always remains opposed to Zola and his tenets. He finds Zola's own
patriotism exaggerated and laughable, particularly in the "Letter to Youth" where
Zola argues that by applying the scientific principle of art, the French will some day
recover Alsace and Lorraine. In refuting naturalism, González Serrano insists that
it will not take hold in Spain, precisely because it is a French movement. On the
other hand, he concurs with Zola that the novel can and should examine social
questions, but he insists that to do so Spanish writers simply need to renew their
own national traditions (*Cuestiones contemporáneas* 156–57). Emilia Pardo Bazán
reveals greater acceptance of Zola and his aesthetic, although she too expresses
reservations. Significantly, she advocates reform of the Spanish narrative along the
lines of French naturalism but then insists that Spanish and French naturalism will
differ, in part because Spain is a distinct cultural entity and in part because
traditional Spanish realism will prevail over a foreign influence. Writing several
years later, after the debate over naturalism had begun to die down, Rafael Altamira
is considerably more open in his defense of Zola, arguing that he is not as
materialistic, pessimistic or obscene as many had charged, but he too underscores
the long realistic tradition in Spanish literature and stresses the continuity of the
novel of the day with that of the past ("El realismo y la literatura contemporánea"
18 Sept. 603).

Numerous critics cite nationalism and patriotism to explain what they perceive as
a Spanish rejection of French nationalism. The danger lies in accepting as the direct
expression of authorial opinion what is more appropriately viewed as a textual
strategy. Throughout the debate, figures on the left and the right call upon a
nationalistic authoritative voice in their attempt to establish solidarity with the
reader. All parties seek to naturalize foreign voices, establishing links between
them and a national past. Menéndez Pelayo conflates Rome and Spain, Latin and
Spanish, and in a curious swerve equates Catholicism – the epitome of the
transnational and the universal – with Spanishness. Pardo Bazán, Valera, and
Altamira argue for the receptivity of foreign influences and then seek to establish
the national roots of these alien movements. The implementation of patriotic
discourse by any single writer is in dialogic relation to its use in the other writers of
the period. The Neo-Catholic and conservative claim of continuity with the past
necessitates a response from writers who advocate an openness to foreign thought
and even after the Neo-Catholic claim to authority has largely disappeared, its
accusation of disdain for the national past continues to echo in the texts and to
demand, and receive, an answer.

Patriotic discourse is one of the more easily isolated elements that make up the
critical debate on naturalism. It is, however, inextricably interwoven with other
voices and discourses, which mark it and on which it leaves a mark. López-
Morillas correctly observes that Menéndez Pelayo's polemic with Azcárate,
Revilla, Salmerón and others regarding the existence or non-existence of a
scientific tradition in Spain really involves the question of the identity of Spain
(203). The same is true for the discussion of the desirability of foreign influences. It
has been impossible to discuss patriotic discourse without mentioning some of the
philosophical and theological debates that took place between 1850–1890, all of
which are inextricably related to the question of "what is Spain?" and even more

importantly, "where is she going?". A significant component of these debates is the validity and desirability of the introduction of German idealism, in particular Krausism, in Spain. The Krausist movement and its gradual evolution toward positivism and naturalism has been studied by a number of scholars (López-Morillas, Diego Núñez Ruiz). For the purposes of this study, it will be useful to briefly review the various philosophical currents that compete for authoritative status during the latter half of the nineteenth century and to identify certain discourses and voices that are pertinent to the reception of naturalism and the form that it takes.

Julián Sanz del Río and his promotion of Krausist philosophy represents one important component of mid-nineteenth-century Spanish thought. From his inaugural address at the opening of the academic year 1857–1858 at the University of Madrid to his death in 1869, Sanz succeeded in winning adepts to his philosophy, largely based on the German philosopher, Karl Christian Friedrich Krause, but adapted to what he perceived to be peculiarly Spanish needs. Key components of Sanz's Krausism are a firm belief in the rationality of human beings and of the world, a view that the world and all that inhabits it is a manifestation of the divine essence which created it, and a conviction that history, literature, and all human activity progress gradually but consistently towards an ideal state. "El racionalismo armónico", the name given to the Krausist movement, captures both the emphasis on reason and on orderly, progressive movement which characterizes Spanish Krausism. The belief in the rationality of the individual and of the universe implies that each individual has the right and the obligation to seek the truth through personal examination. In his *Estudios de filosofía, política y literatura* (1872), the Krausist Francisco de Paula Canalejas insists on questioning all on the basis of reason and rejects tradition in favor of scientific, reasoned demonstration (145–52). The exaltation of reason provokes a strong response from traditional Catholic thinkers, as exemplified by Juan Manuel Ortí y Lara, for whom the only true science is divine science (*Lecciones sobre el sistema* 25). Nicomedes Martín Mateos similarly stresses divine revelation in his article "El catolicismo y la filosofía alemana". The opposition between a belief in divine revelation and reason as the source of knowledge is tied to a fundamental difference in the view of the world and of human nature. For the Krausists, all difference disappears in some future unity:

> La dualidad y la oposición son ley de la vida del espíritu y del universo; pero estas opuestas tendencias no se destruyen entre sí; antes se armonizan en la unidad de la idea. . . . La verdad entre los extremos está, es cierto, en el medio y justo medio; pero en el medio racional, que toca esencialmente a los extremos, y que, siendo como el lazo que los une, debe con ellos estar en unidad esencial y lógica también, y a la vez bajo una unidad superior a que constantemente atenerse y que debe conservar en todo el proceso científico de composición si ha de ser verdadero medio armónico. (Rute, "Breves indicaciones" 53)

This play of paradoxes and of contradictions that resolve in harmonious synthesis is harshly criticized by traditional writers, who insist on a dualistic conception of the human individual and of the world. While Sanz and many of his followers see

humanity and society as essentially good and perfectible, the traditionalist
emphasizes the fall of humanity and the constant and irresolvable conflict between
body and soul, spirit and matter. Sanz and other Spanish Krausists refer frequently
to the harmony that exists in the world and ultimately in the individual:

> La humanidad es la síntesis armónica de la Naturaleza, y el Espíritu bajo la unidad
> absoluta de Dios.
> El hombre debe realizar en su lugar y esfera limitada la armonía de la vida universal
> y mostrar esta armonía en bella forma exterior. (*Ideal de la humanidad*, qtd. in Gómez
> Molleda 51)

This harmony is only possible if the traditional division between body and soul,
matter and spirit, object and subject is rejected and the early Krausists and later
Krausist-positivists address this issue directly. A quotation from Nicolás Salmerón
is representative of the monistic discourse:

> La dualidad radical de cuerpo y espíritu, la división de lo inconsciente y la
> conciencia, la abstracta separación de lo sensible y lo ideal, la contraposición *ex aequo*
> de objeto y sujeto son restos de la antigua escisión entre la realidad y el pensamiento
> que el espiritualismo subjetivo ha entronizado presuntuosamente y que el desco-
> nocimiento de la naturaleza o una superficial observación ha mantenido. (Prólogo to
> H. Giner, *Filosofía y arte* xxv)

The defense of monism comes to occupy a central position in liberal discourse as
one means of marking it off from traditional Catholicism. Thus, it continues to
serve as internally persuasive language even after Krausism *per se* has lost its hold
on moderate and leftist intellectuals. After Manuel de Revilla has openly distanced
himself from German idealism and embraced positivism, he attacks Krausism as
dualistic – and consequently aligned with conservative thought – in comparison
with positivistic monism. ("Revista crítica", 13: 1878, 373)

Catholic writers insistently refer to the dual nature of the individual, with a
marked separation between body and soul. Manuel Alonso Martínez attacks Krause
and his followers for ignoring the human body and human passions; Martínez
stresses that religion, with its mystery and its dogma, functions precisely to remind
human understanding of its limitation and its weakness ("Exposición y crítica" 37,
65). Martín Mateos argues that there is a clear tension between the body and the
soul which can only be explained by the idea of original sin. Furthermore, he states
that the soul is eminently superior to the body ("El catolicismo y la filosofía" 366).

Gómez Molleda points out the difference between the dualistic traditionalists and
the monistic Krausists with respect to the separation of body and soul (59–61). It is
worth noting that a similar difference exists regarding the view of life on earth and
life after death. In traditional Catholic thought, life on earth is constantly described
as "un valle de lágrimas", in which the individual must work and suffer in order to
gain heaven. While opposing fatalism, traditionalists make frequent reference to
"resignation". Nocedal specifically links religion and resignation when he laments
the loss of both: "Al obrero se le ha quitado el pensamiento de resignación cristiana
y el ideal espiritual" (qtd. in Vergés 62) and Martín Mateos expresses the same
idea:

Pero ese orgullo fomenta la insubordinación y la anarquía intelectual, y con esta, cuando llegan momentos críticos, como los presentes [1870], en los que se blasfema contra el trabajo, contra la desigualdad de condiciones, contra todos los que poseen, se conocen la necesidad de las creencias religiosas, absolutas e invariables. ("El catolicismo y la filosofía" 545)

Even the "moderate"[1] Juan Valera echoes the call for resignation and defends the "vale of tears" point of view, albeit with considerably more irony and less passion than his neo-Catholic contemporaries:

Morir tenemos: ya lo sabemos. Este mundo es un valle de lágrimas: en él hay más bocas que pan y más frío que capas, y muchísimo menos dinero del que se necesita. En él hay enfermedades, inundaciones y guerras. Y luego la muerte, como remate de todo. Burlarse de lo serio, melancólico y fúnebre no está bien. Malos hígados tiene quien se ríe de un entierro, pero también es vicio verlo todo negro y complacerse en pintarlo así y no resignarse ni conformarse con nada. (2: 629)

The political implications of the preceding statements are obvious; Christian resignation to human suffering precludes any activity in favor of political change. Valera's statement also has important literary resonances, in that he is here refuting Zola's naturalism. For the moment I will limit my comments to the philosophical and religious issues, leaving the political and literary for later. The publication of the *Syllabus* of 1864 with its condemnation of liberalism and rationalism accredits the traditional Spanish view and serves, along with the declaration of papal infallibility in 1870, to drive Spanish Krausists away from Catholicism (Elías Díaz, Prologue to *Minuta de un testamento* 77; Gomez Molleda 36–37). Gumersindo de Azcárate describes this process in his *Minuta de un testamento* (1876) and illustrates the profoundly religious character of the Spanish Krausists, who move away from Catholicism only after they become convinced that Rome is opposed to what they perceive as modern civilization (*Minuta* 157). For Azcárate and many of his liberal contemporaries, the Unitarian Church comes to embody the beliefs and values that they find lacking in the Spanish Catholic Church. Not surprisingly, the public embracement of a Protestant denomination is met by scandal in a country that had long defended Catholicism as the only true religion. Catholicism clearly continues to be an important authoritative voice and few dare to openly express their conversion to other faiths. Azcárate himself chooses to publish the *Minuta* anonymously, although many of his friends are well aware of his authorship. Fernando de Castro, Sanz del Río, Giner de los Ríos and others generally avoid an open confession of their anti-Catholic stance, unless absolutely compelled to do so. Typically, they stress their Christian faith and avoid a clarification of the non-Catholic nature of this Christianity. Liberal and moderate writers tend to downplay

---

[1] It is difficult to categorize Juan Valera's ideological position over the course of the century. In the 1860s, he espouses a liberal philosophy and aligns himself with Krausists in opposition to neo-Catholics. After the Revolution of 1868, he moves further to the right and over time adopts a moderate and even conservative viewpoint on most issues, although he always maintains his distance from the radically conservative Catholics.

their own heterodoxy and that of their ideological comrades. Palacio Valdés denies that Manuel Revilla is a skeptic, defining him instead as an embarrassed believer ("Manuel de la Revilla", 1877: 767). In a discussion of the novel in 1878, Palacio Valdés glosses over the division between Catholic and non-Catholic, characterizing it instead as a move from Jewish to Christian:

> En nuestra sociedad hay algo que muere, y eso que muere es el dios fulminante, colérico, vengador, el dios asiático que preparó las tragedias religiosas de la Edad Media, el dios que aún alienta el espíritu de intolerancia en las religiones positivas. Hay algo también que renace, y es el sentimiento cristiano, el genio del mártir divino, el espíritu de libertad, igualdad y fraternidad, tan desconocido y humillado por los que usurpan el nombre de cristianos. ("Benito Pérez Galdós" 337)

As late as 1889, Clarín writes that few Spanish authors dare to say openly that they are not Catholic. "Y aun muchos que en realidad no lo son, continúan llamándoselo, y no falta quien, con gran ingenio, está sacando mucho partido de esta doblez" (*Mezclilla* 48).

Clarín's comments illustrate the persistence of an authoritative Catholic voice but they also suggest the growing legitimacy of an open confession of non-Catholic beliefs. By the late 1880s, the Catholic claim to exclusive authority has been considerably weakened. In particular, Neo-Catholic discourse has been largely displaced and has moved from argumentative to demagogic. By the end of the nineteenth century, Neo-Catholic writers who continue to employ Neo-Catholic discourse are addressing a limited readership that is already in agreement with them. They have lost touch with the other voices that are competing for authority and are no longer in dialogue with them. In part, this occurs because the traditionalists perceive the various movements that oppose Catholicism as a single entity. Protestantism, Krausism, and later Positivism are collapsed into one. Nicolás del Alamo attacks Positivism in 1887 by equating it with rationalism, Descartes, Luther, and freethinking ("El positivismo" 208–10). Del Alamo's text distances itself from expository-argumentative discourse because it fails to recognize and thus incorporate, echo, and debate the multiple voices that compete with it for authoritative status. The Krausist movement is obviously not synonymous with Lutheranism or Cartesian Rationalism. Moreover, the existence of a unified Krausist movement is debatable. The belief in an orderly progression and the insistence on a rational questioning of all knowledge encouraged a proliferation of competing discourses. Writing in 1875, Canalejas insists that there is no longer any such thing as a Krausist school and he ties this to Sanz del Río's belief in individual reason:

> Recordemos también que entre los discípulos del ilustre D. Julián Sanz del Río se han declarado tendencias diversas y encontradas. – No hay ya escuela. – Van unos a un theismo racional y cristiano, propenden otros a un positivismo comedido y circunspecto; retroceden algunos, aguijoneados por la duda, a la Crítica de la razón pura de Kant, tomando puerto y sagrado en ella, y esta diversidad de direcciones es muy propia del solícito afán con que el doctor Sanz del Río procuraba despertar en toda inteligencia el sello característico, original e individualísimo, que acompaña al hombre. ("El panentismo" 361)

Subsequent to 1875, the increasing acceptance of positivism in its more extreme forms contributes to an even greater proliferation of voices opposing the neo-Catholic and Catholic. The move from Krausism to positivism is in some sense understandable, but in others, puzzling. A number of factors contribute to the Krausist evolution toward positivism: Krause and Sanz's emphasis on tolerance and on openness to new ideas (Medina 83), their belief in monism, and their faith in an orderly progression toward the ideal. In part as a response to the traditionalists' claims of authority and in part as a natural outgrowth of their own beliefs, Krausists and other moderate Spaniards place a great deal of emphasis on the idea of tolerance, particularly during the 1860s and 70s. With their stress on harmony and orderly progress, these writers attack intolerance as divisive (Revilla, "León Roch" 500) and, in an appropriation of the right's germanophobic rhetoric, "barbarous" (Revilla, "Revista crítica" 3: 1876, 377). Branding the neo-Catholics as fanatic, they seek to accredit their own "tolerant", and by extension, "civilized" position. The idea of tolerance fits in not only with Krausist philosophy but with the middle-class values of order and avoidance of conflict that characterize middle and late nineteenth-century Spanish society (Aranguren, *Moral y sociedad*). Consequently, "tolerant discourse" gradually succeeds in displacing neo-Catholic intransigence as authoritative and internally persuasive. The success of this process is illustrated by the attempt of the right to appropriate tolerance as a feature of its own discourse. Martín Mateus opens his study of Catholicism and German philosophy with a call for tolerance and charity ("El catolicismo y la filosofía") and Balmes dedicates two chapters in his study of Protestantism to a redefinition and justification of intolerance (4: 338ff).

The exaltation of tolerance in conjunction with faith in reason, in orderly progress, and in the individual's right and obligation to arrive at a personal understanding of truth contributes to the breakdown of a Krausist authoritative discourse and explains, in part, the evolution of liberal Spaniards towards positivism. Similarly, the rejection of a traditional dualistic separation of body and soul predisposes these writers to view with some favor the monistic positivistic subordination of the soul to the body. Salmerón's attack on dualism in his prologue to Hermenegildo Giner de los Ríos's *Filosofía y arte* illustrates the early steps in this passage:

> Que todo lo físico es al propio tiempo metafísico, según la profunda afirmación de Schopenhauer; que la evolución de lo inconsciente debe explicar la producción de la conciencia en el mundo, son los dos términos bajo los cuales se mueve toda la ciencia contemporánea, y cuya composición habrá de fundar la alianza definitiva de la especulación y la experiencia. (xxv)

Notwithstanding certain elements that work in favor of the acceptance of positivism, the transition from a philosophy that is unabashedly idealistic to one that largely denies all but physical, empirical data is difficult to reconcile, especially considering the brief period of time in which this transition took place. During the 1860s the primary assault on Krausism and other German philosophies came from the neo-Catholics, but by the middle and late 1870s, moderate, liberal, and more radical thinkers joined in the attack. Furthermore, this was not a question of a new generation with a new perspective; many of those who sought to distance themselves from German idealism had formerly espoused it. Francisco Giner de los Ríos, Azcárate, Salmerón and a good number of their disciples abandoned in varying degrees their earlier positions. The transformation is probably most dramatically and clearly illustrated by Manuel de la Revilla. In 1871 Revilla publishes a review of a book on art by Francisco Tubino and vehemently attacks his positivist and materialist tendencies:

> El señor Tubino es, como hemos dicho, positivista cuando menos (realista suele llamarse sin duda por eufemismo); aunque nosotros por materialista le tenemos. Profesa al "ontologismo" y a la metafísica el más encarnizado aborrecimiento, y no perdona ocasión de manifestarlo en la forma desdeñosa propia de la escuela; considera como la última de las abominaciones cuanto a idealismo se asemeje; cree que es el hombre "materia admirablemente dispuesta, dotada y organizada," cuyo fin será la nada, como espíritu y la circulación por un ameno paraiso de plantas y animales, como cuerpo; cuyo origen es una pareja de "antrópiscos" o de monos "antropomorfos," cuyos retoños tuvieron el capricho de andar en dos pies e inventar una porción de fruslerías que se llaman ciencia, arte, moral, religión, gobierno, civilización y progreso. ("El arte y los artistas" 627)

Revilla's strongly idealistic predilections reveal themselves in his analysis of Tubino's paradoxically non-positivist conception of art, with which Revilla is totally in agreement:

> Pero desgraciadamente para la doctrina del Sr. Tubino (y afortunadamente para él), su clara inteligencia, al ocuparse de arte, reniega de su origen cuadrumano, y en vez de reputar como la suma perfección artística la fiel imitación de la naturaleza (según los doctos cánones de los clásicos galo-latinos) afirma que "la facultad de idealizar es uno de los más preciosos atributos de nuestra naturaleza," a cuya confesión tan espontánea como peligrosa para su idea, añade estas palabras: "unid la más exquisita percepción sensible de la realidad al idealismo más extremado, y tendréis el verdadero genio que se agiganta en la inmensidad de la historia. El gran arte pictórico es la conjunción de estos dos elementos." Afirmación preciosa que suscribe todo metafísico espiritualista serio y reflexivo, y que no debe ser muy agradable para los pontífices de la escuela materialista. (628)

Revilla continues to reveal idealistic tendencies during the next few years, particularly in his discussions of art. But in a review essay published in 1876, he condemns Krausism harshly, advocating a more scientific approach. His text not only incorporates a terminology that echoes positivistic discourse but also appropriates the language and tone of Neo-Catholic writers (accusations of pantheism and of barbarous language) in a clear example of the heteroglot and dialogic character of the essay as it seeks to accredit itself in the face of its diverse readership:

> En cuanto al estudio de Leonhardi sobre la religión y la ciencia, parécenos un trabajo muy poco estimable, absolutamente extraño a todo verdadero carácter científico e impregnado de un misticismo empalagoso, muy propio de la escuela a que pertenece el autor y muy antipático a los verdaderos racionalistas como a los creyentes verdaderos. Todo trabajo de reconciliación entre la ciencia y la fe religiosa es imposible e ineficaz

. . . mientras la primera no renuncie a sus pretensiones teológicas y la segunda a sus intrusiones en el terreno de la ciencia pura. . . . pretender que ésta [la reconciliación] se verifique entre las religiones actuales y los sueños teosóficos de fichtianos o schellinianos, hegelianos o krausistas, dando un barniz cristiano a fórmulas panteistas o una interpretación panteista a los dogmas cristianos y convirtiendo la conciliación en una serie de mistificaciones inaceptables para los creyentes, es empresa vana e insensata que nunca alcanzará el éxito a que aspira. Y menos ha de lograrse semejante intento, adoptando para ello las empachosas fórmulas místicas de Krause, malamente amalgamadas con *un panteísmo vergonzante* y expuestas en *ininteligible y bárbaro lenguaje* (my emphasis) ("Revista crítica" 3: 1876, 505)

The shift from a rather passionate espousal of German idealism to the advocacy of positivism follows different rhythms according to the individual writer. Some continue to espouse the Krausist philosophy, as in the case of Canalejas and Hermenegildo Giner de los Ríos, while others maintain a respectful but increasingly distant posture with respect to Sanz del Río and his ideas, as exemplified by Francisco Giner de los Ríos and Gumersindo Azcárate. Still others, like Revilla, take on an oppositional stance and actively seek to discredit Krausism and other forms of German idealism. During the 1870s and 1880s these various voices coexist, competing with and echoing each other. Their interaction is further complicated by the fact that they develop at a slightly different pace in different areas. Philosophical idealism affects the vision of religion, law, education, human nature, art, and politics but shedding the idealistic outlook and language occurs more rapidly in the political and metaphysical arena than in the artistic. Furthermore, in many areas idealism leaves a residue which continues to affect the manner in which art, politics, human nature and other aspects of human activity are perceived and expressed. Thus, in addition to the echoes of other contemporary discourses, both allied and oppositional, that come into play in any given text, a discourse formerly utilized but now abandoned by a writer continues to resonate in his/her texts and to interact dialogically with the other voices that constitute his/her discourse.

I will explore this complex interaction in greater detail in subsequent chapters but before doing so, I would like to examine further the consequences of German idealism, particularly as it relates to the perception of art and its role in modern society. In some respects, the trajectory of literary theory in late nineteenth-century Spain parallels the shift from idealism to positivism already observed in the discussion of theology and philosophy. However, the positions taken by the conservatives and the liberals are, at specific points along the trajectory, in direct contrast to positions one might expect them to adopt and to positions that they do in fact adopt at other junctures. Moreover, there is no simple correlation between an individual's political stance and his or her view of art.

There are two separate issues involved in the aesthetic debates of the 70s: (1) the conflict between idealism and realism and (2) the legitimacy of *arte docente*. Studies of the debate rarely consider both issues and generally equate liberalism with realism and with opposition to *arte docente*. Traditional writers are depicted either explicitly or by default as idealists and proponents of didacticism. Furthermore, as I have already mentioned in the introductory chapter, the tendency to treat the 70s and the 80s as a single synchronic whole has contributed to misleading and overly simplistic conclusions. Pattison repeatedly ties liberals to naturalism and insists that the polemic surrounding the introduction of naturalism in Spain is but the second phase of the earlier philosophical and religious debates over freedom of conscience (28). Earlier he equates naturalism and liberalism and opposes them to idealism and traditionalism (20) and in another section he quotes Revilla when he states that naturalism is nothing more than the logical outgrowth of realism. The reader of *El naturalismo español* is left with the impression that the proponents of naturalism in the 80s are a somewhat more advanced version of the proponents of realism in the 70s when in fact, as Gifford Davis has shown, in the Ateneo debates of 1875, the vast majority of the participants are best described as "idealists" (1653), whether they are politically liberal, moderate, or conservative. As in the discussion of philosophical discourse, the curious evolution of the liberal position from staunch idealism to the espousal of naturalism has not been sufficiently noted. For his part, Davis focusses primarily on the *arte docente* versus art for art's sake aspect of the polemic and reduces this polemic to a political division between the left, who oppose *arte docente* and the right, who argue for it. As I will attempt to show in this section, this too is an overly simplified depiction of the situation. Neither Pattison nor Davis take into account the shifting of positions that takes place due to historical changes and to the dialogic interaction of the various discourses. In an effort to sort out the different strands that interweave in the debates of the 70s and 80s, I will trace their development and their interaction during this time period.

In the 60s and early 70s, the Krausist philosophy continues to strongly influence the liberal view of art and its role in human activity. This results in an aesthetic that is highly idealistic. Iris Zavala equates this period with realism (173) while other critics see it as a continuation of romanticism (Medina 29–35) but it is more useful to view it as a transitional discourse that moves away from romanticism towards realism without accepting many of the tenets of either. Krausism exalts art as a unifying and harmonizing force, which works in conjunction with science to organize the various aspects of human experience (López-Morillas 123). The firm belief in the gradual evolution of humanity towards an ideal state spills over into a conviction that art is gradually evolving towards new and more perfect forms. Through art, the ideal and the real, the abstract and the material are joined and a transfigured, more perfect and more expressive world is created (Krause in Tiberghien, 567–68). In contrast to Romanticism, Krausism rejects the cultivation of fantasy over reason, advocating a harmonious mix of reason, understanding, and fantasy (F. Giner, "El arte y los artes" 199). The Romantic exaltation of the individual is also condemned; the artist should strive for the universal, the ideal:

> Elevar el individuo a tipo, lo concreto a abstracto, lo particular a general mediante la belleza, es, con efecto, la realización del ideal artístico; expresar el carácter universal por medio de una forma determinada, pasando desde la representación individual a la representación ideal, es el fin del arte y la misión del verdaderamente inspirado por la sagrada llama del genio. (H. Giner, "Acerca de lo armónico" 309)

Non-Krausist followers of German idealism offer a very similar view of art. In a series of articles published in 1875 in *Revista Europea*, the Hegelian Emilio Nieto attacks the use of unrestrained fantasy but he also rejects realism, arguing for an art in which the real is the ideal, without losing its reality ("El realismo en el arte contemporáneo" 532). Nieto condemns the crudities of realism as do many other liberal writers, both Krausist and non-Krausist. The puritanical streak that runs through Krausism and Institutionism leads to the rejection of many classic "realistic" Spanish texts. Salvador Arpa associates the medieval writer Juan Ruiz, Arcipreste de Hita, with contemporary realists and condemns his *Libro de buen amor* as immoral. His judgement of the anonymous *Celestina* is identical (*Historia de la literatura española* 31,72). Hermenegildo Giner de los Ríos and Juan García al-Deguer echo similar sentiments in their *Curso de literatura española*. They praise Juan Ruiz as the best in his century but pass over him with no further analysis or description. Their discussion of *La Celestina* is somewhat more detailed, but they approve of the censorship of certain scenes that they deem obscene (57).

In both its rejection of realism and its puritanism, liberal aesthetics of the 60s and early 70s is indistinguishable from that proposed by the moderates and traditionalists. The tolerant but fervently Catholic writer José Moreno Nieto calls for a return to Christian ideals in contemporary art and defines the mission of art as expressing the ideal through the reconstruction of the "real" world in the light of virtue and exemplarity ("El ideal del arte" 25 Apr. 1875: 319). Valera, in his moderate and later more conservative stages, remains constant in his disdain for realism and naturalism. The neo-scholastic theory of Luis Taparelli, translated into Spanish and published in *Revista contemporánea* in 1878, repudiates the idealism of Victor Cousin and German idealists but remains nevertheless idealistic in orientation. Taparelli condemns realism and the incorporation of the vulgar or the ugly in art:

> Esta imitación no debe ser servil; porque no siendo todas las naturalezas bellas a los ojos del hombre, se necesita elección, deliberación, y la mera imitación podría darnos algo contrario a la verdadera belleza. (19: 310)

His later description of the work of art as an imitation of divine creation, while carefully avoiding any suggestion of pantheism, shares an idealistic orientation with his liberal opposition:

> . . . representar a otros nuestro pensamiento, no es más que transmitir a la ajena mente la forma que existe en la nuestra, en lo cual, como es palpable al lector, el arte puede, según este sentido, nombrarse imitadora de la creación, puesto que, al esforzarse en imprimir el propio pensamiento en la materia preexistente, imita al Creador eterno que estampó el suyo en la materia posible en el acto de reducirlo a la existencia.
>
> En efecto, ¿qué es el universo? Es, dice Santo Tomás, un libro inmenso, del cual son las criaturas otras tantas palabras que expresan un concepto de quien las escribió. ¿Qué es una obra de arte, un cuadro, un grupo, una estatua? Es un librito, una paginita, un palimpsesto, en que el artífice humano, sobre la escritura divina, escribió otro concepto que confía a la materia ya creada. (19: 145)

The moderate and traditionalist rejection of crudity continues throughout the 70s and 80s and leads these groups, like their liberal antagonists, to condemn the immorality and vulgarity of contemporary and traditional texts. It is in this vein that Alarcón assails Sancho Panza and his "vile prose" ("La moral en el arte" 234).

Traditionalists and liberals also concur in their gloomy assessments of the status of the arts in the 1860s. In large part, they all blame the mediocrity of Spanish letters on French cultural imperialism and, in particular, on the proliferation of the serial novel, both in the form of translations of French feuilletons and of native Spanish imitations. A comparison of the views of the liberal Francisco Giner de los Ríos and the reactionary Cándido Nocedal reveals a surprising similarity with respect to the serial novel, the present decadence of Spanish letters, and the perceived remedy. Nocedal's comments were given during his induction into the Royal Academy in 1860 and Giner's appear in "Consideraciones sobre el desarrollo de la literatura moderna", originally published in 1862. Both men lament the negative effects of French literary influence and both decry the popular serial novel as immoral, tasteless, and absurdly implausible:

> Poesías lúgubres, lamentaciones de fingidos desengaños, desatentadas sublevaciones contra Dios, el destino, la moral y el orden social, en nombre de falsos ideales; sarcásticas invectivas contra todos los sentimientos delicados, contra todas las más nobles tendencias; novelas sentimentales, o pseudo-históricas, plagadas de situaciones de relumbrón, de inverosímiles caracteres, de catástrofes inesperadas; dramas interminables, galerías de espectros y crímenes, en cuyos planes desconcertados se falta a un tiempo a los principios del arte y a las conveniencias de la civilización: tal es en su conjunto el fondo general de aquella literatura.

The preceding quote comes from the liberal Giner (*Estudios literarios* 230–31) and not, as might be expected, from the traditional Nocedal. Both writers stress the importance of verisimilitude as an antidote to the abuses of the serial novel, but Nocedal is somewhat more accepting of realistic portrayal than his liberal counterpart. Giner takes pains to distinguish his verisimilitude from that practised by the realists, whom he accuses of equating art with mere duplication or copy and of subordinating the spiritual activity of literary creation to nature (201). Nocedal incorporates the concept of verisimilitude into the very nature of the novel, which he describes as an invented story of cases which generally happen or are probable ("Discurso inaugural" 375). He further believes that the novel naturally reflects contemporary customs and social reality, utilizing terms and concepts later adopted by the proponents of naturalism: "No puede menos la novela de pagar tributo a las costumbres actuales, reflejando al propio tiempo la especial fisonomía de aquella sociedad a quien sirve de recreación y deleite." ("Discurso inaugural" 398). Nocedal's strong defense of verisimilitude provokes a response from Juan Valera, who argues for the incorporation of the extraordinary, the ideal, the bizarre and the avoidance of the commonplace in the novel (2: 191). At this point in his life, Valera espouses a liberal ideology, and although his opposition to realism remains firm throughout his literary career, here he voices an opinion shared by Krausist and non-Krausist liberal writers of the time and in this particular case, at variance with the views espoused by the extremely conservative Nocedal.

The area where Valera and Giner disagree significantly with Nocedal is the question of didacticism in literature. The subordination of invention to instruction characterizes medieval scholastic thinking and continues in nineteenth-century neo-scholasticism. Both in theory and in practice, neo-Catholic Spanish writers advocate *arte docente*, a strongly didactic literature associated with neo-scholastic philosophy. In a letter originally published in 1853, the conservative woman novelist Cecilia Böhl de Faber (Fernán Caballero) vigorously defends her moralizing novels and proudly confesses her ties to Juan Donoso Cortés, the Marqués de Valdegamas and defender of neo-scholastic thought:

> No es Fernán filósofo, señor, ni mucho menos sistemático, pues en la alta esfera en que bebe sus aspiraciones no hay sistemas, sólo hay luz y verdad. Pero si se empeña usted en darle calificación, que sea la de moralista religioso.
> Hay en otros países una clase de literatura amena, que se propone por objeto inocular buenas ideas en la juventud contemporánea; he echado menos una cosa análoga en nuestro país, y he querido, bien que mal, llenar este vacío. . . . Mi instintiva y natural tendencia es espiritualizar el sentir que las novelas modernas han materializado tan escandalosamente. Bajo este hermoso punto de vista admiro y simpatizo con el señor marqués de Valdegamas . . . (qtd. in *Ideología y política*)

Nocedal also advocates the inclusion of a moral lesson in the novel, although he clarifies that the novelist should avoid preaching and communicate the message through the opportune arrangement of the episodes and the story (388). Pedro de Alarcón's induction speech into the Royal Academy in 1877 stridently defends the existence of morality and moralizing in art and attacks those who advocate art for art's sake. Taparelli's neo-scholastic treatise argues for a moral, Christian art (19: 161) and claims for Catholic art the power to convert non-believers (19: 317).

The popular perception of a link between traditional politics and *arte docente* and of liberal ideology and "art for art's sake" is reflected in Galdós's novel, *Doña Perfecta*, where the staunchly conservative Catholic priest Inocencio accuses Pepe Rey of a cult of artistic form with a resultant disparagement of content (2: 432). However, both in Galdós's novel and in the literary debates that take place in mid-nineteenth century Spain, the association of liberal with art for art's sake is more typically an accusation proffered by the right than a reflection of reality. In opposition to the conservative advocacy of didacticism in art and in consonance with the view of art and of the individual espoused by Krausist idealism, moderate and liberal writers condemn *arte docente*. They do not, however, espouse a purely formalist art, the "art for art's sake" of which the writer Alarcón and the fictional character Inocencio accuse them. Writers influenced by the Krausist movement clearly see art as a vehicle for change but they eschew didacticism in literature for a variety of reasons. The belief in reason and in the capacity of the individual to arrive at truth through a rational examination of reality precludes a moralizing stance. Once intolerance is overcome with education and freedom, the individual will recognize the truth and will of his/her own accord progress towards the ideal:

> El arte nos regenera, purifica y engrandece, creando un mundo de aspiraciones en el alma; pero no alecciona, no enseña, no demuestra. Es un efecto mediato, no inmediato; estos efectos son resultados del contacto del espíritu humano con lo absoluto, y por su virtud asciende el hombre algunos peldaños más en la escala de perfección. (Canalejas, *La poesía moderna* 131)

The belief in the transformative effects of art, in the gradual evolution to an ideal and the exaltation of the role of art in the advancement toward the ideal clearly distances Krausism from a purely formalist aesthetic. Francisco Giner laments in 1876 that the art of his time is a mere secondary adornment, a useless pastime (*Estudios* 198). Salvador Arpa repeats the same idea and reveals the underlying link between the liberal opposition to Romanticism and Romantic individualism with the belief that art should play a serious role in the formation of the reader: "el que sólo se revuelve en la movible región de lo individual y particular que le rodea, apenas si puede aspirar a más que a entretener la frívola curiosidad de sus lectores." (*Principios* 182). This will to influence society increases over time and conflicts with the rationalist and idealist origins of Spanish Krausism. It represents an internal contradiction within Krausist and non-Krausist idealism that is resolved in a variety of ways by different writers, in dialogue with themselves, with each other, and with their conservative opposition. Over the course of the 70s there is a shift away from idealism among liberal and leftist writers and at certain moments they move towards positions which are identical to those advocated by writers who are their ideological antagonists. The complex shifting and crossing of positions and their dialogical relationship must be kept in mind in analyzing the various literary polemics of the 70s and 80s.

I mentioned earlier that the initial repudiation of *arte docente* on the part of the left relates to their faith in the power of reason. Additional contributing factors can be located in their recognition of the authoritative stature of Catholic didactic discourse, which they seek to undermine, and their tendency to foreground tolerance over direct confrontation. Leftist writers work to undermine the authority of conservative literary theory not so much by entering into debate with it as by describing it as limited, narrow, sectarian, calling on the same internally persuasive discourse that operates in the philosophical and theological debates. Ricardo Blanco Asenjo avoids any direct mention of *arte docente* in his 1873 study of realism and idealism but he successfully invalidates it by presenting certain "catch words" of the left as invested with indisputable authority. Words such as "modern", "impartial", "moderation", "progress toward truth", "reasonable and beneficial teaching" are played against "frivolous", "the spirit of the sect", "the perturbing passion that causes only confusion and differences" in a continued assault on intolerance and traditional intransigence (386–91). As liberal discourse acquires greater authority, the attacks on didactic literature are both more direct and more frequent. In the mid 1870s, several writers speak out against *arte docente* and seek to discredit it precisely because of its association with traditional religious discourse. Canalejas refers to *arte docente* as "arte por la iglesia" (*Poesía moderna* 167), thus foregrounding the conflict which previous writers had generally played down. Luis Vidart's attack in 1877 utilizes a language and a tone that reflect a more confident and belligerent attitude:

> El arte, esclavo de la religión: he aquí el sueño de los ultramontanos y para conseguir este resultado, se comienza pidiendo que el arte tenga por fin último la manifestación de la ley moral, después se dice que no hay más moral que aquella que reconoce como fundamento la verdad religiosa, que el dogma revelado; y de consecuencia en consecuencia, o mejor dicho, de absurdo en absurdo, se llega a

sostener que el dogma de la religión es el criterio infalible para juzgar de las creaciones artísticas. (''El arte por la belleza'')

It is this quotation that prompts Gifford Davis to assert that ''the real clash in this polemic had come to be between liberal and ultramontane'' (1655). However, it is precisely at this moment that the liberal point of view reveals the fissures and contradictions that its own evolution in interaction with the cultural ambience and other discourses has brought about. The gradual displacement of traditional authoritative discourse, as well as the liberal and leftist belief in the transformative power of art, leads some progressive writers to an increasing didacticism in art as a means of hastening the demise of traditional authority. Davis is correct in identifying José de Navarrete as a defender of didacticism in art, but he fails to point out that Navarrete is not advocating the *arte docente* of the traditionalists; to the contrary, he is quite radically anti-Catholic in his speech before the Ateneo. As reported in the *Revista Europea*, he responds with considerable energy to Moreno Nieto's discourse and seeks to discredit him by comparing his definition of the Christian ideal with that proposed by an ignorant village priest. He further accuses Moreno Nieto of a very narrow Catholicism, akin to that developed in the *Syllabus*. Navarrete wants an art that is in touch with contemporary problems and that will spread democratic ideals to the reader/public:

> Atribuyó el Sr. Navarrete a los oscurantistas gran empeño en negarle al teatro la grandiosa importancia que en su concepto tiene, porque saben que si desde la tribuna se difunde por las inteligencias la luz de la democracia, mucho más honda impresión han de producir estas ideas cuando se revelen en hechos, levantándose en cada pueblo un templo del arte dramático, en el que cual se vean, con los ojos de la cara, los talleres donde forjan sus planes liberticidas los explotadores del humano linaje . . . (''El ideal en el arte'' 76)

Significantly, at the same time that Navarrete is calling for a didacticism that will confront the traditional, conservative message communicated in *arte docente*, Galdós is publishing his thesis novels, which deal with the religious question from a liberal point of view. The association of traditionalism/*arte docente* and liberalism/ art for art's sake is clearly untenable in the face of the shifting attitude of the progressives towards the end of the 70s. Writers of the time are aware of the changing views on didacticism in art and seek to clarify the contradictions and the overlapping points of view of the right and the left. Liberal writers labor to disassociate progressive didacticism from traditional *arte docente* and to reconcile this new didacticism with their previous opposition.

An analysis of the reviews of Galdós's ''thesis novels'' is instructive in this respect. Francisco Giner de los Ríos remains firmly opposed to didacticism in art and criticizes *La familia de León Roch* for sacrificing the work to the ideological goal, although he consistently praises various aspects of Galdós's narratives (*Ensayos* 67). Leopoldo Alas (Clarín) also combats *arte docente*, which he claims is destructive of art in his review of the conservative Pereda's *El buey suelto* (*Solos* 205–06). However, he defends the incorporation of philosophy in the novel of his day as a means of communicating abstract and difficult ideas to a readership which would otherwise remain uninformed or uncomprehending. In his review of Galdós's *Gloria*, Alas reveals both a new tolerance for didacticism in art and a clear awareness of the growing authority of liberal over traditional discourse. He discusses three examples of the "novela tendenciosa": Alarcón's *El escándalo*, Valera's *Pepita Jiménez*, and Galdós's *Gloria*. All deal with the religious-moral issue and all are artistically meritorious, in Clarín's opinion. However, he dismisses *El escándalo* as being outdated, "the solution of the past", and *Pepita Jiménez* as not really addressing the religious question directly. Alas criticizes a lack of clarity in the latter's discussion of the religious problem and laments the imprecise impact that it leaves on the reader with its excessive use of reservation and circumlocution. On the other hand, he has nothing but praise for Galdós, whom he sees as confronting the religious-moral problem head-on and leading the battle against the traditional and now out-moded Catholic solutions:

> ' Pero sí nos es lícito, y hasta obligado, celebrar la aparición de otro escritor de no inferiores vuelos, que sabe y quiere sin ambajes [sic], perífrasis ni pretericiones colocarse en nuestro campo enfrente del enemigo, peleando por una bandera conocida y desplegada a todos los vientos: este escritor es el inspirado autor de *Gloria*. ("Gloria" 209)

In conjunction with this praise for Galdós's polemical and didactic stance, Alas struggles to distance the novelist from the traditional moralistic writers who sacrifice the coherence and reality of the literary work to a preconceived idea. His defense of *La familia de León Roch* incorporates a variety of discourses and echoes of discourses which come together in a not entirely harmonious confluence: a disassociation of the tendentious novel from cheap propaganda, and by extension, the inferior works of *arte docente*; a defense of the realism of Galdós's work; a linking of this realism with aesthetic idealism and the priority of beauty over all other artistic effects; and then a return to the justification of the didactic character of the text. These conflicting voices are all evident in the following paragraph:

> Las novelas contemporáneas del Sr. Pérez Galdós son tendenciosas, sí, pero *no se plantea en ellas tal o cual problema social*, como suele decir la gacetilla, sino que como son copia artística de la realidad, es decir, copia hecha con reflexión, no de pedazos inconexos, sino de relaciones que abarcan una finalidad, sin lo cual no serían bellas, encierran profunda enseñanza, ni más ni menos, como la realidad misma que también la encierra, para el que sabe ver, para el que encuentra la relación de finalidad y otras de razón entre los sucesos y los sucesos, los objetos y los objetos. (*Solos* 181)

Manuel de la Revilla undergoes a similar transformation, moving from a stalwart rejection of *arte docente* in his 1877 "La tendencia docente en la literatura contemporánea" to a moderate defense of it in his article on Galdós in 1878 to a full acceptance in his 1879 review of *La familia de León Roch*. In making his transition, Revilla gradually drops the use of the words *arte docente*, undoubtedly because of their traditional connotations and because of his own previous disapproval, and adopts the term "arte trascendental". In the 1877 essay he uses both expressions interchangeably, but *arte docente* is by far the most frequent. In the 1878 study of Galdós, Revilla begins to establish a distinction between the two terms:

Sin sacrificar jamás la forma a la idea ni caer en los extravíos del arte docente, en todas ellas [novelas] ha sabido encerrar su autor un pensamiento filosófico, moral o político, de tanta profundidad como trascendencia. ("Don Benito Pérez Galdós" 123)

The review of *La familia de León Roch* does not contain a single mention of *arte docente* although it makes oblique allusions to the old debate between art for art's sake and moralistic art in the closing argument:

Presentar a los ojos de la humanidad el espectáculo de la belleza, es sin duda empresa meritoria; pero ¡cuánto más grande es llevar una piedra al magnífico edificio del progreso y contribuir al glorioso triunfo de la verdad y del bien! (510)

Earlier in the text, he praises the novel both for its artistic qualities and for the "transcendencia del pensamiento" (507). The change in Revilla's attitude is not shared by all liberal writers, as evidenced by the mocking comments it provokes in the young Palacio Valdés in *Revista Europea* in 1879. In refuting Revilla's "conversion", Palacio Valdés points out the rather surprising shift in Revilla's position:

En este momento llega a mi noticia que el Sr. Revilla no es el inventor del arte docente. Aún más, que el Sr. Revilla lo ha combatido personalmente con gran encarnizamiento hace muy pocos años. ("Manuel de la Revilla", 1879: 638)

In contrast to the view held by many critics and fostered by nineteenth-century conservatives, liberal and progressive opposition to *arte docente* never implied support of art for art's sake. The early Krausist belief in the transformative power of art evolved rather quickly among certain writers to a moderate and then more vigorous support of didacticism in literature. A similar fragmentation of the supposed homogeneity among liberal writers is evident in their attitude towards realism. On this issue, traditional writers also display a noticeable lack of uniformity. I pointed out previously that in the early 60s, the conservative Cándido Nocedal emphasizes verisimilitude in the novel and theater as a means of combatting the influence of the serial novel and late Romantic excess. In the 1875 Ateneo discussion of realism and idealism, the *Revista Europea* publishes a summary of the intervention of a certain Mr. Rayón, whom Gifford Davis has tentatively identified as Damián Menéndez Rayón, an archivist for the Department of the Treasury (1652). Rayón's participation is reported on two separate dates, the 27th of March and the 3rd of April. On the first occasion, Rayón defends a moderate form of realism, as when used in combination with idealism, and insists that the great Spanish artists such as Lope de Vega, Tirso de Molina, Velázquez and Cervantes have always maintained a balance of the two:

. . . el realismo en el teatro no es ventaja ni inconveniente, mientras se contiene en los justos límites, como han hecho y realizado los grandes artistas; pero que, fuera de ellos, puede llegar a ser una aberración, una monstruosidad. ("El realismo en el arte dramático" 58: 197)

While Rayón's political outlook is not apparent in the summary of the March 27 debates, in that of April 3 it is much more obvious. Rayón asks for the floor to respond to Luis Vidart and Manuel de la Revilla, both allied at that time with liberalism and Krausism. In his speech, Rayón denies Vidart and Revilla's assertion of the superiority of the nineteenth century and decries the rationalist destruction of traditional ideals. In an increasingly emotional appeal, he insists that only Rome has the moral force to restrain modern materialism ("El realismo en el arte dramático" 50: 274). This combination of a traditionalist political credo and an acceptance, albeit moderate, of realism arises in part as a dialogic response to the liberal espousal of an idealistic aesthetic. In opposition to Vidart and Revilla, who defend foreign and contemporary ideas and values, Rayón – and before him, Nocedal – evoke the realism espoused by Cervantes, Velázquez, and other canonical Spanish writers. Other conservative writers distance themselves from realism, emphasizing its crudity and voicing a preference for literary idealism, as illustrated earlier in the cases of Alarcón and Taparrelli. Over the next decade, the promotion of realism, and then naturalism, will gradually pass to the left while the right will adopt an increasingly antagonistic position. Within each group, however, residual voices and echoes of previously enunciated viewpoints will continue to resonate and evolve in dialogic interaction within and between members of diverse political alliances. As in the discussion of *arte docente*, the shifting of alliances often results in a curious similarity of argument in ideologically opposed individuals.

An early call for realism in literature from a progressive writer comes in 1874 from Francisco Pi y Margall, a leader of the Spanish Democrats and a former president of the First Republic. While his more moderate liberal colleagues continue to espouse a highly idealistic aesthetic, Pi y Margall advocates an art that reflects the doubts, disillusions, and problems of contemporary society and will awaken the reader to the urgency of these issues:

> He aquí por qué condenamos la marcha actual de la pintura, la escultura, la arquitectura, la poesía: he aquí por qué hace veinte años venimos esforzándonos en reconciliarlas con nuestro siglo. No rechazamos en ellas el idealismo, pero queremos el idealismo hoy posible; no queremos que, por aspirar a un idealismo, hoy quimérico, pierdan su espontaneidad y carácter. Todo lo real es ideal: queremos, no que el arte prescinda de lo real para llegar al idealismo, sino que vaya y llegue al idealismo por medio de la realidad, que más directamente pueda conmover los espíritus y agitar los corazones. ("Del arte y su decadencia" 449)

The emphasis on an art that reflects contemporary reality is closely linked with the desire to effect change in the reader and in the 1870s, Krausist writers echo Pi y Margall's call for relevancy in art with increasing frequency. In Salvador Arpa's *Principios de la literature general* (1874), he combines a strongly idealistic aesthetic with the exhortation that the author always draw his materials from the present and depict protagonists with which the public can identify (289–90). Early in his writing (1863), Francisco Giner de los Ríos defines art as the natural manifestation of the society in which it is created and rejects Romanticism and other artistic movements which emerge from a nostalgia for the past or a cult of the future (*Estudios* 122). In an article on the state of the Spanish theater published in 1870, Giner reaffirms his view of the necessary contemporaneity of good art and goes on to urge the incorporation of pressing social issues in literature:

El artista que así comprenda sus deberes procurará, en cuanto al fondo de sus obras, tomar sus asuntos de algún grave problema, algún interés real y humano, digno de preocupar su espíritu y el de la sociedad. (15: 338)

Many of the writers of the period express a strong conviction that the genre most adequate to exert an influence on the reader is the novel. Revilla acclaims Galdós as the originator of the modern Spanish novel and praises his realistic portrayal of contemporary society. In defining the modern novel, Revilla stresses that it is a portrait of contemporary society, a masterly depiction of the characters, an astonishingly truthful representation of life ("Don Benito Pérez Galdós" 118). Urbano González Serrano continues to echo these sentiments into the 1880s and although he rejects the crudities and the determinism of naturalism, he applauds Zola and the movement in so far as they fulfill the requirement of a realistic portrayal of society and of the moral standards that govern social relations:

El único dato positivo, aportado por el naturalismo al progreso del arte, y que quedará como verdad rejuvenecida y vigorizada por él para la literatura universal, es el dato exactísimo, innegable, de que el poeta ha de moverse en el medio social y tomar el pulso a la atmósfera moral que le circunda. (*Cuestiones contemporáneas* 160)

González Serrano's medical terminology and the general thrust of his message are strikingly similar to Cándido Nocedal's earlier defense of the novel as a reflection of the physiognomy of contemporary society designed to entertain and instruct ("Discurso inaugural" 398). There is obviously no need to take the pulse of the moral atmosphere if there is no intent to influence or transform the social and moral attitudes of the reading public. In much liberal discourse in the late 1870s and early 1880s, advocacy of an art that influences human behavior is increasingly evident and the novel is uniformly seen as the genre which best realizes this goal.

González Serrano and other liberals who write on the subject of art and its purposes in the late 70s and early 80s reveal a dramatic shift in attitude as compared to the late 60s and early 70s. The change is evident in the use of the term "idealism" itself. In the 1860s and early 1870s, "idea" and "ideal" are exalted as the primary aim of art in opposition to the "real" and the "individual" (Arpa, *Principios* 182). Francisco Giner rejects both romanticism and realism in art and proposes literary idealism as the antidote. He praises Plato as the initiator of the true concept of art, in which the ideal and the real are joined through the purification of the form (*Estudios de literatura y arte* 199). By the later 1870s and early 1880s, idealism is being used not as an antonym but a synonym for Romanticism. In an 1879 review, Manuel de la Revilla speaks of the literary debates between the proponents of the new French realism and the idealistic, Romantic, or national school, remarking sarcastically that in the interests of greater clarity it is known by all of these names (*Críticas* 12). In the mid-1880s, Altamira writes that there is no consensus on how to describe the school that opposes realism, with some preferring romanticism and others idealism ("El realismo y la literatura contemporánea" 24 Apr. 1886: 262). Literary idealism is now seen as antiquated and discredited, equivalent in value to the moribund Romantic school.

It is imperative to remember that the liberal acceptance of realism in the 80s is preceded in many liberal writers by a strongly idealistic and anti-realistic stance in previous years, although some progressives begin to distance themselves from an idealistic aesthetic and even coincide with very traditional writers in their consideration of the purposes of art. A similar transformation occurs regarding the question of didacticism in art. Not all writers follow the same trajectory and many of them evolve according to different rhythms, urged on by the competing voices that enter into dialogue with the right and more and more frequently, within the left itself. Consequently, the transition from the 70s to the 80s is considerably more troublesome than previous studies have indicated and the difference between the right and the left is not nearly as clear cut as many critics have asserted. The literary debates of this period reveal a number of curious swerves, inversions, and subversions that need to be recognized. The move from idealism to realism among liberal writers and the early acceptance of some forms of realism by some conservative writers, followed by the absolute rejection of naturalism, are indicative of the complex weaving and crossing of voices and discourses that come into play at this time in Spanish history. In this chapter I have traced this evolution and attempted to explain some of the forces that contribute to the transposition of traditional and progressive writers in relation to specific issues. The shifting and swerving remains, however, perplexing and is compounded by a sudden and, in many ways, unexpected brake/break in the evolution of moderate and liberal thinkers. Having effected the move from idealism to realism, the rather tepid acceptance of naturalism is somewhat surprising. In comparison with the differences between philosophical and aesthetic idealism, those that distinguish realism and naturalism are relatively minor and the transition from realism to naturalism would appear to be less conflictive than the transition from idealism to realism. In Spain, however, as critic after critic has confirmed, the critical (and many would say, practical) reception of naturalism by liberal writers is fraught with disclaimers. There are many causes for this qualified and often wary endorsement of naturalism, not the least of which is the continuing echo of the previously espoused idealism. Other significant contributing factors can be found, however, not in the voices and echoes of the voices that resonate through the various discourses, but in specific silences and in the paradoxical echoes that they produce, a subject which I will consider in Chapter 3.

III

SILENCES AND ECHOES

As already indicated in the Introduction, critical studies of naturalism and its reception in Spain generally avoid or sidestep a discussion of political issues. This silencing of political factors relates in part to the predominance of New Critical and formalist views of literature during the first half of the twentieth century, when many of these studies were written. In a period when texts were perceived as autonomous objects of study and literature was deliberately cut off from its context, little or no attention was paid to the political and social implications and causes of naturalism. This omission was also encouraged by the fact that the debates and texts produced during the discussion of naturalism in the 1870s and 80s similarly suppressed the mention of social and political factors. Proponents of naturalism in nineteenth-century Spain continually stress that they are endorsing only the literary component of the movement. Rafael Altamira insists repeatedly that non-literary considerations should not come into play in discussions of Zola and his novels ("El realismo y la literatura" 15 May: 312–15). In a series of exchanges with Luis Alfonso in *La época*, Emilia Pardo Bazán defends her participation in the debates over naturalism by pointing out that even though it does not have political implications, there is a great deal of public interest in the polemic ("Carta magna" 6 May, 1884). In the opening paragraphs of *La cuestión palpitante*, Pardo Bazán reiterates this same idea and attributes some of the interest to the moral scandal that naturalism has provoked. Her own declared intent is to return to a purely literary focus and an impartial analysis of this most recent literary phenomenon (3: 577). An article by "Orlando" in *Revista de España* accepts as logical the prevalence of the naturalistic novel and the victory of science over idealism but also emphasizes that first and foremost writers should strive to create works of art. In passing, Orlando mentions that it is erroneous to believe that the novel can contribute to a nation's progress (606–07).

Orlando's comments are significant in that they echo, although faintly and almost unidentifiably, Zola's repeated references to the political and social goals of the naturalistic novel. In "Le roman expérimental" (1879), Zola clarifies that the novelist is both the observer, who collects data, and the experimentalist who interprets, produces and directs (*OC* 46: 18). Like the medical doctor, the naturalistic novelist seeks to understand the causes in order to effect the cure. Although Zola concedes that a great deal still remains unknown, ultimately the experimental novelist will be able to take the human machine apart and then reconstruct and transform it:

C'est ainsi que nous faisons de la sociologie practique et que notre besogne aide aux sciences politiques et économiques. Je ne sais pas, je le répète, de travail plus noble ni d'une application plus large. Etre maître du bien et du mal, régler la vie, régler la société, résoudre à la longue tous les problèmes du socialisme . . . (*OC* 46: 28–29)

In the light of the baldly political and social aims of Zola's literary manifesto, the repeated exclusion of non-literary considerations among Spanish proponents of naturalism is surprising. It is perhaps understandable that Spanish writers would seek to tone down Zola's radicalism but the insistence on the purely literary aspects of naturalism is a rather extreme response. The silencing of any political or social motivation is all the more perplexing in view of the gradual acceptance of the "transcendental" novel and of the polemical treatment of contemporary social problems by liberal writers of the period. Zola provides a theory and a practice that enable a progressively inspired narrative and yet, for the most part, Spanish progressive writers either reject naturalism or argue for its adoption in a muted and strictly literary sense. The rejection of naturalism can not be explained simply by the influence of Catholicism, as certain critics would have it, in that liberal and progressive Spaniards have been evolving away from the Church since the 1860s. Although specific voices and discourses already analyzed in the preceding chapters, notably philosophical and literary idealism and its residue, contribute in some fashion to brake the liberal evolution toward positivism and naturalism, the increasingly strident repudiation of idealism and the growing acceptance of realism and the transcendental novel would suggest a more open acceptance of Zola, his theory and his novelistic practice. A better understanding of the factors behind the resistance to naturalism and Zola can only be attained by examining extra-literary factors, and in particular the insistent silencing of political issues by those involved in the critical reception of naturalism. In line with Pierre Macherey's theory of literary production, this silence leads us to the work's unconscious (94) and points to a significant contradiction in the Spanish critical reception of naturalism. In a paradoxical extension of Bakhtin's theory of language, the silence is perceptible through the echoes and resonances that it produces in the dialogic interplay of the various texts and discourses. In order to better identify this particular discourse, I will retrace briefly the political history of Spain from the early 1860s, emphasizing specific events which are relevant to this study. In particular, I will focus on cantonalism, a movement whose profound effects on late nineteenth-century Spanish culture have been largely ignored by all but a handful of historians.

The years preceding the Revolution of 1868 are characterized by diverse competing political ideologies[1]. The older political parties – the Carlists, Moderates, and Progressives – persist alongside newly-formed groupings such as the pragmatic, middle of the road Liberal Union, and the Democrats, who are themselves split between monarchists, federalist republicans, and nonfederalists. With the fall of Isabel II in 1868, the competition for power among the different groups continues and intensifies. A coalition of monarchists composed of

[1] My principal sources for this section are Carr, Gil Cremades, Hennessy, and Fernández Almagro.

Unionists, Progressives, and Democrats drafts the Constitution of 1869 and names
Amadeo of Savoy as king. Radical Democrats and Republicans, as well as Carlists
and monarchists loyal to Isabel II or her son Alfonso resist Amadeo but, according
to most historians, it is the internecine feuding of those who had drawn up the
Constitution of 1869 that precipitates his abdication. The Republicans, equally
divided between Federalists and Radicals, who want a unitary republic, are called
on to form a government. In an effort to calm the fears of moderate and
conservative parties, Republican leaders defer on the issue of federalism, thus
weakening much of their popular support. Furthermore, the Republican opposition
to military conscription and the increasingly democratic rhetoric lead to a decline in
military discipline (Carr 330–31). The rapid succession of governments and the
internal division of the various political parties is compounded by the existence of
the Carlist threat to the north. The declaration of the Republic in 1873 prompts
renewed Carlist military action, which the weakened army and divided government
are unable to control:

> By 1874 Carlism was at its most powerful in terms of occupied territory. There was
> an organized Carlist state in the north with its own administration, postal system,
> electric telegraph, and newspapers. The capture of Eibar had given it a small arms
> factory and its agents abroad were buying surplus French arms and greatcoats to equip
> an army of 20,000 men, paid by levies on the countryside, customs duties, and
> payments by the railway companies whose lines went through Carlist territory. (Carr
> 339)

At the same time, in the south and along the southern Mediterranean coast of
Levante, a number of local governments surface and declare independent republics.
Valencia, Málaga, Sevilla, Cádiz, Almansa, Granada, Castellón, Avila, Salamanca, Bailén, Algeciras, among others, declare themselves independent cantons.
Although many of the cantons are orderly and reflect a middle-class regional spirit,
others are more violent[2]. The Cartagena canton demands money and foods from
nearby communities and engages in military combat with those towns that do not
contribute. In Alcoy, the mayor is assassinated, homes of those considered
reactionary are burned, some fifteen people die, and the rioters parade through the
streets with the remains of their victims. A declaration promulgated by local leaders
calls for total social revolution:

> . . . el deber de cada uno y de todos los trabajadores consiste en marchar siempre
> adelante, sin detenerse en el camino de la revolución, y pasando por encima de todos
> los obstáculos que nos opongan los individuos que en los más supremos instantes de la
> vida de los pueblos, en las grandes crisis de la organización social presente, sólo
> pronuncian la palabra "orden", que en su boca no significa otra cosa que la
> continuación del agiotaje inmoral, causa de la esclavitud, de la miseria y de la
> ignorancia que pesa sobre la clase obrera. (Gascón Pelegri 224)

---

[2] I have relied on Gascón Pelegri, Hennessy, López-Cordón, Medioni, Puig Campillo and
others for this section.

This same document calls for the triumph of anarchism and collectivism and the creation of a world in which there will be no popes, kings, bourgeoisie, priests, soldiers, lawyers, judges, clerks, or politicians (Gascón Pelegri 225–26).

Historical and literary studies of the nineteenth century in Spain place great emphasis on the Revolution of 1868 and its relation to the political and literary figures of the period. In contrast, much less mention is made of cantonalism and its impact. Although the cantonalist movement was a brief interlude, lasting from as little as a few days to six months – in the case of Cartagena – its effects on Spaniards of all political persuasions was profound and long-lasting. It marks a watershed in nineteenth-century evolution and greatly complicates the ongoing dialogue between the conservatives and the liberals and within the liberals and progressives. With cantonalism, a new voice and a new discourse enter into competition for authoritative status and force a realignment of the other voices and discourses. The anarchist call for radical social and political change had existed in isolated pockets but with the cantonalist movement, it gains national attention. The introduction of the anarchist voice adds new intricacy to the ongoing debates between the left and the right and radically changes the configuration of the various political groupings as well as the nature of their dialogue.

Historians debate the extent of the Anarchist International Association of Workers' intervention in Alcoy and in the cantonalist movement in general and it may well be that there is little or limited anarchist influence. Whatever the historical reality, the local perception at the time of the events insistently identified cantonalism with anarchism and the International. Engels accused the Bakhunists of backing the cantons and thus contributing to the eventual failure of the Republic and the triumph of the reactionaries (Jutglar 282). In the parliamentary debates of the day, the terms "cantonalist" and "internationalist" were frequently used interchangeably (Jutglar 285–86). Not surprisingly, the Spanish right and center responded to cantonalism with great uneasiness. The establishment of the Republic was in and of itself enough cause for alarm and the Cantons, with the specter of the International in the background, created a hysterical reaction. The memory of the recent Paris Commune only increased fears of widespread revolution. "Commune", "Canton", and "International" enter conservative rhetoric in the years that follow in association with the discredited Revolution of 1868 and the First Republic. In arguing for *arte docente*, Alarcón equates the separation of Art, Morality, and Science with "cantonalismo cerebral" (227) and later goes on to link those who defend art for art's sake with the International:

> . . . sabréis que la teoría de *el arte por el arte* está hoy relacionada con otras a cual más temible, y que juntas socavan y remueven los cimientos de la sociedad humana. Comenzóse por pedir una Moral independiente de la Religión: pidióse luego una Ciencia independiente de la Moral: en voz baja empieza ya a exigirse que independiente de la Moral sea también el Derecho, y a grito herido reclaman los *Internacionalistas*, dejándose de contemplaciones y yendo derechos al bulto, que se declaren asimismo independientes de la Moral las tres entidades sociales; el Estado, la Familia, el Individuo. ("La moral en el arte" 236)

In his discussion of the political events of the early 1870s, Menéndez Pelayo writes that the socialist revolution was roaring at Spain's doors, proclaimed by the one hundred mouths of the International Association of Workers (*Historia de los heterodoxos* 772).

Progressive politicians and writers generally respond to the conservative reaction with silence. With the downfall of the Republic in 1873 and the restoration of the Bourbon Alfonso XII, state and self-imposed censorship certainly effect a suppression of political debate, but an additional contributing factor is the political disillusionment of many leftist intellectuals that is brought on by the cantonalist movement and their concerns regarding the breakdown of central authority during the First Republic. Vicens Vives has described how many military leaders move to a more conservative stance in response to the democratic character of the revolution of 1868 and the republican and federalist beliefs of many of the rank and file (qtd. in Jutglar 200–04). Carr notes that the cantonalist revolt causes a decided shift to the right in the Republican leadership (334–35) and Jover observes that collective Spanish memory during the entire Restoration equates federalism with disorder, socialism, separatism, and atheism ("La imagen" 34). A similar process can be observed in the vast majority of intellectual and literary figures of the period. Intellectuals who had been or continue to be closely tied to Krausism or the Institución Libre de Enseñanza are especially driven to disassociate themselves from the violence that erupts after the Revolution and during the Republic because their whole philosophy is based on moderation and evolutionary change and also because so many Krausists and Institutionists played major roles in Amadeo's government and in the First Republic. Segismundo Moret, an early disciple of Sanz del Río and collaborator in the founding of the ILE, served as Minister of Finance under Amadeo; Francisco Canalejas was an active participant in the Republican Parliament; Emilio Castelar, an early Krausist who later evolves toward Hegelianism, was one of the presidents of the Republic as was Nicolás Salmerón; and Gumersindo de Azcárate served in Salmerón's government, as Minister of Justice (Gómez Molleda 183–89). During the parliamentary debates concerning the status of the International in Spain, Salmerón defended their right to exist and was the only speaker to earn the approval of the Internationalists (Vergés Mundó 70). While it is true, as Gil Cremades argues, that Krausism is essentially antirevolutionary, the political activity of many Krausists and Institutionists during the early 70s, in conjunction with the hysteria brought on by cantonalism, lead many observers to equate Krausism/Institutionism with radical politics. In response to these charges and to the political events themselves, the discourse of the Krausists and other liberals takes a new direction. The faith in idealism is profoundly shaken in the light of the violence and the upheaval that liberal and Krausist policies set into play. In his study of the relationship between Krausism and the Revolution of 1868, Gil Cremades correctly points out the liberal recognition of the failure of idealism. "Los apóstoles de la concordia, la reforma y la armonía se veían superados por la guerra civil, la revolución y el cisma. Una venganza de la praxis sobre la teoría (115)."

The political events of the early 1870s greatly accelerate the fragmentation of Krausism and contribute in large part to the curious swerve away from idealism that I have traced in the preceding chapters. Revilla's harsh repudiation of Krausism and

its leading proponents in the mid-1870s reveals his impatience with idealistic
abstractions that fail to take into account political realities. In his review of Giner de
los Ríos's *Estudios jurídicos*, the horror of cantonalism constitutes an obvious
subtext:

> El idealismo utopista de esta escuela, sus esperanzas casi mesiánicas en un porvenir de
> perfección que nunca llegará, sus vacilaciones entre la dirección individualista y el
> socialismo a que la arrastran con igual impulso, por una parte su concepto del
> individuo y por otra su concepto del derecho del Estado, revélanse en este libro, que
> encierra caústicas y amargas críticas de lo presente y risueñas esperanzas sobre lo
> futuro. No domina en él, por cierto, el sentido práctico y político. . . . en la
> organización de los poderes del Estado descúbrese aquella vaga nebulosidad en que
> gusta de envolverse la escuela krausista . . . ("Revista crítica" 4: 1876, 123)

The repudiation of idealism is, however, complicated by a number of other
factors and takes place within an arena of multiple and competing discourses. It is
misleading to assume that the fear of revolution led to a wholehearted adoption of
Cánovas and his politics of order[3]. While a very palpable fear of the new radical
left, consisting of anarchism and socialism, contributes to the adoption of more
conservative political, or apolitical, even antipolitical stances, this tendency was
counterbalanced by the need to combat Carlism and neo-Catholicism[4]. The
dilemma facing those progressives who oppose cantonalism is precisely how to
salvage their own program for social and political change in the light of the threat
from both the right and the left. Writing in 1873, Juan Valera specifically addresses
this issue in response to the work of the neo-Catholic Antonio Aparisi y Guijarro:

> Como españoles, como liberales, como aceptadores de la revolución de 1868,
> estamos llenos de dolor, profundamente lastimados en el alma; estamos moralmente
> peor que Job. Nadie extrañe, pues, que se nos acabe la paciencia cuando, con la
> publicación de las obras del señor Aparisi, surge este Eliú para atormentarnos e
> insultarnos en nuestra caída, en la pérdida de la revolución y para justificar en cierto
> modo a los que la pierden. En efecto, si el liberalismo y el espíritu del siglo y las ideas
> modernas, según pretende el señor Aparisi, implican la negación de Dios, la
> indiferencia entre bien y mal y virtud y vicio, la guerra a la propiedad, la
> desmembración de la patria, la profanación de la familia, la violenta rotura de todos
> los lazos sociales, el olvido de todo respeto y el desconocimiento de toda autoridad
> humana y divina, entonces los incendiarios de Alcoy, y los internacionalistas
> andaluces, y los forajidos de Cartagena, tienen razón contra nosotros; no nos queda
> más recurso que escondernos, llenos de vergüenza, y dejar expedito y libre el camino
> al señor don Carlos VII[5] para que suba al trono de sus mayores y tienda desde él, sin
> piedad, su látigo sobre nuestras espaldas y encadene a nuestos hombres de acción y
> haga colocar por mano del verdugo una mordaza en nuestra boca blasfemadora.
> (2: 1554-55)

---

[3] Gómez Marín (37) suggests a strong turn to the right among liberals, Krausist and non-
Krausist, and Gil Cremades insinuates the same.

[4] Jutglar comments on the military's need to counterbalance the Carlists to the right and
the cantonalists to the left, but previous studies have not observed how the pressures from the
two extremes affected other areas of Spanish cultural life.

[5] Valera alludes here to the Carlist contender.

Those who had occupied the left in the 1860s now find themselves displaced to the center and engaged in a complex dialogue with other more radical voices as well as with their old conservative antagonists. The relations between and within the various groups become increasingly complicated; there is inevitably greater overlap of the different discourses and at the same time, an attempt to maintain their differences. The unfolding of this new dialogic interplay continues throughout the 1870s and is an essential component of the reception of naturalism.

In the early years of the Restoration, progressives and liberals who had advocated change and welcomed or at least accepted the Revolution of 1868 now find themselves excoriated by the right and reduced to silence by their own guilt and fear of exacerbating the social conflict that had surfaced during the Republic and in particular, during the cantonalist revolt. Throughout the 1870s and well into the 1880s, liberal and more radical writers seek to disassociate themselves from violence and revolution. Explicit references to the political events are rare and often surface as afterthoughts or asides within texts that purposely emphasize non-political issues. Azcárate's *Minuta de un testamento* largely relates the theological and philosophical evolution of the text speaker, who glosses over the events of 1868–1874 in three pages of a one hundred and fifty page manuscript. In his brief discussion of his political activities during these years, the text speaker refers to the "movimiento cantonal criminal" (164) and repudiates "la República revolucionaria y desorganizadora de los que intentan reproducir las luchas de clases y resolver en un día cuestiones delicadas que piden detención y madurez de juicio" (165). He concludes by stating that he has now retired from politics. Francisco Giner de los Ríos rarely comments on political events and when he does, it is in texts that deal primarily with literary or philosophical topics. In the article "Biblioteca de autores aragoneses" he condemns the early 1870s with extraordinarily harsh language: "época nefanda, vitanda y olvidanda, y a favor de aquella perversa excitación que nos puso a dos dedos de nuestra cabal ruina" (15: 303). Giner's disgust with the Republic and its consequences leads him to turn against politics entirely and to castigate his old friend Nicolás Salmerón for his "criminal pasión política" (Pablo de Azcárate 235). Revilla also decries demagogic cantonalism in an article on Galdós, intermixing his literary analysis with praise for the conservative victory over license and disorder (*Críticas* 115). Galdós himself condemns the Canton of Cartagena in his letters and refers to the federal experiment as absurd (Shoemaker 173, 185).[6] Even Gómez Ortiz, who is characterized as radically revolutionary in politics (*La Epoca*, 23 June, 1882), and who sympathizes with the desire for change and social reform in his *El naturalismo: Naturalismo en el arte, política y literatura* calls for moderation and hopes that once naturalism has passed beyond "el peligroso período de su '93 literario" (70), it will contribute positively to art. For the Spanish reader of the period, the emphasis on moderation and the allusion to the distant French revolution (Louis XVI was executed in 1793 and the sans-culottes gained control of the revolution) calls to mind the more recent

---

[6] Although Galdós later adopts an objective and even sympathetic view of cantonalism in his *Episodios nacionales* (*De Cartago a Sagunto* 1911), in the years immediately following the cantonal uprising, his judgment is much harsher.

French commune and the even more recent cantonalist movement. The numerical similarity of the dates, '73 and '93, further encourages the association.

The repudiation of violence and conflict constitutes a localized voice of authority in the middle and late 1870s and is exploited by writers of diverse ideological conviction. It leads to a reaccentuation of harmony and gradualism, and to an avoidance of extremes, all of which are present in the Krausist discourse of the previous decade but now receive new emphasis and take on new resonances in dialogic interplay with the various components of contemporary political discourse. The aspiration to sidestep politically divisive issues and to emphasize harmony and tolerance is exemplified by the polemic between Francisco Canalejas and Ramón de Campoamor. At the request of Manuel de la Revilla, Campoamor wrote a prologue to a collection of Revilla's poems. The prologue appeared in advance of the book on May 2, 1875 in the *Revista Europea* and contained a harsh attack on Krausism, with several veiled allusions to Krausist political radicalism. Early in the prologue, the text speaker equates Krausism with communism ("Dudas y tristezas" 322) and later encourages Revilla to avoid politics, and the horrors of social conflict (325). López Morillas attributes Campoamor's attack on Krausism to his own personal pique at Krausist indifference to his poetry and to his desire to ingratiate himself with the Restoration government (196–97). Whatever his motives might have been, his attempt to disparage Krausism by linking it, however subtly, with the discredited politics of the preceding years is strategically astute and dismays the liberals and Krausists. In a note accompanying the prologue, the *Revista Europea* emphasizes the importance of Campoamor's attack on Krausism and invites the defenders of the Krausist system to respond. Campoamor himself anticipated responses from the leaders of the movement and later expresses surprise at their silence ("A la lenteja" 441).

The disarray of former Krausists and the general disavowal of the Revolution and the Republic precludes an impassioned defense but, at the same time, the need to prevent a return to neo-Catholicism and traditional philosophy and social policies necessitates a reply. The tension between these two motivations informs the texts that respond to Campoamor as well as many of the publications that appear in the following years. Both Canalejas and Revilla rebut Campoamor's assertions and significantly, both begin by disavowing any present connection with the Krausist school. It is precisely in this essay that Canalejas describes the fragmentation of Krausism into various tendencies ("El panentismo" 361; see previous reference on page 38) and then describes himself as a follower of Leonhardi and the religious, rationalist school. The speaker's insistence on the religious question is a clear attempt to sidestep the political issues and center the debate on less divisive topics. Throughout the article, he insists on tolerance and respect for all beliefs and only introduces political commentary when, in an attempt to recuperate antipolitical authoritative discourse for his own ends, he accuses Campoamor of writing "en un momento de pasión política quizá, y por tanto en un momento desgraciado" ("El panentismo" 364).

In Campoamor's response, the text speaker attempts to accredit himself by evoking both liberal and conservative authoritative voices. He begins by praising Canalejas and then proceeds to echo liberal discourse by defending his own right to express his opinions. Subsequently, he reverts to a more traditional rhetoric, reiterating the nationalistic attack on Krausist language as contributing to the ruin of the state. For the moment he totally avoids any mention of political issues and concentrates on the religious questions of pantheism and atheism. Having established his own authority in the first five sections of the article, in the sixth the text speaker denies the accusation of political opportunism and then applauds the actions of Cánovas and his Minister in expelling certain liberal professors[7]. In an increasingly hostile attack, he then states that it is impossible to write about Krausism without appearing to write about politics and, in particular, socialist politics. Utilizing military terminology, he evokes the violence of cantonalism and the civil war and thus suggests a direct link between Krausism and social upheaval:

> . . . es imposible ocuparse del Krausismo sin que parezca que se escribe de política, y de política socialista, pues desde el baluarte del sistema armónico siempre están preparados contra todo orden social cañones apuntados por artilleros llenos de buenas intenciones, pero buenas intenciones de aquellas de que se dice que está empedrado el infierno. ("A la lenteja" 443)

In response to Campoamor's article, Canalejas and Revilla's texts travel a circuitous path, alternately distancing themselves from Campoamor and Cánovas to the right and the radical and violent Anarchists and Socialists to the left. Canalejas's speaker condemns the recent university expulsions and marvels at the ultraconservative tone of Campoamor's article. In an ironic undermining of Campoamor's authority, Canalejas's text speaker quotes from the former's text and turns it against him. Campoamor had alluded to those who accused him of plagiarizing and linked them to the Krausist leaders, whom he referred to as "hipocentauros" (441). The speaker in Canalejas's text feigns incredulity that Campoamor could have penned such melodramatic, bourgeois prose and surmises that one of those Centaurs that conspire against his reputation must have inserted the political diatribe in an effort to discredit him ("El panentismo" 67: 529–30). Canalejas then proceeds to ridicule the association of Krausism and violence and of Krause and Bakunin ("El panentismo" 67: 530–31). In Revilla's letter to Campoamor, published in the same issue of *Revista Europea* as Canalejas's second response, he clarifies that he no longer considers himself a Krausist but feels that Campoamor's attacks are intemperate and polemical. He equates Campoamor's attack on scientific freedom with neo-Catholic discourse and calls for tolerance and a "scientific" treatment of the subject. He neatly sidesteps a discussion of the political issues by alluding repeatedly to his own lack of freedom to address the subject ("Carta a Campoamor" 533–35). Although there was some state censorship in the early years

---

[7] The second "University question" involved the dismissal of several well-known Krausist university professors and the arrest and deportation of others who refused to submit to the Royal Decree of 1875, which proscribed any teaching not in accordance with Catholicism and required professors to surrender their texts and materials for approval by the University president and the appropriate government officials. Among those fired and imprisoned were Giner de los Ríos, Laureano Calderón, Augusto González de Linares, Nicolás Salmerón, and Gumersindo Azcárate. For more information, see López-Morillas (168ff) and Jiménez-Landi (431ff).

of the Restoration, Revilla's silencing of political discussion reflects more the liberal disillusionment with political solutions and the need to fashion a discourse that is neither revolutionary nor traditional than fear of official censure. The fact that Canalejas and Campoamor had escaped censorship in their previous discussions indicates that Revilla had little to fear.

The impulse to avoid political issues but to sustain the drive for change leads to a curious displacement of revolutionary discourse. During the 1870s, liberal writers revert to the philosophical and theological debates of the preceding years but their discussions contain a silenced political subtext which makes itself heard in several different ways. The calculated suppression of political topics in the years immediately following a period of political turmoil represents a gap that requires filling. Contemporary readers obviously "heard" the political echo behind the silence and today's readers, in spite of their distance from the events, sense the intrusion of politics in the repeated insistence on the non-political nature of literary, philosophical, and theological matters. Furthermore, the language used to discuss both religious and literary questions is replete with revolutionary political rhetoric that signals the repression, rather than the suppression, of political concerns. Writing on Galdós's religious thesis novels, José Palacio Valdés employs a rhetoric that verges on the apocalyptic and although it largely addresses the question of religious tolerance, it obliquely makes reference to political reform:

> La estrella del dogmatismo palidece. Esa estrella, rojiza como la sangre que alumbró el suplicio de Savonarola y de Servet, pronto dejará de lucir. Mas volved los ojos al Oriente y veréis los destellos de un sol que levanta. Volvedlos a la vida política de las naciones, a sus ideas y a sus costumbres, y percibiréis cómo acude la libertad a su organismo, cómo se encarna la tolerancia en sus reformas.
>
> El genio de la Edad Media murmura y brama como un torrento [sic] que, a su pesar, va a perderse en los cóncavos senos de la tierra, huye de los espíritus fuertes, va a refugiarse en los débiles y les promete, como la serpiente del Paraíso, a cambio de una ciega sumisión, toda la ciencia de la tierra y toda la gloria de los cielos. ("Don Benito Pérez Galdós" 337)

In his 1879 review of *La familia de León Roch*, Manuel de la Revilla also employs revolutionary terminology and radical rhetoric, but he too applies it to the question of religious rather than political freedom:

> La intolerancia religiosa es un foco perenne de perturbaciones en la familia y en la sociedad. Separando a los hombres en dos castas enemigas e irreconciliables, compuesta la una de los poseedores de la verdad, elegidos de Dios y destinados a la dicha eterna, formada la otra por los secuaces del error, sectarios de Satan, condenados a perpetuo castigo, la intolerancia rompe la unidad humana y lleva la división y la lucha a las conciencias, a las familias y a los pueblos. ("León Roch" 500)

Later in the same essay, Revilla refers to Galdós as the champion of the holy cause of progress (502–03). The application of a radical rhetoric to the question of religious freedom serves to salvage the progressive spirit of the 1860s in texts that simultaneously disassociate the speaker from the revolutionary political positions of cantonalism and the first Republic. The language calls for change but the topic represents a return to the theological debates of the 60s, which even under Cánovas and the Restoration are a "safe" subject of discussion. Although the Constitution of 1876 was a clear retreat from that of 1869 in the area of religious freedom, Cánovas refused to accede to conservative and Catholic demands and in the end, Article 11 guaranteed that no one would be persecuted for his/her beliefs provided the appropriate respect for Christian morals was shown (Jiménez-Landi 542). If the liberals had initial fears that the Restoration would totally abolish the policies of the Revolution of 1868, by the late 70s Cánovas's policy of compromise was apparent to all. In the emphasis on religious tolerance and harmony in the essays and thesis novels of the late 1870s, liberals appropriate the authoritative discourse of accomodation but also struggle to sustain a more progressive and at times radical vision.

The tension between a desire for change and a fear of radical violence and the resultant displacement of political topics accompanied by a radical rhetoric continues well into the 1880s. Clarín's "El libre examen y nuestra literatura presente", published in *Solos* in 1881, focuses on the religious question in the title and in the text itself but political commentary surfaces frequently. The text opens with a discussion of the Revolution of 1868 and an expression of faith that the Restoration has not been able to erase the revolutionary spirit that took root during the preceding years. In the speaker's view, the revolutionary spirit survives precisely because it was not limited to the political sphere, but was extended to literature, science and religion (52). Early in the text he distances himself from the collective violence of the revolution but seeks to salvage other aspects of the movement:

> Vista de cerca, con los pormenores prosáicos y mezquinos que a todo esfuerzo colectivo acompaña en la historia, esta gran fermentación del espíritu en España puede perder algo de su grandeza, sobre todo, a los ojos del observador ligero o pesimista: mas de lejos, y en conjunto, al que atiende bien y sin prevenciones, la historia de estos pasados años tiene que parecerle bella, grande, digna de la musa épica. (53)

The reference to the epic muse is strategic, in that political factors recede or are redefined as literary in the next paragraph. It is in literature that the "ferment of thought and passions" are best expressed and it is through literature, in particular the novel, that the concepts of freedom and religious tolerance will find acceptance in Spain. Clarín ties the resurgence of the modern Spanish novel to the Revolution of 1868, and then immediately clarifies that these novelists are non-political and totally opposed to violence: ". . . no son por cierto espíritus aventurados, amigos de la utopia, revolucionarios ni despreciadores de toda parsimonia en el progresar y en el reformar" (57). Speaking specifically of Galdós, the speaker assures that he is neither a social nor a literary revolutionary and belongs to no sect (57).

The liberal dialogue with the left and the right impacts on the reception of positivism and naturalism in several different ways. As I mentioned earlier in this chapter, Zola provides a theory and a practice that enable a progressively inspired narrative. His theoretical essays stress the need to understand the reciprocal influence of the individual and society in order to thus regulate society and ensure social justice ("Le roman expérimental"). However, for most liberal Spanish writers, the image of the cantons and the social disorder of the early 1870s as well as the residue of their own previously held philosophical and literary idealism preclude an unqualified acceptance of Zola's political program and consequently of naturalism; hence, their insistence on the literary character of the movement and their continued silencing of its political ramifications. On the other hand, the rightwing condemnation of positivism and naturalism, as well as the liberal desire to provoke change in combination with their own disillusionment with literary and philosophical idealism, compel liberal writers to adopt an increasingly favorable position with respect to Zola and his literary theory. In the dialogic interplay between these groups and their different discourses, the lines of demarcation are sometimes indistinct and, on occasion, naturalism and neo-Catholicism appear as a common antagonist, irrespective of their ideological differences. Paradoxically, Spanish liberals who are committed to social and political change oppose positivism and naturalism because the doctrine of biological determinism is dangerously similar to neo-Catholic fatalism. As early as 1873, Urbano González Serrano attacks positivism because it can only lead to a fatalistic conception of the world as subjected to a blind mechanism and a place where justice, freedom and progress have no role:

> Negando lo absoluto, reduciendo la realidad al puro fenómeno, siendo la Ciencia el conocimiento de apariencias pasajeras, y la vida el número indefinido de existencias fugitivas, la justicia es una palabra vacía de sentido, la libertad una noción inconcebible y el progreso una vana ilusión. ("Estudios sobre el positivismo" 279–80)

The fear of political conservatism as a consequence of this fatalism is exposed in the following paragraph, where the text speaker links positivism's exclusive reliance on experience with Aristotle's justification of slavery on the basis of his own social reality. In subsequent essays, González Serrano warns against the dangers of pessimism in philosophy and art and advocates realism rather than naturalism precisely because of a continuing belief in the perfectibility of the individual and the progress of the species (*Cuestiones contemporáneas* 82, 147–51).

Gumersindo de Azcárate echoes very similar sentiments when he attacks pessimism. However, he argues that philosophical pessimism as exhibited in Schopenhauer and Hartmann is less detrimental to contemporary Spanish society than the more popular, religiously inspired vision of life as a vale of tears. Although he does not name neo-Catholicism or even Catholicism as the source of this other class of pessimism, the mention of a mystic in the desert as its originator and the use of the "coded" expression "vale of tears" leaves little doubt as to his meaning. In contrast to a view of life that leads to apathy and a complacent acceptance of the *status quo*, the text speaker insists on the need for action, struggle, and change. ". . . vivir no es padecer, como tampoco es gozar; *vivir es luchar*, y por tanto gozar y padecer" ("El pesimismo" 264). In the essay on pessimism, Azcárate does not mention positivism directly but in his study "El positivismo y la civilización" written at about the same time (1875–76), he draws a comparison between positivism and Catholicism and points out how both can lead to inaction and quietism (*Estudios filosóficos* 117-18).

Revilla differs from Azcárate in a greater acceptance of certain forms of positivism – what Azcárate calls critical as opposed to dogmatic or ontological positivism – but his attempt to find an intermediate position between traditional Catholicism and the radical left is equally representative of liberal thought in the 1870s. Revilla condemns pessimism and denies the inevitability of evil, distancing himself from both positivistic and neo-Catholic fatalism. Like Azcárate and González Serrano, he emphasizes the need to continue in the struggle to improve the human condition ("Revista crítica", 12: 1877, 506). However, he accepts critical positivism precisely because it enables change while at the same time avoids the extremes of revolution:

> El positivismo crítico es a la vez liberal y conservador: liberal porque reconoce la imperfección de muchas instituciones jurídicas y aspira a reformarlas y ponerlas en armonía con las necesidades de la naturaleza humana y de la justicia, que no es más que la conformidad entre las relaciones jurídicas y esta misma naturaleza; conservador, porque reconociendo el carácter relativo de todo lo que es humano, sabe muy bien que el derecho ha de amoldarse a condiciones históricas, que lo mejor es enemigo de lo bueno, que cada pueblo requiere distintas instituciones políticas, y que las reformas han de ser suaves transformaciones y no revoluciones violentas. Por eso no menosprecia la tradición, ni anticipa revolucionariamente el porvenir, ni olvida las exigencias del momento histórico, sacrificando la paz de las naciones a utopias idealistas y delirantes sueños. ("Revista crítica" 12: 1877, 502)[8]

The liberals' resistance to positivism/naturalism as deterministic and dangerously akin to the neo-Catholic "vale of tears" fatalism and their desire to salvage a progressive, but non-revolutionary program, constitutes an important strand in the debates regarding naturalism and has important repercussions for the general critical response to Emilia Pardo Bazán's entry into the debate. As many critics have observed, Pardo Bazán's participation in the discussion of naturalism provokes a vehement reply in those who oppose naturalism (Pattison 99; Shaw 222; Clemessy 97). The intense reaction is surprising, not only because the discussion of positivism and then naturalism had been going on for almost a decade when Pardo Bazán publishes her comments on naturalism in the prologue to *El viaje de novios* and then in *La cuestión palpitante* but because she essentially reiterates what others have said before her. Shaw (222) and Clemmessy (98) link the reaction to Pardo Bazán's position as an aristocratic wife and mother. For traditional Spanish writers, Pardo Bazán's tolerance and even discussion of a movement associated with pornography and heterodoxy is clearly a scandalous event. Less understandable and less commented is the trepidation with which moderate and liberal writers meet the publication of Pardo Bazán's critical and literary texts. The presence of a woman in the discussion of naturalism impacts on both the left and the

---

[8] Not only does Revilla use "idealistic" with negative connotations in this passage, but he associates it with violence (contrasting idealistic utopias with the peace of nations) and lack of contact with reality (raving dreams).

right and changes the nature of the debate, adding yet another voice to those competing for space and authority.

The responses to this new voice vary considerably, with some writers addressing the issue of the female speaker directly and others swerving away from any explicit recognition of the entry of the feminine voice. Some texts display a vociferous enunciation of opposition to women and the female speaker while others disguise their antagonism behind a rhetoric of acceptance and welcome. In all cases, the underlying anxiety at the appearance of the female speaker and the causes for this anxiety are silenced in much the same way and for many of the same reasons which contribute to the silencing of political issues. The silence is, however, audible in the echoes and the subtexts that surface within and between the various texts that deal with naturalism and its reception in Spain. In opposition to the female voice, both as represented by Pardo Bazán and by other anonymous women who figure in the background of the debate, there is an identifiable anti-female voice and discourse that enters into dialogic interplay with the female voice and the many other voices that I have identified in this and previous chapters. Contemporary feminist literary theory provides a fruitful perspective for locating and analyzing the silencing and at times vociferous enunciation of the anti-female voice but before a discussion of the relevant feminist theory, I will review the status of women in late nineteenth-century Spain and its relation to the political events discussed earlier in this chapter.

During the latter part of the eighteenth century, the subject of the education of women began to draw the attention of the government and leading figures of the Enlightenment. Over the next century, free public elementary education for both sexes increased and the need for trained women teachers led to the establishment of the Escuela Normal in 1858 (Jiménez-Landi 35–37). Among liberal and progressive thinkers, emphasis on the dignity and perfectibility of the individual accompanied a reevaluation of the treatment of women and children and the lower classes and gave rise to calls for the abolition of slavery. In Spain, the Krausist movement was actively involved in both the anti-slavery movement and the reevaluation of the role of women. Sanz del Río's *Ideal de la humanidad*, a loose translation of Krause's *Urbild der Menscheit*, calls for the eradication of differences and oppositions in general in order to foster the progress of humanity as a whole (2–3). The text speaker decries the subordination of certain sectors of society, of certain professions, of certain age groups to others. Women, in particular, should be treated as equal and marriage is only to be recommended as an institution if it fosters equality (93).

The Krausist movement in Spain worked actively to increase women's access to education during the 1860s and 70s. The Revolution of 1868 provided additional impetus and during this period, several important events took place. As president of the University of Madrid, the Krausist Fernando de Castro encouraged a series of lectures and classes that were open to the public. From February until May of 1869, he sponsored weekly lectures on the topic of the education of women. Also in 1869, Castro organized the Ateneo Artístico y Literario de Señoras and at his initiative, the School for Teachers and the Association for the Education of Women were established in 1870 and 1871. Many Krausists and Institutionists participated in the

Association, including Giner de los Ríos, Azcárate, and González Serrano (Cacho Viu 276–77, Scanlon 30–37).

As Geraldine Scanlon has pointed out, Krausist and Institutionist support for greater educational opportunities for women were predicated on their social function as mothers (32). In Azcárate's *Minuta de un testamento*, the text speaker enunciates a view that is common to all of his liberal contemporaries when he criticizes the cold, distracted, and disinterested instruction he received in his primary schooling and laments that his mother's lack of education prevented her from playing a larger role in his early instruction (102). Manuel Ruiz de Quevedo, in his address at the 1879 opening ceremonies for the Women's School of Commerce and the Teacher's College emphasizes the need to educate women as a direct consequence of the mother's pivotal role in the formation of her children:

> Partiendo, en efecto, del sentimiento divino y misterioso que identifica a la madre con el hijo, lo que hace falta es capacitarla, ilustrándola de modo que reconozca al hijo como pedazo de la madre patria y de la madre humanidad, y que vea con evidencia que le mutila y le rebaja y le deforma en lo que de más real y precioso tiene si omite en la crianza del niño esos lados superiores de su ser; que, en una palabra, no le ama con plenitud de amor si no ama en él al ciudadano y al hombre. ("La instrucción de la mujer" 11)

A number of structures and lexical choices indicate that for Ruiz de Quevedo the "hijo", Spanish for male or female child is, in reality, the son. In the preceding quotation and in several other paragraphs devoted to a discussion of the mother as educator, Ruiz de Quevedo refers to the child exclusively by means of the singular male pronoun. Although Spanish, like English, routinely utilizes the masculine form to refer to a mixed gender group, the choice of the singular masculine pronoun rather than the more ambiguous plural and the total lack of any reference to daughters while addressing a female audience connotes a masculine referent. The antithetical play of mother – first as a biological entity and then a figurative one, mother country and mother humanity – and child, also conjures up the image of a biologically male child. Furthermore, the mention of the child as a future citizen and "hombre" virtually erases any possibility of a feminine referent. While the masculine "man" can arguably communicate "human" or "male and female", the use of "citizen" evokes an adult male figure in nineteenth-century Spain, where women had rather limited legal and civil rights (Scanlon 122ff).

The rather constrained "liberation" envisioned by Krausists and other liberals is evident in the Sunday conferences on the Education of Women organized by Castro. Speaking on "La educación literaria de la mujer", Francisco Canalejas emphasizes sentiment and fantasy as feminine traits and portrays women as living vicariously through their husbands (7). Due to their primarily affective character and to the natural subordination of their own needs and dreams to that of their husbands and children, women readers should judge the quality of the literary works that they read by their sentimental appeal and their ability to inspire sacrifice and self-denial:

Si después de leer un libro, si después de asistir a la representación de un drama, de
una comedia o de una tragedia, en la secreta comunicación de vuestra conciencia no os
sentís mejores, más aptas para el sacrificio que el deber impone, más prontas a la
abnegación, y no experimentáis ese sacudimiento eléctrico que parte del corazón y que
despierta mística sed de perfecciones en el entendimiento, arrojad sin escrúpulo aquel
libro, reprobad sin temor aquella escena, porque ni el libro es poético ni la escena
bella. (15–16)

While some of the other Sunday lectures employ a less exalted language, the
subordination of women to the role of mother and wife remains constant. The
rhetoric fluctuates between encouraging independence and change and containing
this liberation through the insistence on dependence and servitude. Women should
cultivate their emotional-sentimental character, but always in the service of others:
"Sentir, sí; pero sentir para conocer y para convertiros en instrumentos dóciles y
apasionados, en enérgicas sacerdotistas de vuestros deberes" (Canalejas, "La
educación literaria de la mujer" 17)[9].

The move toward increased educational and professional opportunities for
women is further constrained by the events of the Revolution of 1868 and
cantonalism. The Anarchist advocacy of a society free of institutions and authority
as well as the suggestion of free love and the abolishment of marriage astounds and
horrifies traditional and also liberal Spanish writers. During the 1871 parliamentary
debates on the legalization of the Anarchist International Association of Workers
(AIT), conservative opponents argue that the International is a foreign organization
that opposes the concept of God, nation, private property, and the family (Vergés
51, 56). Within the conservative community, the term "family" is part of the
ideologically charged sociolect and connotes opposition to free love, women's
emancipation, the legalization of divorce, and any change in the traditional sex
roles. While the parliamentary debates of 1871 focus on the International as a
foreign body and see its involvement in the Paris Commune as a still distant threat
in terms of the Spanish social experience, the establishment of the Republic in 1873
and the subsequent cantonal uprising change this perception. Women are involved
in many of the violent acts that occur in the early 1870s. In Montilla, women and
men lynch a rural guard on February 12, 1873, the day the Republic is declared
(Fernández Almagro 164–65). In Alcoy, the Anarchist promise of a full social
revolution involves institutional and social changes that radically alter the role and
position of women. The Declaration of the AIT of Alcoy, promulgated on February
24, 1873, abolishes marriage and all other institutional control, thus tacitly
advocating free love. Furthermore, by expelling all prostitutes (Medioni 31), the
Alcoy government eradicates the accepted Spanish means for controlling male
sexuality and opens the door to sexual freedom for all.

[9] A much later text echoes in even more obvious language the view that women's entry
into education is a function, not of women's rights or needs, but of the needs of men and in
particular, the male child. In "Misión docente y misión social de la mujer", 1914, Juan
Barcía Caballero defines education as a four part process consisting of teaching, correcting,
scolding, and punishing, all in a loving environment. In this context, he writes that while a
man can be instructed by another man, every man should be educated by a woman (8).

Conservatives and neo-Catholics had long associated the emancipation of women with revolutionary activity and in particular, French culture. In Nocedal's address to the Royal Academy, he attacks the serial novel – of French origins – for its incorporation of radical political topics, in which he includes the treatment of political economy, civil and criminal legislation, penal systems, the emancipation of women, the organization of work, history, philosophy, and religion (381). He condemns the utopian authors who lead their female readers to impossible dreams and is particularly disturbed by attacks on marriage and the family. In referring to one text which recommends against marriage as the only means by which a women can retain her dignity, Nocedal calls it a horrible blasphemy (384). By associating the emancipation of women with the defense of adultery, Nocedal seeks to discredit the movement as immoral and antisocial (384).

Following the Revolution of 1868 and the Second Republic, conservative writers seek to blame Republicans, liberals, and in particular, Krausists, for the breakdown of the family and the "lamentable" shifts in the position of women in Spanish society. Krausist participation in the Revolution of 1868 and in the Republic and the active role of Castro and other Krausists in fostering educational and professional opportunities for women are exploited by the opposition. Moreover, Krause, Sanz del Río and their followers advocate divorce, a position which enables their Conservative opponents to link them to Anarchism and to other groups seeking to restructure society. Writing in 1876, Alonso Martínez calls Krause "impío, anárquico, socialista" and then moves immediately to attack Krausist support for divorce as an attack on the weakness and dignity of women and on the Christian family ("Exposición y crítica" 34). Alarcón's "La moral en el arte", 1877, makes constant reference to the family in the context of social stability. He stresses that even in pagan Rome the sanctity of the country, the family, and the home was protected (231). He then equates Krausism with atheism and with the negation of society, property, the home, women and children and with the call for universal anarchy and free love (236). Similar charges appear in Campoamor's "¡A la lenteja! ¡A la lenteja!" (534). Menéndez Pelayo's discussion of the Revolution makes frequent reference to the establishment of civil marriage, which he refers to as "concubinato civil" (Heterodoxos 770). In his condemnation of Anarchism and of Nicolás Salmerón's defense of the AIT he notes as his example of radical, revolutionary activity the speech of Guillermina Rojas, in which she advocates free love (772).

As in the debate over political revolution, liberals and progressives largely respond to the conservative attack on women's emancipation with silence. However, in contrast to their evident desire to distance themselves from both the radical left and the right in the discussion of other aspects of social and political change, in reference to the emancipation of women, liberal discourse assimilates and echoes that of the conservative opposition. In the aftermath of the cantonalist movement, liberal and Krausist disenchantment with German idealism and with revolution leads them to adopt a more defensive tone and the already moderate defense of women's educational and professional opportunities grows increasingly tepid. The political disillusionment with radicalism and the resultant swerve to the right is repeated in the treatment of women's issues, but in this case, it is both more prolonged and more pronounced. In 1869, Carlos Rubio responds to conservatives who blame the revolution for fostering women's liberation, insisting that the problem is of long standing and that while the Revolution is trying to resolve it, its origins and cause predate 1868. Writing during the pre-Republican years, Rubio is generous in his praise for women, and cites their intelligence and decisiveness, alluding to their active participation in the political conspiracies that preceded the Revolution (452-55).

In the following years, liberal commentary on women and their role in society is increasingly disapproving and often indistinguishable in form and content from the writings of traditionalists. Both groups use terms associated with masculinity and maleness to communicate positive attributes, while adjectives and nouns associated with women have a pejorative connotation. Clarín's praise of Galdós and Pereda is typical:

> Y si se me dice quienes son los artistas de pluma menos vanidosos, menos mujeres, más sinceros, llanos, modestos, y de veras cariñosos, respondo: Galdós, Pereda ("B. Pérez Galdós" 25).

Clarín's ideological antagonists use a very similar rhetoric. In describing the philosophy adopted by mid-nineteenth-century conservative politicians, Menéndez Pelayo writes that it was easily accessible, that even educated women could read it. He then contrasts it with other more legitimate philosophies that satisfy the needs of serious and logical spirits and the manly pleasure of systematically investigating the truth (*Heterodoxos* 696). In the same vein, Campoamor praises "el talento varonil" of Manuel de la Revilla ("Dudas y tristezas" 324).

The conservative hysteria that women's emancipation will lead to sexual liberation and free love is echoed in liberal writings. As numerous feminist studies of the patriarchy and partriarchal family structure have argued, the control of female sexuality is essential for male control of women, the family, and power[10]. The fear of a loss of this control is an important factor in the male response to feminism and female writers in late nineteenth-century Spain. Numerous writers have commented on the puritanical streak that runs through Krausism and Institutionism (López-Morillas 112; Cacho Viu 378-80) but its relation to the Krausist-Institutionist view of women and in particular, the liberal and progressive reaction to naturalism and to Emilia Pardo Bazán and her study of naturalism requires further comment. Writers of the period who encourage sexual equality or call for increased education and professional opportunities for women consistently falter in the face of a stated or implied fear of sexuality and in particular, female sexuality. In his exaltation of the family, the text speaker in *Minuta de un testamento* condemns prostitution and adultery and advocates premarital virginity for both sexes. While he describes the early sexual education that he provided for his sons as a means to inculcate the values of male chastity, his daughter's education is left to her "discreet and virtuous" mother and consequently, to a more traditional

---

[10] For an overview of the subject, see Hester Eisenstein, Chapters I-III. Juliet Mitchell and Susan Brownmiller provide more detailed studies.

sexual education (Azcárate 174–79). Liberals and Krausist-Institutionists repeatedly express the view that women and particularly young girls should not be exposed to certain materials and certain kinds of art. Canalejas warns his female public to avoid books that only mirror misery and to refrain from attending indecent plays ("Sobre la educación literaria" 18). Manuel de la Revilla objects to Eusebio Blasco's drama *Soledad* because it falsifies and romanticizes the purity of lower class women when, in reality, feminine virtue, even when protected by a loving mother and a proper education, is always at risk (*Críticas* 1884: 110). Giner de los Ríos objects to the depiction of female sexuality in Galdós's *La familia de León Roch* (*Ensayos* 69) and finds it "shocking" that Pepa Fúcar, in her anger and despair at the marriage of León Roch to her rival, bites off pieces of a rose bud and its stem and spits them at León (73–74). He also criticizes what he sees as the influence of French literary style in Galdós's descriptions of León and his wife's honeymoon and expressions such as "besos húmedos" (74).

Giner's objections undoubtedly are inspired not only by the novelistic portrayal of sensual and impassioned women but also by the knowledge that the reading public for Galdós's novels was heavily female. For Giner and many liberal writers, the novel in general plays an important role in presenting appropriate models of behavior, particularly for women readers. In the specific case of *La familia de León Roch*, the text presents the conflict of religious fanaticism and religious tolerance but it does so in terms of a male versus female confrontation. Significantly, many of the critics who deal with this and other of Galdós's novels and with the question of religious freedom, expect or encourage a strong religious faith in women but also expect and encourage that the wife's religious faith be subordinated to the husband's right to a peaceful and harmonious homelife. León Roch himself states that he wanted a Christian wife (Pérez Galdós 4: 801). In Azcárate's *Minuta*, the strong Catholic faith of his wife is accepted and respected. The liberal Armando Palacio Valdés praises Fernán Caballero's conservative Catholic novels as appropriate reading material for young women in contrast to the racier French novels, which "predican la rebelión a los jóvenes y muy particularmente al sexo femenino" ("Fernán Caballero" 244). Later in the same article, Palacio Valdés writes that women shouldn't participate in the contemporary theological debates and recommends that women writers continue to publish in the service of religion as long as they avoid fanaticism:

> Mas aparte de estas intransigencias y exageraciones [sic], no puedo negar que me complace más ver una pluma femenina al servicio de la religión, aunque sea ésta una religión petrificada, que sirviendo de intérprete a las vacilaciones y combates de nuestro siglo. El espíritu de la mujer es esencialmente receptivo, conservador, se amolda fácilmente a toda realidad, aun la más dolorosa, y extrae de ella los elementos de belleza y armonía que contiene. La mujer no debe participar de nuestras dudas y sufrimientos, porque se quebraría como se quebró *Gloria*[11].
>
> Esperamos para introducirla en el mundo agitado de nuestra conciencia religiosa, a que hayamos conseguido arrancar a la duda su cabellera de sierpes para

---

[11] The reference is to Galdós's thesis novel in which the female protagonist dies in the struggle between her religious faith and her love for the Jewish hero.

ofrecérsela, al modo de los antiguos guerreros de la América, como trofeo de nuestro
combate. (245)

In the same year, Alas publishes his review of *La familia de León Roch* and
identifies intolerance and fanaticism as the causes of León's unhappy marriage,
accusing the intransigent María Egipciaca of thwarting León's right to "la paz del
hogar, al natural dominio . . . del esposo sobre el espíritu de la familia propia"
(*Solos* 182–83). He goes on to attack the church for perverting María's natural
docility and turning her against her husband. Clarín, like Giner, expresses his
puritanical views of sexuality when he suggests that without spiritual and moral
harmony between husband and wife, marriage is no more than concupiscence
(184). In the campaign to liberate women from the control of the church, the enemy
of liberalism, the emphasis is very clearly on maintaining her subordination to her
liberal husband and family. One of the Sunday lectures on the education of women
emphasizes this fundamental contradiction in indirect but revealing language.
Speaking on "La educación social de la mujer", Joaquín María Sanromá stresses
the need to improve the education of women so as to prepare them better for their
domestic role and in particular, to protect the family from outside influences, that
is, from the church:

> Sobre todo, es preciso acostumbrar a la mujer a no admitir en el seno de la familia más
> que aquellas influencias *legítimas* y *naturales* que deben rodearla constantemente.
> Que no haya sombras, que no haya oráculos que vengan a interponerse entre los
> esposos y las esposas, entre los padres y los hijos. No vengan fuerzas extrañas a
> contener las corrientes de cariño con pretexto de encauzarlas. (16–17)

The dominant themes running through liberal discourse on women in the 1870s is
freedom from fanaticism for the benefit of matrimonial harmony, education in the
service of motherhood and sexual constraint. In all cases, the impulse toward
freedom is contained by a fear of the consequences of this freedom and a baldly
paternalistic view of women. As more and more women successfully compete for a
voice in the public discourse of the period, the fear of female freedom grows more
intense. Gilbert and Gubar have pointed out the rage with which men of letters
greeted female literary achievement in England, which they saw as a threat to their
own control of language and culture (199). A similar response can be observed in
Spain. In addition to the better known figures such as Concepción Arenal and
Emilia Pardo Bazán, a number of other women participate in the debates on
women's education and attempt to gain entry into the literary world. The increasing
hostility is evident in two liberal thinkers who were closely allied to Krausism or the
Institución Libre de Enseñanza: Manuel de la Revilla and Leopoldo Alas. Revilla's
antifeminism is apparent early in his writings and increases in hostility over time. In
1876 he criticizes "la mujer sabia" as vain, proud, and cold. "Creer, sentir, amar:
he aquí la ciencia necesaria para la mujer" ("Revista crítica" 6: 1876, 114). In a
review of Echegaray published that same year, he opposes the choice of a woman as
a dramatic protagonist because women are enigmas and there is no room for
enigmas in the theater ("Revista crítica" 6: 1876, 476). While discussing Galdós's
Marianela, he writes "la mujer fea no tiene derecho al amor, y la mujer sin amor

no tiene más esperanza ni destino que la muerte" ("Revista crítica" 14: 1878, 507). Early in a review of the play *Rienzi el Tribuno* by the female playwright Rosario de Acuña, Revilla reiterates his belief that women's sole function is to love and subsequently, he attributes the play's success to the presence of masculine qualities in Acuña's writing. Consequently, he is surprised to find that the playwright is an attractive young woman and confesses that her appearance dissipates his fears that her liberal ideas really hide radical feminist doctrines:

> Esperábamos, con efecto, ver salir a la autora, y presumíamos hallarnos enfrente de alguna solterona empedernida, vieja y fea por añadidura, cuyas ideas liberales fueran la máscara con que encubría feroces doctrinas emancipadoras y cuya inspiración varonil se explicara por su misma fealdad y desabrimiento. (*Críticas* 1885: 345)

The coded use of masculine for praise and feminine for condemnation is apparent in a later short review of Acuña's poetry, in which Revilla dismisses the collection as typical of the feminine poetic tradition, melodious and sweet, but lacking in grandeur and masculine emphasis ("Revista crítica" 4: 1876). The persistent use of this sexually bound terminology reveals the latent hostility of the male critic to the women writer. She can only succeed by adopting literary attributes viewed as inherently male, but as soon as she does, her female identity is called into question, as is her virtue and the political correctness of her position. "Masculine" and "feminine" participate in two separate semantic codes in late nineteenth-century Spain: cultural, in which masculine is positively valued and feminine is denigrated, and biological, in which both terms are viewed positively as long as individual behavior corresponds to biological sexual identity. The semantic ambiguity of the terms is exploited by the male discourse of the period to mask hostility towards women and apprehension in the face of an increasingly vocal feminine voice. When applied to women, the normally positive attribute "masculine" retains its positive value at the same time that it introduces a negative connotation. In that masculinity is associated with sexual prowess, the suggestion of a woman's "maleness" carries with it the much-feared image of unrestrained female sexuality, which in turn threatens the patriarchy by nullifying the husband's control of the wife's production and thus his ownership of the children.

The arrival of positivism and naturalism, with its emphasis on biological determinism, only reenforces a rigid interpretation of sexual identification, which is appropriated by those who oppose women's emancipation. The thesis of biological determinism is adopted to argue the inevitable inferiority of women. Again, Revilla provides one of the clearest examples in his two-part article entitled "La emancipación de la mujer", which appears in 1879 in *Revista contemporánea*. In one of the most open endorsements of naturalism to appear during the period, the text speaker specifically links determinism and sexual inequality:

> La herencia, la adaptación, la selección natural, el medio ambiente, son las fuerzas y factores a que corresponde el cumplimiento de estas leyes, y merced a ellas cada individuo viene a la vida destinado fatalmente a cumplir una determinada función. . . . De la acción de estas leyes no se libran los sexos. Creados por la naturaleza para hacer posibles las formas superiores de la reproducción de la especie, a este fin se

subordina su organización entera . . . el destino de ambos sexos es tan diverso como su organización. Hablar, pues, de igualdad, tratándose de hombres y mujeres, es dar prueba de desconocer por completo las leyes de la naturaleza. ("La emancipación de la mujer" 18: 451)

The text speaker then proceeds to argue the natural inferiority of women, based on their smaller brain and body size, and the exclusivity of their interest, which is limited to the immediate family. He argues that women are not fit for most professions and defends their exclusion from politics on the basis of their fundamental conservatism. Given their attachment to tradition and their religious fanaticism, they would be a reactionary influence in political affairs (164). Although he feels that women generally make poor writers, he does not object to women artists and writers, as long as they "evite(n) el riesgo de hacerse varonil" (463). The fact that he and many of his contemporaries essentially define good art as "masculine" is silenced in this as in many other texts.

In the second part of "La emancipación de la mujer", the text speaker discusses the question of morality and the contradiction between theoretical ethics, in which adultery and licentiousness are condemned irrespective of sex, and social ethics, in which women are held to a much harsher standard than men. Revilla justifies the double standard on numerous grounds: the male sex drive is stronger than the female, women are naturally more chaste, sex and love are inseparable in the female experience, the family can not exist without the presence of the supreme authority of the father (167–69). He also defends the honor code, by which the adulteress is punished with much greater severity than the adulterer, because while men cannot conceal their illegitimate offspring, women can "engendra(r) hijos ilegítimos que roban al padre su apellido, su amor y su fortuna y son ladrones de sus proios hermanos, a quienes usurpan el cariño y los bienes de su padre " (175). In keeping with the view that the male sex drive cannot be harnessed, the text speaker argues that prostitution is a social necessity, required to protect wives and daughters from daring and uncontrolled young men (178). It is significant that over half of Revilla's discussion of the emancipation of women is devoted to questions of sexuality and the protection of female purity. The two issues are inextricably linked in both conservative and liberal discourse of the period and surface either explicitly or in echoes in texts dealing with the works and activities of contemporary women, and in particular, with Emilia Pardo Bazán.

Manuel de la Revilla's review of Pardo Bazán's first novel opens with a long discussion of his views on women writers and his fear that Pardo Bazán would be a writer of the same style as Clemencia Royer, a woman geologist who translated Darwin and writes, in Revilla's opinion, with a materialistic crudity that competes with the worst of the naturalists (*Críticas* 1884: 107–08). Although the text speaker admits to being pleasantly surprised upon reading Pardo Bazán's novel, the allusions to naturalism and crudity continue to echo and thus influence the reader's perception of both the work and the author. Furthermore, while commending the quality of Pardo Bazán's narrative, Revilla invokes the ambiguous code words – masculine, feminine – which serve to deflate his praise:

Al leer aquella narración llena de color y de verdad, al ver aquellos caracteres tan bien trazados, y sobre todo al saborear aquel estilo y aquel lenguaje tan castizos y elegantes que no estarían fuera de lugar en uno de nuestros estilistas clásicos, cesó toda prevención y no pudimos menos de celebrar los méritos de la nueva escritora, la cual, por lo viril de la concepción y el lenguaje de la obra, debe ser fruto de una equivocación de la naturaleza, que encerró el cerebro de un hombre en un cráneo femenino. (108)

Although Leopoldo Alas is initially more favorable to Pardo Bazán as a novelist, some of his early commentary and much of his later language is remarkably similar to that of Revilla. In his 1881 review of *Un viaje de novios*, Clarín identifies Pardo Bazán as a traditionalist of the same school as Pereda and Alarcón but more tolerant and less intrusive. He praises the novel but denies that it is naturalistic and implies that Pardo Bazán does not fully understand naturalism and that she does well – presumably owing to her sex – to not read all that has been written by French naturalists. He ends the review commenting specifically on those details that reveal the hand of a woman author, such as the description of clothing and the idealized male protagonist (Beser 271–79). Clarín published two reviews of *Los pazos de Ulloa*: some rather general comments on Pardo Bazán as a novelist and a personality that are published in *Nueva campaña* and a bona fide review that appears in *La Ilustración Ibérica*, 1887. Although the general tone of both texts is positive, certain allusions and echoes introduce a negativity that undermines the expressed praise. The "Los pazos de Ulloa" appearing in *Nueva campaña* opens with a discussion of the new series initiated by the Cortezo publishing house, which intends to publish novels by the best Spanish writers. The text speaker identifies Pardo Bazán's *Los pazos de Ulloa* as the first of the collection and then proceeds to express doubts as to the success of the series, in that the best Spanish novelists, such as Galdós and Pereda, would demand prohibitive royalties and other important writers, such as Valera and Alarcón, are no longer writing novels. After several pages regarding the improbable success of the enterprise, the speaker acknowledges that the publishers started off on the right foot by inaugurating their series with a work by Pardo Bazán. He then proceeds with several pages of commentary on the autobiographical notes that appear as a prologue to the first edition of *Los pazos*. He describes Pardo Bazán as a woman of admirable moral and material health but his praise is often interwoven with words that carry a negative semantic charge. He refers to her as "agarrada a la superficie de la tierra" (220) and then seeks to dispel a possible association of "superficie" with superficial by clarifying "de la realidad, quiero decir". The same rhythm of assertion and self-correction with persistent negative echoes occurs in his discussion of Pardo Bazán's intellectual curiosity:

Se trata, al fin, de una mujer *que quiere verlo todo* en la ciencia, como otras quieren verlo todo . . . en un almacén de ropa blanca. Nada de eso quiere decir, y es en rigor ocioso el advertirlo, que se trate de un espíritu superficial, en el sentido corriente de estas palabras, sino de un temperamento de exuberante fuerza asimiladora, que necesita mucho alimento, que consume mucho y vive a expensas del ambiente que busca afanoso, y no de su propia sustancia. (221, 236)

The text continues to point out how Pardo Bazán's sex and her social position impede her treatment of certain topics and distance her from naturalism. To really write an experimental novel, she would need a first-hand knowledge of individuals and environments that she neither can nor should acquire (227). Throughout the review, the text speaker seeks to prove that Pardo Bazán is not and can not be considered a naturalistic writer and suggests a certain insincerity in her desire to be taken as such. In his view, she refuses to reveal her true spirit in her novels and her insistence on separating the corporal and the spiritual and on silencing the spiritual is both erroneous and deleterious to her art (235). While he insists that he will refrain from offering advice, Clarín strongly suggests that Pardo Bazán would do well to abandon naturalistic topics and techniques and pursue a more spiritual and perhaps even Catholic form of expression.

The review published in *La Ilustración Ibérica* similarly seeks to distance Pardo Bazán from naturalism and to stress her conservative and feminine temperament. In the opening sections, the text speaker associates Pardo Bazán with Pereda and likens her descriptions of the rural Galician landscape and its peoples to those of the conservative Cantabrian novelist. The review closes with warm praise for the character of Perucho, the young illegitimate child, and underscores Pardo Bazán's motherhood:

> . . . creación tiernísima en que han colaborado un pintor que imita bien a Murillo, un estilista emulista de los Goncourt . . . y una madre. (Beser 287)

Although *Los pazos de Ulloa* is generally seen as the most naturalistic of Pardo Bazán's writing, Clarín associates it with realism and with traditional Spanish writing. In conjunction with his stress on her maternal instinct and her political and religious conservatism, Clarín clearly perceives a Pardo Bazán who is well within the limits set by liberal thinking of the period: religious, sexually constrained, motherly.

Pardo Bazán herself had cultivated this image in her early publications, which consisted of a poem to her son Jaime, an essay on Feijoo, a rather traditional novel, and a biographical study of Saint Francis of Assisi. During the 1880s and early 1890s, Pardo Bazán publishes a number of novels and short stories which are considerably more radical in content, moving from the debatable naturalism of her early *El viaje de novios* to the apparent naturalism of *La madre naturaleza* to the more openly feminist novels, *Insolación* and *Morriña* and her feminist essay "La mujer española". Furthermore, during this same period, Pardo Bazán separates from her husband, adopts a feminist life style, and enters into a series of extramarital affairs with well known figures such as Benito Pérez Galdós and José Lázaro Galdiano. Clarín was clearly aware of these events and his horror at her sexual liberation and his increasingly hostile repudiation of her feminism surface as at times apparent and at other times disguised subtexts in his reviews of her work. Writing on *Morriña* in 1889, he objects to the detailed description of household and other feminine chores and he is clearly uncomfortable with the female protagonist's decision to commit suicide at the end of the novel. In "Emilia Pardo Bazán y sus últimas obras", (1890), Clarín reiterates traditionalist and liberal antifeminine discourse, declaring that he will never be able to truly comprehend Pardo Bazán because she is a woman, and furthermore, a woman who writes like a man (*Nueva campaña* 56). He also seeks to cast doubt on her religious sincerity, describing her as the perfect example of a lay spirit (62), a clear attack in a society where both liberals and conservatives view religious faith as paramount to feminine virtue. His discussion of *Insolación*, republished in *Folletos literarios*, is a subtle attempt to suggest the author's immorality and the autobiographical character of the narration, all the while denying any such intention[12]. He begins by praising Pardo Bazán's conversational style, which he compares to that of a man of the world. He then proceeds to distinguish between a "man of the world" and a "woman of the world" and to insist that the latter has no relation to his intended meaning:

> . . . multitud de cualidades que en doña Emilia concurren como hablista, erudito, hombre de mundo (porque mujer de mundo es, aun en la acepción más inocente, otra cosa, que no lo que yo quiero dar a entender). (71)

On the heels of this denial, Clarín moves into a consideration of the immorality of the novel and then clarifies that it was surely not Pardo Bazán's intent to corrupt the morals of her readers (73). He classifies the work as somewhere between pornography and a disinterested presentation of concupiscence (75) and then subtly suggests the autobiographical nature of the text by remarking that the author did not distance herself sufficiently from the materials (76). He alludes to inexperienced novelists who think that their own sentimental experience is good material for literature and then points out that women readers tend to believe that what is written is autobiographical (77–78). Clarín condemns the love affair depicted in *Insolación* as pure carnal love and absolutely sinful:

> No hay más remedio: el que trata materia pecaminosa, si no sabe elevarse a la región de la poesía, deja ver el pecado como pecado. El amor sensual, objeto de un libro, cuando no muestra una trascendencia artística, es . . . escandaloso, en la rigorosa acepción de la palabra. (*Folletos literarios* 83)

Although Alas's comments on *Insolación* appear in 1890, several years after the height of the debate over naturalism, they confirm the connection between the liberation of women and fears of female sexuality that surfaces in a less blatant but still apparent manner in texts that precede and participate in the discussion of naturalism in Spain. Pardo Bazán's *La cuestión palpitante* is a central text in the critical reception of naturalism and the fact that it is written by a woman significantly changes the nature of the discussion. It provokes a variety of responses, depending on the political and social views of the respondents. Some fear that Pardo Bazán's appropriation of naturalism will contribute to undesirable social and literary change and to the escalation of the emancipation of women. Others identify Pardo Bazán with traditional Catholic feminine discourse and fear that her intervention in the debate and her definition of naturalism will strip it of its

[12] The novel was apparently inspired by Pardo Bazán's affair with Lázaro Galdiano and many contemporary readers, at least among the intellectual 'inner circle', would have read Clarín's comments with an awareness of the negative implications of his innuendo.

progressive character and impede social change. Still others seek to appropriate naturalism in some form as a vehicle for change but strive to locate Pardo Bazán within traditional discourse as a means of separating women's emancipation from other forms of social change. In all cases, *La cuestión palpitante* enters into dialogic interplay with the texts that precede and follow it and is itself a response to past and projected voices. The combination of these various texts creates its own larger text with its own enunciations, echoes, and silences.

The critical reception of naturalism represents a confluence of the various voices and discourses that compete for public space in late nineteenth-century Spain. The nature and definition of the Spanish nation, of its religious, philosophical, literary, political, and social character are debated and reexamined in the continual coming together of patriotic, philosophical, theological, literary, and political discourses. Although some of these voices and discourses are present only in traces and echoes in the texts that constitute the nineteenth-century critical reception of naturalism in Spain, it is clearly necessary to give voice to these silences in a critical study of Spanish naturalism. In the previous chapters, I have tried to identify the various voices and discourses that inform the discussion of naturalism in Spain. In order to clarify the many resonances that each voice or discourse carries with it, it was necessary to reinsert them in their historical context and retrace a variety of polemics and developments that took place in Spain from 1860 on. In the remaining chapters, I will look at the texts that specifically address and debate the issue of naturalism and will seek to identify the dialogic interplay that exists between these texts and to locate and give voice to the silences

IV

VOICES, SILENCES AND ECHOES:
THE CRITICAL RECEPTION
OF NATURALISM IN SPAIN 1879-1882

The subject of naturalism dominates Spanish literary discourse during some
fifteen years, surfacing initially in the late 1870s, peaking during the 1880s, and
gradually ceding to other topics in the 1890s. Walter Pattison has already identified
and described the texts that constitute the critical reception of naturalism in Spain in
his classic study *El naturalismo español*. Building on that work, in this and the
following chapter I will study the complex interweaving of the various discourses
and voices that come into play in the discussion of naturalism. My analysis will take
into account local social and historical developments as well as the nature of the
essay and the important role of the reader in essayistic discourse. I will focus on
certain pivotal texts in the debate in order to illustrate the manner in which
argumentative structures, essayistic textual strategies and the dialogic character of
language condition the expression and production of meaning. I will pay particular
attention to the confluence of multiple and sometimes opposing discourses in the
critical reception of naturalism, with emphasis on the silencing or muting of the fear
of radical political action and of women's emancipation.

The first major study of naturalism is written by Manuel de la Revilla and appears
in *Revista de España* in May of 1879. At this stage in his development, Revilla has
moved away from philosophical idealism and has clearly distanced himself from the
revolutionary events of the early 1870s which are linked in the collective memory
with Krausism and German idealism. However, his aesthetic continues to reveal a
strongly idealistic orientation and the tensions between these various forces mark
"El naturalismo en el arte". The essay opens with a justification of its relevancy,
responding to the obviousness precondition by answering the reader's question,
"why are you telling this to me?" The speaker emphasizes how a new doctrine
tends to spread from one area of human activity to another, as in the case of
positivism, which has now invaded all areas of life, and in particular, art. The
pervasiveness of the phenomenon justifies its study, as does its new, revolutionary
character. Furthermore, the text emphasizes the struggle that is taking place in the
area of the arts and the profound transformation that is bound to occur.

The emphasis on the revolutionary nature of the movement is almost immediately
palliated, in keeping with the anti-revolutionary authoritative discourse of the
Spanish 1870s. The traditional character of the new school is suggested by
underscoring its similarities with Romanticism and Neoclassicism. Like the former,

79

it opposes blind subjection to rules and like the latter it insists on imitating nature, thus opposing Romanticism's "idealismo desenfrenado" (148). Not only is the "revolutionary" movement presented as rooted in tradition, but the text speaker swerves away from any endorsement of radical extremes:

> . . . se ven aunadas la fórmula clásica en lo que al concepto y finalidad del arte se refiere, y la romántica en lo que a la regla de conducta del artista atañe. Síntomas felices todos ellos de que, pasada la exageración propia del movimiento y depuesto el radicalismo que a todo movimiento de revolución acompaña, la nueva escuela, conciliando lo que hay de razonable en la doctrina clásica y en la romántica, podrá encontrar al cabo la fórmula de lo porvenir. (150)

A further indication of a mitigated vision of naturalism can be found in the opposition to Zola's declaration of authorial impersonality and the defense of realism with its insistence on the intrusion of the writer's personality:

> Los realistas afirman todo lo contrario. Para ellos, el arte ha de arrancar de las entrañas mismas de la realidad; ha de ser la realidad percibida y sentida por el artista, y reproducida por su libre actividad en formas sensibles, tal como ella es, pero marcada con el imborrable sello de la original personalidad del que la reproduce. (149)

The insistence on the personality of the artist is a constant in the Spanish debate on naturalism, although its relationship to other elements of the debate changes over time and varies according to the individual author. In Revilla it introduces a subjective note which can be related to a residual literary idealism, to the Krausist emphasis on personality, and to a discomfort with the impersonal, scientific world advocated by the naturalists.

In keeping with essayistic discourse, Revilla spends the first pages of his text establishing his authority to speak on the subject. He bolsters his established reputation as literary critic with a quick review of literary history and largely avoids the presence of the "I" through the use of the third person with only an occasional first person plural. He remains on relatively neutral grounds, discussing the absence or limited presence of naturalism in architecture, sculpture, painting, and only in the sixth page of the twenty-one page article does he begin to address the controversial areas of poetry and finally, the novel. Still speaking of contemporary literature in general, the text speaker signals two characteristics: the prevalence of transcendental or instructive art, about which he makes little evaluative commentary, and the substitution of truth and reality for fantasy, fiction, and sickly idealism, about which he is frankly enthusiastic (153). The emotional note quickly recedes, however, and the favorable comments regarding naturalism are balanced by a more "objective" consideration of its excesses and rigidity. Once more the rhetoric of moderation and the echoes of literary idealism surface. The text speaker argues for a broader definition of art so as to not exclude all idealism and insists that art can never be limited to mere imitation or copy. The artist always creates:

> El arte no es, pues, mera idealidad ni copia servil de lo real; es idealización de lo real por la fantasía creadora, la emoción viva e intensa y la personalidad activa y

vigorosa del artista, y también realización sensible de lo ideal que el artista, con mirada escrutadora, sabe adivinar en el seno mismo de la realidad. (161)

All exclusive and extreme doctrines are to be rejected in favor of a harmonious reconciliation. Pure idealism errs in falsifying reality and in attempting to correct its imperfections. Here the text speaker alludes to and rejects the neo-Catholic moralizing literature defended by Alarcón and produced by Fernán Caballero and Alarcón himself. In the same vein, he justifies the presence of the ugly and the immoral in art. On the other hand, he attacks Zola's naturalism, which he describes as ''la demagogia del realismo''. He condemns the naturalists' emphasis on the repulsive and obscene and on the coarse language of the lower classes, which – although legitimate in art – should always remain in the background.

Throughout this section of the text, what might be called the ''rhetoric of the middle'' predominates. Pressured by the neo-Catholics and the conservatives to the right and the radical French naturalists to the left, the text speaker seeks to provide avenues for change while at the same time he continually warns against the dangers of excess. He appeals to a variety of localized authoritative voices and sociolects to create solidarity with the reader and to avoid the appearance of an excessive imposition of his own personal authority. In a constant rhythm of denial and assertion, the essay moves slowly and cautiously towards the introduction of a new voice. After condemning the predominance of risqué topics in naturalistic works, the speaker clarifies that he is not among those who oppose all presence of evil and immorality in art nor does he require that the artist always depict the victory of virtue over vice. On the other hand, he cautions against art that idealizes vice and portrays it as attractive. Although Revilla condemns Zola's lack of form and his cultivation of repulsive topics, he is careful to clarify once more that these defects are not intrinsic to naturalism; rather, they represent the typical exaggeration that accompanies revolutionary movements. In the end, the revolutionary excesses will give way to the harmonious synthesis of idealism and realism.

Revilla's article incorporates many of the discourses that interweave in the discussion of philosophy, religion, literature and politics during the preceding years. Furthermore, as the first text to specifically address the subject of naturalism in art, it occupies a pivotal location. Subsequent texts enter into dialogic interplay with it, echoing, refuting, clarifying and qualifying its points. In that it is an early consideration of the topic, it is to be expected that it falls considerably short of a wholehearted endorsement of naturalism. However, given Revilla's rather harsh condemnation of Krausism in several other essays of the period (''Revista crítica'' 3: 1876), the strong defense of literary idealism and of a harmonious reconciliation between idealism and realism is surprising. Whereas philosophical idealism quickly loses ground in the aftermath of the Revolution of 1868 and cantonalism, as I discussed in Chapter 3, in the area of aesthetics, echoes and residues of idealism persist well into the 1870s and 1880s. Although no direct mention is made of politics or political events, the use of politically charged terms such as ''demagoguery'', ''revolutionary'', ''radicalism'' reveal a silenced subtext which continues to surface, at times subtly and at times more blatantly, in subsequent studies of naturalism.

Urbano González Serrano's 1881 *Ensayos de crítica y de filosofía* include several texts that deal with naturalism. As in Revilla's articles, the text speaker adopts the rhetoric of the middle, arguing against didactic art but favoring a reflection of the social medium (73). He accepts the presence of evil and pessimism as a means of throwing virtue into relief (84) and defends the presence of the ideal, which he sees even in Zola (94). In a review of Galdós's *Doña Perfecta*, he expresses his belief in the novel as the genre most appropriate and adequate to deal with the problems and needs of the present (202). In another essay "El arte y la poesía", the speaker affirms that true artistic inspiration has its source in the collective spirit and in popular poetry. Both of these ideas will be reiterated often in the discussion of naturalism and conjoin in various ways with other aspects of the debate.

Emilia Pardo Bazán intervenes in the discussion of naturalism for the first time in her prologue to her novel *Un viaje de novios* (1881). Although only a few pages long, it reveals a complex play of various and sometimes conflicting discourses. The text speaker echoes other intellectuals in their condemnation of the serial novel – a product of fantasy which aims to distract the reader for a few hours – and exalts the novel of observation and analysis – the social, psychological, and historical study (3: 572). On the heels of this endorsement of realism, the speaker immediately retreats to a less controversial position, condemning the contemporary French novel for its systematic choice of repulsive and indecent subject matter as well as its emphasis on sadness and despair (3: 572). Writing as a woman, Pardo Bazán seeks to distance herself from any possible association with sexuality or with echoes of George Sand's calls for free love. Although she does not specifically mention Sand in the prologue, she very definitively repudiates her calls for free love in the later *La cuestión palpitante*. The emphatic repudiation of the French novel and of the treatment of sexuality in the French novel which appears in the prologue suggests that Sand is the French model from which she seeks to differentiate herself.

In addition, writing as a women who was strongly identified with Catholicism due to her sex, social position, and previous writing, she veers away from an exclusive emphasis on the negative and consequently, on determinism and fatalism. To underscore the difference with the French, the text speaker makes use of patriotic discourse, applauding the tradition of Spanish realism as exemplified by the *Celestina*, Cervantes, Velázquez, Goya, Tirso de Molina and Ramón de la Cruz. In the speaker's view, Spanish realism does not disdain idealism, but successfully unites the material and the spiritual (3: 572–73). This final emphasis on a balance of matter and spirit echoes Krausist-Institutionist discourse and serves to separate the patriotic discourse from traditional neo-Catholic nationalistic exaltation. The swerve is increasingly evident in the closing paragraphs, where the speaker expresses a desire to answer anticipated criticism from those who might see her as endorsing moral didacticism in the novel:

> Aun pudiera curarme en salud, vindicándome anticipadamente de otro cargo que tal vez me dirija algún malhumorado censor. Hay quien cree que la novela debe probar, demostrar o corregir algo, presentando al final castigado el vicio y galardonada la virtud, ni más ni menos que en los cuentecicos para uso de la infancia. Yo de mí sé

decir que en arte me enamora la enseñanza indirecta que emana de la hermosura, pero aborrezco las píldoras de moral rebozadas en una capa de oro literario. Entre el impudor frío y afectado de los escritores ultranaturalistas y las homilías sentimentales de los autores que toman un púlpito en cada dedo y se van por esos trigos predicando, no escojo; me quedo sin ninguno. (*OC* 3: 573)

Like Revilla and others, Pardo Bazán follows a circuitous path through the competing discourses but as a woman, her journey is all the more hazardous. Furthermore, the shadow of Fernán Caballero, the major Spanish woman novelist prior to the appearance of Pardo Bazán, necessitates additional swerving and clarifying. In the passage quoted above, Fernán Caballero's insistence on the moralizing function of art echoes through the text even as Pardo Bazán's text speaker refutes it. The reference to the little stories destined for children and the sentimental homilies evoke a feminine literature that is here denigrated and negated while at the same time the association with the French George Sand and her open treatment of sexuality is precluded. As one of a still small number of women writers who successfully competes in the male world of the realistic and naturalistic novel, Pardo Bazán constantly seeks to claim her own ground and to silence the echoes and projected echoes of other women writers in her work and in her aesthetic.

During the winter of 1881–1882, the Ateneo in Madrid sponsored a discussion on the topic of naturalism. Among the various participants in the debate was E. Gómez Ortiz, who began publishing his speeches in *La América* and then in book form under the title *El naturalismo en el arte*, which appeared in 1882 (Pattison 41). Although conservative critics described *El naturalismo en el arte* as revolutionary (Pattison 41), the text reveals only a moderate endorsement of naturalism and a clear disassociation from revolutionary tactics and ideologies. In the early pages, the speaker praises Romanticism and the political and literary liberation that accompanied it (21). He then applauds the appearance of the art of observation and the abandonment of imaginary art for the serious study of humanity and modern society (37). The rhetoric employed at this point in the text is truly progressive, with radical resonances:

Nos hallamos en el siglo de las grandes luchas y de las grandes adquisiciones; el horizonte de las ciencias es inmenso; el campo de la filosofía es dilatado; los descubrimientos son cada día más temerarios e imprevistos; la necesidad de la civilización se nos impone y nuestras frentes se hallan aun enrojecidas por el fuego de la revolución. Hay necesidad de acudir con remedios enérgicos a la curación de graves dolencias; los problemas sociales se multiplican cuanto más se resuelven; los errores no han desaparecido ni los fanatismos han dejado la tierra; por esto los medios de progreso no descansan, el ansia de la verdad no cede, y la inteligencia y el pensamiento vigilan cuidadosamente los espacios como si escrutaran el porvenir. (36–37)

Gómez Ortiz clearly advocates progress and defends significant social change but even in the passage just quoted, antirevolutionary discourse surfaces. The mention of ''descubrimientos temerarios'' suggests that the allusions to the fires of revolution which follow immediately contain more unease than enthusiasm. This is confirmed by a subsequent declaration that some naturalists have taken their exaggerations to the extremes of demagoguery (43) – an obvious echo of Revilla – and by the expressed doubt as to whether naturalism has passed the dangerous period of its literary "93" (70. See page 59 of this study). There is a schizophrenic quality to Gómez Ortiz's text, as it develops textual strategies that seek to form a coherent readership in a society that is increasingly divided and subjected to competing discourses. *El naturalismo en el arte* wavers between a discourse that, on the one hand, advocates change and on the other, argues against revolution. The speaker wants a democratic, popular literature while at the same time, he censures the naturalists' systematic preference for lower-class characters and themes (45). He condemns Menéndez Pelayo and the official antagonism to liberal writers, but he also decries Zola's emphasis on pure physiology to the detriment of art and of free will. In the opposition to Zola, the discourse echoes the conservative and even neo-Catholic defense of individual responsibility and free will but with the co-presence of the call for change and the radical rhetoric, the condemnation of determinism becomes also a condemnation of neo-Catholic fatalism. The insistence on individual liberty carries with it echoes of Krausist/Institutionist faith in the human capacity for growth and seeks to salvage the possibility for change even while repudiating violence and revolution. Resonances of literary and philosophical idealism continue and clash with Zola's emphasis on the physical, the lower class, the unpleasant. The following quotation contains traces and echoes of all of these discourses, which enter into dialogic interaction and thereby redefine and modulate each other as they seek to redefine and modulate the collective Spanish reader:

> La fisiología, aplicada ciegamente a las letras, la observación y experimentación de sus fenómenos . . . desarrollarán hábilmente una tesis científica, adornada con formas literarias y fantásticas, pero no llegarán a la obra de arte porque es uno solo su camino; no alcanzarán la realidad porque no reside ésta en lo inverosímil; lograrán, sí, mostrarnos el espectáculo triste y luctuoso de una vida ignorada y tenebrosa, sobre la cual surgirá el fatalismo fisiológico arrastrando sin responsabilidad nuestras acciones al crimen y nuestros hábitos al vicio, sin que por un instante la conciencia del hombre se le imponga ni la voluntad le refrene. (42–43)

The text proceeds to emphasize the nihilism that underlies naturalistic determinism and to clarify that it leads to a view of life that is significantly more hopeless than that derived from the Greek or Christian concepts of destiny. In this respect, Gómez Ortiz echoes Azcárate and other writers who had previously condemned pessimism and positivism precisely because they lead to a passivity that precludes change. Notwithstanding the use of a radical rhetoric in the initial pages and in some other places within the text, Gómez Ortiz's *El naturalismo: Naturalismo en el arte, política y literatura* differs very little from Revilla's "El naturalismo en el arte", published some three years earlier. Naturalistic discourse enters into the text but it continues to be pinched off, qualified, or negated by the residues of idealistic discourse and by the pressures to reach a readership that accepts that discourse as authoritative.

The liberal acceptance of French naturalism is somewhat more marked in several articles published in 1882, and the catalyst for this increased tolerance is at least in part Emilia Pardo Bazán's *El viaje de novios.* Contemporary feminist criticism repeatedly points out the silencing of women in patriarchal cultures. In a now classic essay, Elaine Showalter writes that "women have been denied the full resources of language and have been forced into silence, euphemism, or circumlocution" (Abel 23). She and the anthropologists Shirley and Edwin Ardener describe women as a "muted" group (Abel 29). Sandra Gilbert and Susan Gubar also link female submission with silence and argue that women writers are traditionally viewed as a daemonic force that must be silenced (35–36). In a study of Renaissance theories of rhetoric and creativity, Ann Rosalind Jones examines the male view that female access to speech is linked to sexual promiscuity: ". . . a women's accessibility to the social world beyond the household through speech was seen as intimately connected to the scandalous openness of her body" (76). It is worth noting that the association of silence and the female continues in the psychoanalytic theories of Jacques Lacan and Julia Kristeva, both of whom identify the acquisition of language with entry into the symbolic order or Law of the Father and the loss of the imaginary (Lacan) or the semiotic (Kristeva), which is linked to the mother and is expressed through absence, silence, or incoherence (Moi 99–101, 161–67; Jacobus 12). The fear of female possession of speech and the desire to retake the word from the woman speaker is extraordinarily evident in the responses to Pardo Bazán. Her word is constantly challenged, restated, or negated by male writers. The speakers enter into a dialogue with Pardo Bazán with the desire to muffle if not silence her voice or to appropriate and redirect it. At times, especially in the early years, male writers intervene to assure that her word will be interpreted more liberally than they feel she intends and at other times, generally in the late 1880s and early 1890s, they move to preempt a liberal or feminist interpretation.

The effect of Pardo Bazán's presence can be observed in Leopoldo Alas's changing position with respect to naturalism in the early 1880s. Palacio Valdés and Alas publish a series of reviews in their collection *La literatura en 1881,* and in Alas's articles he makes several important references to naturalism. In his study of Galdós's *La desheredada,* he endorses naturalism but with specific reservations regarding the use of indecent words (136) and a caution not to renounce Spain's own glorious past (132). The review of Pardo Bazán's *Un viaje de novios* moves further in the direction of an unqualified acceptance of French naturalism, in large part as a response to Pardo Bazán's prologue. Alas's text speaker classifies Pardo Bazán as a traditionalist, a tolerant version of Alarcón and Pereda but an opponent to liberty and progress. The association of Pardo Bazán with conservative, if not reactionary, attitudes has its roots both in her own past activities and in the collective perception of women as essentially more religious and more conserva-tive. I mentioned previously that her initial publications include a poem to her son and several studies of religious figures. Furthermore, in 1877 she had published a refutation of Darwin's theory of evolution in *La Ciencia Cristiana*, a conservative Catholic publication whose editor was the neo-Catholic Ortí y Lara (3: 715). Although she clearly was moving towards increasing openness to new ideas, the male reading and writing public continued to identify her then (as well as now) with conservatism. In this context, Pardo Bazán's moderate endorsement of realism/naturalism threatens to redefine the movement in a manner totally unacceptable to the left and consequently, provokes a series of responses that seek to impede the readers' return to older authoritative models which echo through Pardo Bazán's text and exert an appeal on the strength of their familiarity. Whereas the speaker in Alas's review of Galdós's *La desheredada* expresses a qualified acceptance of naturalism and defends the "glorious national literature", in response to Pardo Bazán he insists that French naturalism is the only true, legitimate form of realism (184). He clearly fears a conservative appropriation of naturalistic discourse and seeks to recuperate the movement for the liberals:

> La señora Pardo Bazán, discreta siempre, ha visto mejor que los más; pero no ha querido verlo todo. El naturalismo francés es precisamente el verdadero, el legítimo, el que tiene la clave, el que da la norma; el naturalismo español, a que ella se acoge, apenas acaba de nacer, y su existencia es todavía tan precaria que los más niegan aún que viva. (184)

He further remarks that her understanding of naturalism is not exact and argues that Zola is not as pessimistic as Pardo Bazán describes him. The constant reminders to the reader that as a woman she would do well not to read all that French naturalism has produced and the suggestion that she is somehow incapable of portraying a male character (he conjectures that she is in love with her protagonist and wants to save him) serve to undermine her authority to define naturalism as well as to write novels.

Luis Vidart also seeks to recuperate naturalistic discourse from possible conservative appropriation but he does so, not by marginalizing Pardo Bazán's narrative, but by reclaiming it as progressive. In "El naturalismo en el arte literario y la novela de costumbres", the text speaker opens with an enthusiastic description of naturalism, which is described as a vigorous and necessary protest against art for art's sake and frivolous literary productions, presumably the serial novel. In reviewing Pardo Bazán's prologue to *El viaje de novios*, he agrees with her condemnation of naturalism's proclivity for licentious subject matter but then refutes her charges that naturalism is pessimistic and moves to preempt a potential return to traditional Spanish realism. He quotes her exaltation of Cervantes, Velázquez, Goya, Ramón de la Cruz and then argues that the Quijote and the Celestina are no less pessimistic than some of Zola's works. He also disagrees with her defense of art for art's sake and argues that the presence of a thesis is not necessarily injurious to art. The discussion of Pardo Bazán's prologue is clearly designed to neutralize her attacks on naturalism and to nullify a return to former literary models as an alternative to naturalism. It is only in the matter of licentious language and behavior that Vidart echoes Pardo Bazán.

The remainder of the review deals specifically with the novel *Un viaje de novios* and here the text speaker strives to illustrate that, irrespective of her theory, Pardo Bazán's narrative practice is clearly naturalistic. He commences by insisting that she can in no way be associated with those who oppose progress and offers as proof her novelistic depiction of an atheist who is honorable, attractive, and morally without reproach (186–87). Furthermore, he contends that her text provides a convincing argument in favor of divorce (188). In keeping with naturalistic tenets, it is a serious study of contemporary customs, with the requisite objectivity and even a certain social determinism (189).

Vidart's review offers a reading of *Un viaje de novios* that places it within a liberal tradition and within the naturalistic canon. In this way it seeks both to influence Pardo Bazán as a writer, encouraging further development along progressive lines by an acceptance of her narrative and its implications, and to influence readers of the novel, by suggesting a liberal interpretation. Although "El naturalismo en el arte literario" works to impede a conservative appropriation of Pardo Bazán's theory and practice, in the area of female sexuality, it promotes traditional patterns of conduct. Several critics had commented previously that *Un viaje de novios* sacrifices plausibility to an imposed morality, asserting that the prolonged co-presence of the young and attractive protagonists in an unsupervised relationship would lead inevitably to sexual relations while in the novel, the young woman's purity is dutifully respected by the hero. Vidart goes to some lengths to prove that adultery and sex were not the inevitable outcome of the narrative action and even quotes a ladies' man acquaintance of his who invokes general educational, social and moral values to prove the verisimilitude of the protagonists' sexual purity (193).

The persistence of a puritanical attitude towards female sexuality clearly serves to brake the acceptance of naturalism and impacts significantly on the acceptance of Pardo Bazán and her subsequent works. It figures heavily in Aureliano J. Pereira's response to the Vidart review, in which the text speaker insists on distinguishing between realism and naturalism and classifies Pardo Bazán as a realist, both in theory and in practice. In order to disprove the authorial indifference alleged by Vidart, Pereira quotes Pardo Bazán's own declaration that the writer always contributes his/her peculiar manner of seeing reality (513). Pereira stresses Pardo Bazán's condemnation of lewd scenes and cites her patriotic discourse in an effort to tie her to traditional Spanish literature and thought (517). In a previous review of *Un viaje de novios*, which he quotes here, he had lamented the fact that Pardo Bazán depicted an atheist, and thus a hardened sinner, as honorable and attractive (521–22). Although he would clearly prefer a more orthodox characterization, with the appropriate punishment of evil and rewarding of virtue, he concedes that Pardo Bazán has chosen to distance herself from moralizing art in favor of a more modern approach. While he accepts this in the name of good art, he insists on highlighting the fundamental contradiction between her aesthetic and her political and religious beliefs. In direct refutation of Vidart's comments, he asserts that Pardo Bazán is politically and theologically conservative and, thus reclaims her for conservative Spain. Notwithstanding the obvious ideological differences between Vidart and Pereira and their attempts to reappropriate Pardo Bazán for two opposing political ideologies, the two critics coincide in their judgment of the plausible sexual behavior of the protagonists. Pereira agrees that the heroine's purity is completely believable and his commentary, like Vidart's, is designed to encourage a narrative that portrays women and female sexuality in traditional, constrained terms. The two critics differ only in that Pereira's study offers the heroine's purity as proof of the novel's realism and convincing disproof of a naturalistic influence. The association of female sexuality and naturalism will surface again in subsequent articles and is a constant in the critical reception of naturalism.

Pereira's opposition to naturalism has its roots in a conservative political and religious stance that had previously opposed Krausism, positivism, and other modern currents of thought. In previous chapters I discussed the gradual evolution of Krausist/Institutionist thought from philosophical idealism towards positivism and naturalism. In Revilla and others, I have pointed out a residual idealism that remains particularly strong in the area of aesthetics. Urbano González Serrano, an active collaborator in the Institución Libre de Enseñanza, exemplifies even more clearly the Institutionist resistance to naturalism and the persistence of an idealistic discourse within liberal writers well into the 1880s. In March of 1882, González Serrano began publishing the first of a series of articles entitled "El naturalismo artístico" in *Revista Hispanoamericana*. The study was subsequently republished in *Cuestiones contemporáneas* (1883).

The text opens with certain grudging concessions to naturalism's modernity and Zola's talents, but immediately makes reference to such negatives as its crudity and the baring of "impurities" (127–28). It then continues to present a balanced view of the movement, alternately identifying its merits and its defects. Calling forth the late nineteenth-century authoritative voice of "impartiality", the text speaker concedes that naturalism does produce art and beauty and is not solely limited to the gutter (128). On the other hand, he strongly condemns naturalistic determinism, arguing that without freedom, there can be no art (136). In defense of Zola, he asserts that in his novelistic practice, he does depict the struggle of his characters with their destiny and argues that it is precisely this struggle which produces beauty (137). The essay then attacks Zola's declaration of authorial impersonality and the limited world depicted by naturalism. The text speaker declares that much of reality is irrational and remains outside of material phenomena (141). In both language and essayistic strategy, González Serrano is careful to avoid any confusion between his opposition to naturalism and that of neo-Catholicism. His language is scientific, clear, direct – purposely devoid of the dense, convoluted Krausist language but also of the emotionally charged rhetoric of the neo-Catholics. Furthermore, he praises Zola for separating the question of morality and art and defends the secularization of art that has been developing since the Reformation (145, 181).

It is precisely the presence of liberal discourse and the belief in progress which lies at the core of González Serrano's opposition to French naturalism and in particular to determinism and pessimism, echoing here his own previous study on positivism and those of other Krausist/Institutionists:

> La belleza es la realidad viva, pero la vida, que no se observa sólo en el límite pesimista, ni se contempla en extáticos y optimistas deliquios, sino la vida en acción, luchando incesantemente. (162)

In line with the insistence on struggle and change, the text speaker combats the exclusive reliance on observation and on the present, insisting that human lives are defined by their memories of the past and their hopes for the future (152); it is this ability to conquer rigid temporal division that enables humanity to cancel the inalterability of temporal succession (152). González Serrano's text clings to idealism but with a desire to study and capture human reality and then to transform it in the name of progress. In the final pages of the essay, the speaker refers to a harmonic reconciliation of the two tendencies, which he designates as realistic idealism or ideal realism (195). True to the Harmonic Rationalism of his Krausist formation he seeks to accommodate observation and invention, physiology and ethics (196–97). In keeping with Krausist/Institutionist discourse and with authoritative patriotic discourse, he underscores the foreign character of naturalism and recommends a return to the "glorious traditions" of Spanish literature (157).

González Serrano's defense of idealism and his efforts to extend Krausist/ Institutionist discourse into the 1880s constitute an important voice in the critical reception of naturalism and are echoed in the studies of Luis Alfonso (*La Epoca* 1882) and, to some degree, in Emilia Pardo Bazán. However, among most liberal and progressive writers, the trend is more and more towards a growing enthusiasm for naturalism as a means to social change. José Alcázar Hernández talks openly about the popularity of the contemporary novel and its suitability for influencing society (112). In a similar vein, José Ortega Munilla calls for its acceptance. "Aceptemos, pues, la moda, ya que esta vez va a servir de auxiliar a una transformación necesaria" ("Madrid").

Leopoldo Alas continues to study and endorse naturalism in "Del naturalismo", a series of articles that appeared in *La Diana*, 1882. Although never finished, it is Clarín's most complete study of the literary movement and it represents a response to González Serrano and to others who oppose the introduction of naturalism in Spain or who propose an excessively moderate reading of the movement. As Clarín and other writers move towards a greater advocacy of French naturalism and thus distance themselves more and more from their readership, the presence of the tact maxim (see page 19 of this study) becomes more evident and circumlocution and other strategies to minimize confrontation increase. To this end, the text speaker opens with a discussion of the relationship between literary naturalism and metaphysics and argues that it is a purely artistic theory with nothing to say about either the natural or the spiritual world (Beser 110). On another occasion, he denies that it originates in a specific philosophical system:

> Esta advertencia le quita toda afinidad con determinado sentido filosófico y científico; pues ni con éste, a que el nombre empleado parecía inclinarle, ni con otro alguno, tiene el naturalismo relación de dependencia.
> Ha nacido por la evolución natural del arte y obedeciendo a las leyes biológicas de la cultura y de la civilización en general, y en particular del arte. (119)

The same idea is reiterated continually throughout the essay with the obvious intent of undercutting conservative opposition by excluding from discussion philosophical, theological, and other non-literary aspects of the question. In response to both the conservative opposition, including French critics of naturalism such as Brunetiére, Sarcery, and Bigot, and to liberal critics like González Serrano, the speaker admits that naturalism is not new and asserts that it never claimed complete originality (119). He also denies as silly the accusation that naturalism advocates or practices mere photographic reproduction of reality (121). Like Pardo Bazán and others, he insists that artistic reproduction always requires the intervention of the artist's intention and of his conscience and ability (121). The principal defense of naturalism stems from its liberating effects on the novel. Whereas previous aesthetics had largely ignored the novel as genre or limited it to a reduced and artificial treatment of life, naturalism opens up all of reality to the novelist, with no limitations or exceptions (136).

In Clarín's study, as in those of other proponents of naturalism, the role of this new novel in the transformation of contemporary society is voiced but muted and almost imperceptible. Tucked in between the repeated assertions that naturalism is a purely artistic movement, with no relation to specific metaphysical systems, and the equally strong insistence that naturalism opposes the tendentious novel, the following definition of the aim of the naturalistic work surfaces with barely audible traces of Zola's socialist message:

> Esto, en cuanto al objeto y al medio; respecto al fin, es éste: hacer que el arte sirva, mejor que hasta ahora, a los intereses generales de la vida, hacerle entrar seriamente, como elemento capital, en la actividad progresiva de los pueblos, para que deje de ser vago soñar, y haciéndose digno de su tiempo, sirva más en adelanto de la cultura, consiguiendo que las facultades humanas por el arte se educan, recojan en éste la mísera enseñanza que en todos los órdenes impera, la verdad, tal como es, el conocimiento profundo, seguro, y exacto de la realidad . . . (127)

A few pages later, the speaker cautions against the intrusion of fantasy or authorial intent in the gathering of data, but once the novelist reaches the experimental stage – the composition of the work – then he/she can arrange the facts so that they provide some teaching ("alguna enseñanza") on the point the writer seeks to elucidate (130). Towards the end of the essay, the text speaker goes to some lengths to prove that the naturalistic novel is much more than a mere study of character; it should always include the natural surroundings and the social world, a complete morphology of life (142).

The conflicting discourses that come into play in this essay and the diverse and often oppositional forces that bring them together lead inevitably to textual tensions and contradictions. The increasingly strong incorporation of naturalistic discourse conflicts with the muting and often the silencing of the political resonances of naturalism. The endorsement of French naturalism as the single, most appropriate means for modernizing the novel and addressing contemporary literary and social needs falters in the face of naturalistic determinism, which runs counter to the Krausist/Institutionist belief in individual freedom and comes dangerously close to the long-opposed neo-Catholic fatalism. Naturalism's insistence on the impersonality of the author interweaves and at times collides with two distinct phases of Spanish liberal aesthetic discourse: the art for art's sake of the 1860s and early 70s, with which it partially coincides, and the defense of the tendentious novel of the later 70s, which it opposes in the name of authorial impersonality and scientific objectivity but encourages in terms of the construction of the experiment and the transformation of society. The overlaying and interweaving of the various discourses, voices, and echoes produces a text that is multilayered, contradictory, and signally reflective of the conflicts and contradictions that exist in late nineteenth-century Spanish culture. The confluence of competing discourses is not static, however, and in a slow but perceptible manner, new voices intrude and gradually displace or reconstitute the discourse. In the case of Alas as well as many others, a fundamental force for the transformation of the discourse is located, paradoxically, in the silences that are created by the conflicts of the competing discourses but that resonate in textual gaps and contradictions. Naturalism is increasingly accepted as a means for literary and social change but the tact principle and authoritative anti-revolutionary discourse militate against the voicing of this impulse.

Similar tensions and silences characterize Emilia Pardo Bazán's famous study of naturalism, but *La cuestión palpitante* reveals an even greater discursive complexity due to her social position and to the precarious position of the woman writer in late nineteenth-century Spain. Originally published over several months in *La Epoca* during the winter of 1882 and the spring of 1883, it was reissued as a book in 1883. Although it represents a greater acceptance of naturalism than that expressed in the prologue to *Un viaje de novios*, in comparison with studies by Alas, Gómez Ortiz, and other male writers, it is somewhat more moderate in its endorsement. Previous critics have attributed this to Pardo Bazán's Catholicism or conservatism. My own reading of *La cuestión palpitante* suggests that the dialogic character of the essay as a response to past voices and an anticipation of future responses contributes to specific silences in the text, which are, however, perceptible. *La cuestión palpitante* is a pivotal text in the debate on naturalism because it not only suggests change, but also exemplifies it. The text advocates new literary modes but more importantly, the presence of a woman writer in an intellectual debate of considerable importance gives evidence of social and political changes that are already in process. We have seen how the prologue to *Un viaje de novios*, with its moderate defense of naturalism, provoked a response from both the right and the left. The much longer and less constrained study of naturalism in *La cuestión palpitante* incites an even greater outcry and permanently alters the direction of the discussion. Writing from the vulnerable position of a woman in a man's world, and in a society that is increasingly hostile to female success, Pardo Bazán is even more obliged than Clarín and other liberal advocates of French naturalism to employ textual strategies and rhetorical devices that seek to minimize conflict and to slowly accredit her voice.

In the early paragraphs of *La cuestión palpitante*, the text speaker echoes Clarín and seeks to exclude non-literary considerations in order to deal with naturalism purely as an artistic curiosity. More than the expression of sincere authorial belief, this affirmation can be read as a textual strategy in the intricate construction of the speaker's authority. Throughout the study, the potential influence of literature on social and political reality is played down. Literature is presented as a reflection of society rather than an influence on it. The speaker ridicules those who blame art for corrupting society when it is the immorality of society that contaminates art (3:577) and subsequently refutes Zola's contention that literature is destined to regulate society's course (3:580–81). The thesis and tendentious novel are consistently criticized and Galdós's shift towards the new novel is applauded:

> Por fortuna, o más bien por el tino que guía al genio, Galdós retrocedió para huir de ese callejón sin salida, y en *El amigo Manso* y en *La desheredada* comprendió que la

> novela hoy, más que enseñar o condenar estos o aquellos ideales políticos, ha de tomar nota de la verdad ambiente y realizar con libertad y desembarazo la hermosura. (3: 642–43)

In terms of the metaphysical, theological, and ethical implications of naturalism, the speaker works similarly to establish the neutrality of art. In the following quote, echoes from Clarín's study of naturalism are clearly audible:

> En cuestiones religiosas y sociales, los naturalistas proceden como sus hermanos los positivistas respecto de los problemas metafísicos; las dejan a un lado, aguardando a que las resuelva la ciencia, si es posible (3:633)

By denying any political or theological heterodoxy, the speaker invokes contemporary authoritative discourse. The silencing of the political on the heels of the perceived failure of the Revolution of 1868 and the First Republic constitutes a generational "sociolect" and establishes a relationship of solidarity with the reader. The opposition to heresy evokes the tradition of the Counter Reformation and Spain's particular brand of Catholicism. For readers familiar with Pardo Bazán's previous publications, it reaffirms the image of a staunchly Catholic, if not neo-Catholic writer. This is further cultivated through the explicit condemnation of Zola's determinism early in *La cuestión palpitante* and repeated protestations of absolute religious orthodoxy (3: 578–79; 631–32). These protestations are, however, only one of many strands that come together in the text, and many of the other discourses and discursive traces collide with and undermine the declared conformity with established authority.

Early and repeated references to impartiality and neutrality, to the imperative to be informed regarding contemporary trends, and to the avoidance of extremes and sectarianisms, echo a liberal discourse that enters into conflict with the Catholic authoritative voice and opens it up to new interpretations. The text even makes ironic use of the neo-Catholic code words "valle de lágrimas" to further emphasize its distance from conservative Catholic discourse:

> Si no hubiese más vida que ésta; si en otro mundo de verdad y justicia no remunerasen a cada uno según sus merecimientos, la moral exigiría que en este valle de lágrimas todo anduviese ajustado y en orden; pero siendo el vivir presente principio del futuro, querer que un novelista lo arregle y enmiende la plana a la Providencia, téngolo por risible empeño. (3: 631–32)

Like Clarín, Gómez Ortiz, and other liberal writers, Pardo Bazán seeks to distance herself from neo-Catholic literary practices by condemning works that reward virtue and punish vice. Unlike her liberal contemporaries, however, Pardo Bazán's previous writing had created a perception of her persona and her writing that conflicts with progressive, liberal discourse and *La cuestión palpitante* alternately exploits and negates the conservative image. In discussing the alleged immorality of naturalistic writing, the text speaker argues that it is no worse than many Romantic novels. By reminding the reader at this specific point that as a young Catholic woman she was not allowed to read Hugo's *The Hunchback of Notre Dame* nor certain works by Espronceda, her defense of the morality of naturalism is made to appear all the more acceptable, as is the literature she is defending. If she, as a Catholic woman who was subjected to the traditional Spanish education for women, has read these texts and is not scandalized, then they can not really be as offensive as others charge[1].

The text speaker utilizes a very similar strategy to strip naturalism of any revolutionary political motivation. In addition to the emphasis on the movement as purely literary, the essay points to the radical propaganda contained in much Romantic literature and insists that by comparison, naturalism's neutrality in political and metaphysical matters is much less hazardous: "Abstención mil veces menos peligrosa que la propaganda socialista y herética de los novelistas que les precedieron" (3: 633). It is significant that this portrayal of naturalism as a corrective to the politically radical and theologically unorthodox literature of the preceding period occurs towards the end of *La cuestión palpitante*, after the speaker has gradually constructed a personal authority. The early condemnation of Zola as heretical distances the speaker from his brand of naturalism, as do the calls for a broader definition of realism. However, over the course of the text, a number of strategies work to reintegrate naturalism and Zola into the mainstream. On several occasions, the speaker reminds the reader that idealism, the accepted mode of literary expression, was also once cause for scandal (3:585–86). Patriotic discourse surfaces to nationalize naturalism, as when the text speaker points out that at one point in time people used the same language presently employed to combat naturalism in order to oppose such national institutions as the lottery and bullfighting. Echoing the prologue to *Un viaje de novios*, *La cuestión palpitante* defines Spanish literature as essentially realistic and asserts that with the return of realism, Spain is recovering her own true, pure character. In tracing the history of the novel in Spain, the speaker strives to establish the foreign origins of the novels of chivalry, which are then associated with literary idealism. The Quijote, on the other hand, is depicted as an autochthonous product and is tied to the Celestina and other Spanish creations.

The description of French literary history places emphasis on the great diversity of writers who fall under the rubric of realism/naturalism. In a clear desire to sever the reader's association of naturalism with Emile Zola, the text discusses the stylistic and philosophical variety of Diderot, Stendhal, Balzac, Flaubert, the Goncourt brothers, Daudet, and then finally, Zola. The text speaker specifically makes reference to this strategy in the opening paragraph of chapter XIII:

> Reservé adrede el último lugar para el jefe de la escuela naturalista, y hablé primero de Flaubert, Daudet y los Goncourt, no tanto por ceñirme al orden cronológico, cuanto por no emprenderla con el discutidísimo novelista, sin estudiar antes las variadas fisonomías de sus compañeros, cuya diversidad es argumento poderoso a favor del realismo. (3: 619)

[1] The passage functions on various levels and communicates more than one meaning. There is also a suggestion of the absurdity of the kinds of controls placed on young women readers but one of the pragmatic effects is to accredit the voice by aligning it with traditional authority.

This strategy of deferral or postponement is employed repeatedly in *La cuestión palpitante*. Before describing Zola, the text presents other French novelists in detail; before discussing Zola's literary production, the text stresses the bourgeois character of his life, his prosaic appearance and his devotion to his wife and family. The obvious goal is here an attempt to dispel the vision of a revolutionary. Before entering into a discussion of Zola's novels, the speaker makes repeated references to his success, which is attributed to his being at one with the surrounding culture.

Through the strategy of deferral, controversial subjects are typically put off for later sections of the text when the reader has been brought into the text speaker's sphere of influence. This is particularly true of the discussion of the alleged immorality of naturalism. Having condemned naturalistic determinism early in the text, the speaker avoids dealing with the much talked about issue of morality. Early in chapter 1, passing mention is made of the topic but merely to point out that many of those scandalized by the movement have never read a naturalistic novel or condemn the entire school on the basis of one or two works (34). Subsequently, in the chapter on Flaubert, the speaker mentions the scandal created by *Madame Bovary* but immediately defers a full treatment of the "delicate question" of the moral issue until a later chapter (3: 608–09). In the discussion of Zola, the text speaker devotes a full chapter to his life and character, another to his tendencies, the following to his style, and finally, in the last chapter on the novelist, enters into a discussion of the morality of his works. Given the social and political context and the position of women in late nineteenth-century Spain, the question of morality overlaps not only ethical issues, but also such other matters as social transformation and the emancipation of women. The deferral of a direct discussion of this topic has its origins in the tact maxim, which is also related to the silencing of the topic of women's emancipation throughout *La cuestión palpitante*. Before considering Pardo Bazán's discussion of morality in Zola and in naturalism in general, it will be useful to retrace the muted allusions to women and the general silencing of women's issues in order to show how they interweave with the overall treatment of naturalism.

The avoidance of the imposition of the "I" which is characteristic of the essay is understandably exaggerated in Pardo Bazán's writing, given the status of women and women writers at the time. Various forms that contribute to the deletion of the agent abound in *La cuestión palpitante*: the first person plural, the passive, the impersonal "se", and agentless verbal forms such as "conviene" or other impersonal expressions. The presence of a "feminine I", with specific reference to the sex of the speaker, is negligible and when it appears, generally swerves away from a direct consideration of women's issues. In Chapter 1, the text speaker alludes to an anonymous article appearing in the *Révue Britannique*, in which the author comments that a woman writer, in *Un viaje de novios*, is trying to introduce the naturalistic novel in Spain. After remarking ironically on the anger and disdain revealed by the French critic in the face of a woman who dares to make such an attempt, the speaker veers to avoid a confrontation on the question of women writers. Instead, the following sentences include a qualified denial of any attempt to introduce naturalism in Spain and a back-handed attack on the French writer on the basis of his bungled translation of the title *Un viaje de novios as Voyage de fiancés*

(3: 576)[2]. Towards the end of Chapter 1, the female "I" reappears to justify the treatment of the topic, clarifying that although it had been dealt with the previous year in oral debates in the Ateneo, it had not been treated in written form. The speaker alludes to the exclusion of women from the Ateneo and its sessions but mutes any sustained criticism of the practice, commenting that her lack of time prohibits the investigation of causes other than simple custom. A third intrusion of a female speaker occurs in the previously mentioned references to the prohibitions of such texts as *The Hunchback of Notre Dame*, where the speaker flaunts her conventional upbringing with only a very subtle criticism of its limitations.

Other appearances of a textual "I" are devoid of any specific sexual identifying markers and generally seek to forestall any association of the speaker with feminism and other radical groups. The first person singular is noticeably present in the discussion of the Goncourt brothers, with whom the speaker clearly wishes to be identified. The text emphasizes their differences from Zola, in particular, their love of color, and their avoidance of exclusively vulgar types and scenes in favor of a certain ideal of beauty that they identify with contemporary society (3: 612–13). The "I" also surfaces in the discussion of Zola, but the language employed consistently plots out the distance between the text speaker and the novelist. The first person singular intrudes in the discussion of Zola's scientific method and points out the positive appeal of such a method in contemporary society but also signals with great force the error of the method (3: 623). Later in the same chapter the "I" surfaces to identify Zola's defects: "En cuanto a sus efectos, mejor diré a sus excesos, ellos son tales y tanto los va acentuando y recargando, que se harán insufribles, si ya no se hicieron, a la mayoría" (3: 625).

In the representation of the "I" as well as in the surface arguments of the text, *La cuestión palpitante* silences the subject of social change and in particular of the emancipation of women. The topic is not, however, absent from the essay and forms a significant subtext which advocates a new role for the woman writer and, in turn, a change in the status and power of women. This muted discourse is evident in repeated allusions to the limits placed on women and also in the version of literary history presented in the text. Early in chapter 1 the speaker refers to the public outcry in response to Echegaray's theater and comments that for the general public it came down to the fundamental argument over the morality of his plays and whether unmarried women should be allowed to attend performances of *Mar sin orillas*. In the following sentences the text ridicules the entire scandal and the proposed exclusion of the female public by pointing out that after the initial hysteria, prudent judgment has come to the conclusion that the subversive dramatist is really no more than a reactionary who retreats not only to Romantic theater but to the much older theater of Calderón and Lope (3: 574).

This early allusion to the subject of morality and the female literary public will reappear later in the text, but over the next chapters the focus shifts to the importance of women writers in the history of literature. The text speaker takes

---

[2] It is significant that Pardo Bazán strives to correct a translation that conveys an image of her novel as erotic. The patriarchal association of female access to speech and authorship with sexual liberation requires that she defend the sexual orthodoxy of her narrative.

every available opportunity to applaud the valor and value of female precursors, both anonymous and known. In discussing Romanticism, the text refers to the "bandada de dulces y valientes poetisas" (3: 586) and in tracing the origins of the novel, it emphasizes the role of grandmothers and wet-nurses in the oral transmission of the narrative (3: 591). The discussion of the French novel not only stresses the inferiority of Rabelais to Cervantes, but also points out that while Rabelais never really formed a school and had no imitators, Margaret of Navarre initiated the much cultivated "nouvelle". The same valorization of the female writer appears in the discussion of Madame de Staël, whose realistic portrayal of herself and of her contemporary world is contrasted favorably to Chateaubriand's idealized invention (3: 600). George Sand is depicted as another major landmark in French literary history and is judged far superior to her contemporaries, Alexandre Dumas and Eugène Sue (3: 603). In the discussion of Daudet, the text speaker alludes to the feminine character of his talent (3: 619) and suggests that the collaboration of his wife contributes to his moderated, poetic version of naturalism.

The repeated positive references to female writers signal the vindication of women as an important subtext of *La cuestión palpitante*. There is, however, a large subset of women writers from which the text speaker very specifically distances herself and whose value she strives to diminish. In Chapter 8, dedicated to the French literature of the late eighteenth and early nineteenth centuries, the text speaker condemns the moralistic novel and is especially harsh in the judgment of Stéphanie-Felicité de Genlis for her "chorro continuo, igual y monótono de narraciones con tendencia pedagógico-moral" (3: 599). The treatment of the English novel reiterates the same criticism. Calling on the authoritative Catholic voice, the text speaker seeks to undermine the prestige of the British literary tradition by pointing out its Protestant, puritanical character. English women novelists are depicted as daughters of Protestant ministers who use the proceeds of their literary works to finance missionary expeditions and sacrifice literary value to please their mass readership. The closing sentences of the section invoke conservative patriotic discourse, with a Counter Reformation bias, to invalidate the English novel as a possible model for Spain:

> Por añadidura trae la novela inglesa – aun cuando es superior – tan fuertemente impresa la marca de otra religión, de otro clima, de otra sociedad, que a nosotros, los latinos, forzosamente nos parece exótica. ¿Cómo nos ha de gustar, v. gr., la predicadora metodista, heroína de *Adán Bede*? (3: 637)

In contrast to the prudish English moralists with their puritanical platitudes, the text speaker applauds the literary achievements of George Sand but very specifically excludes those early works which contain "propaganda anticonyugal y antisocial" (3: 602). Citing the French critic Latouche, the speaker suggests that these extravagant philosophical theories did not really originate with Sand; rather, she borrowed them from others. While her ideas are no longer taken seriously and are in no way offensive to anyone, her literary talents continue to be admired (3: 602). As in so many texts involved in the critical reception of naturalism, the speaker adopts the rhetoric of the middle, seeking to define a moderate position that is distant both from the neo-Catholic right, here portrayed as the British puritanical tradition, and the radical left, exemplified in this instance by several of George Sand's early novels.

The establishment of a valid feminine tradition that is not limited to a narrow, prudish outlook nor can be confused with calls for free love and revolutionary social transformation animates the literary history delineated in *La cuestión palpitante* and also motivates the defense of the morality of naturalistic novels. Returning to Chapter 16 and the discussion of the alleged immorality of Zola in this context, the underlying desire to open the literary canon to women writers and to women readers is apparent. The chapter contains a very strong apology of naturalism with an unusually strong presence of the textual "I" serving to make the argument even more forceful. The text speaker stresses the need to differentiate between immorality, as that which leads to vice, and vulgarity, or that which conflicts with certain ideas of social decency (3: 630–31). While reiterating the condemnation of determinism, the speaker ridicules those whose most serious charge against naturalism is that its novels are inappropriate for unmarried women. The response to this much repeated objection is extraordinarily emotional and marks one of the few moments in the text where the speaker sheds the tact principle in favor of a combination of ironic discourse and the imposition of personal authority:

> ¡Válanos Dios! Lo primero habría que empezar por dilucidar si conviene más a las señoritas vivir en paradisíaca inocencia, o conocer la vida y sus escollos y sirtes, para evitarlos; problema que, como casi todos, se resuelve en cada caso con arreglo a las circunstancias, porque existen tantos caracteres diversos como señoritas, y lo que a ésta le convenga será funestísimo quizá para aquélla, y vaya usted a establecer reglas absolutas. Es análoga esta cuestión a la del alimento; cada edad y cada estómago lo necesita diferente; proscribir un libro porque no todas las señoritas deban apacentar en él su inteligencia es como si tirásemos por la ventana un trozo de carne bajo pretexto de que no la comen los niños de teta. Désele norabuena al infante su papilla, que el adulto apetecerá el manjar fuerte y nutritivo. ¡Cuán hartos estamos de leer elogios de ciertos libros, alabados tan sólo porque nada contiene que a una señorita ruborice! Y sin embargo, literariamente hablando, no es mérito ni demérito de una obra el no ruborizar a las señoritas. (3: 631)

The argument for expanded opportunities for women readers and women writers immediately precedes and is clearly related to the defense of naturalism, which appears at the end of the chapter (3:633). In the context of women's changing role, naturalism is here viewed as the most appropriate vehicle for literary liberation. It considerably increases the field of study and with its insistence on authorial neutrality, frees women writers from the narrowly moralistic literary subgenres to which they had been previously limited. Although the text speaker sidesteps a specific clarification of the consequences of naturalism for women writers and readers, the assumptions governing the reconstruction of literary history and the emphatic condemnation of certain kinds of women's literature, followed almost immediately by a qualified but strong endorsement of naturalism, suggest a silenced subtext.

While the discussion concentrates almost exclusively on literature and indirectly on women and their relations to literature, the implications for social and political change follow logically. The tact maxim, the dialogic character of the essay, the precarious position of the woman writer in late nineteenth-century Spain, the general muting of political questions during the 1870s and 1880s all contribute to the silencing of the political ramifications of naturalism. The underlying impulse for political and social change does not, however, disappear entirely and as mentioned earlier, while the attempt to remove literature from political and theological concerns is sustained throughout *La cuestión palpitante*, it collides with other discursive strands that underscore the presence of the non-literary. One final example of these discursive collisions can be found in the examples and metaphors presented in *La cuestión palpitante*. Frequently, the text speaker employs metaphors that introduce the very political and theological issues that have been declared irrelevant to the discussion of naturalism. The first sentence of the text declares that naturalism and realism are to literature what the Duke of la Torre is to politics. The reference to Francisco Serrano y Domínguez carries with it reminiscences of the Revolution, the Republic, and more recent progressive political activism. Serrano had been the president of the provisional government formed after the Revolution of 1868 as well as the last president of the Republic. When the conservative government of Cánovas del Castillo fell in 1881, the Liberals under Sagasta took power. In protest over Sagasta's support of the Restoration and the Constitution of 1876, Serrano formed the Leftist Dynastic party which called for a return to the more liberal Constitution of 1869, universal suffrage, and the introduction of jury trials (F. Almagro I 386–87; Ossorio 440, 808). The mention of this controversial figure, whose recent political manifesto revived the memories of the silenced revolutionary period and called for a return to its principles, clearly inserts the political into the discussion of naturalism even as the following sentences assert the exclusively literary nature of the question. Other metaphors or examples gratuitously poke fun at conservative political or religious behaviors, as when the text speaker compares Moret y Prendergast's condemnation of Zola to a small town preacher's sermon:

> El proceder del señor Moret me recuerda el caso de aquel padre predicador que en un pueblo se desataba condenando las peinetas, los descotes bajos y otras modas nuevas y peregrinas de Francia, que nadie conocía ni usaba entre las mujeres que componían su auditorio. Oíanle éstas y se daban al codo murmurando bajito: "¡Hola, se usan descotes, hola, conque se llevan peinetas!" (3: 575)

In a later chapter, introducing the "Victors", as the chapter title refers to them, the speaker employs yet another metaphor which ties discredited idealism with religious orthodoxy: "Conocidos ya los padres de la Iglesia idealista, ahora nos toca trabar amistad con los jefes de la escuela contraria" (3: 603).

The use of terms such as "strike up a friendship" applied to those who are metaphorically and literally depicted as unorthodox collides with the insistent professions of religious orthodoxy that appear on the surface of the text. Furthermore, these political and philosophical metaphors link the text to ongoing debates on the subject of naturalism and thus introduce echoes of those silenced discourses. Zola's contention that the novelist is like a doctor who seeks the causes of disease and then proceeds to effect the cure (*OC* 46: 28) is specifically refuted in *La cuestión palpitante*, where the text speaker emphasizes the distinction between art and science and condemns politically motivated literature. However, in the closing paragraphs of the text, Zola's silenced voice echoes quite clearly in the metaphoric language used to describe and justify realism: "Así el realismo, que es un instrumento de comprobación exacta, da en cada país la medida del estado moral, bien como el esfigmógrafo registra la pulsación normal de un sano y el tumultuoso latir del pulso de un febricitante" (3: 647). The use of medical terminology and the representation of illness echo the idea of literature as science and the goal of social cure enunciated in Zola's manifesto.

The silencing of controversial political and social issues in *La cuestión palpitante* has its roots in the nature of essayistic discourse – its dialogic character with preceding and succeeding texts as well as with the contemporary reader – and in peculiar socio-political features of late nineteenth-century Spain – the collective memory of the Revolution of 1868 and cantonalism, social unease at the changing role of women, the conflicting pressures of neo-Catholicism, liberalism, and the radical left. All of these factors enter into play in the production of *La cuestión palpitante* and contribute to a complex interweaving of discourses and textual levels. Although the text works to mute suggestions of radical and even moderate social and political change, the presence of a female voice and a female speaker represents a change that is already in process and provokes a series of responses that continue into the 1890s. In Chapter 5 I will analyze these texts to demonstrate the transformative effects of the female voice on the critical reception of naturalism in Spain.

VOICES, SILENCES AND ECHOES:
THE CRITICAL RECEPTION
OF NATURALISM IN SPAIN 1882–1891

In spite of the muting and silencing of controversial issues in *La cuestión palpitante*, its publication provokes a series of responses from both the right and the left which alternately seek to refute, appropriate, or redefine it. Typically, the writers react more to the figure of Pardo Bazán as an example of change that they fear or resent than to the information communicated in her text. As author of the prologue to the book version of *La cuestión palpitante*, Clarín is the first of many respondents. In keeping with his early articles on Pardo Bazán's theory of naturalism, he stresses her Catholicism (*Los prólogos* 138) and suggests that she does not fully understand the movement she is describing (134). Notwithstanding generous praise of her abilities, the text speaker seeks to undermine her authority by emphasizing her marginality as a woman writer. He refers to many that abhor her, to the resentment that her success causes in others, and in the closing sentence, manipulates the semantically ambiguous "masculine"/"feminine" attributes in a manner that deconstructs his expressed admiration. Having discussed literary envy in the previous paragraphs, the speaker suggests that many will respond with irritation, not at Pardo Bazán's defense of certain doctrines, but at her praise of certain people. He then goes on to express his hope that his own praise of Pardo Bazán will turn certain male and female writers green with envy. The specific mention of female writers is followed by a final description of all of these envious writers as members of the "weaker sex", in that there is something of the everlasting feminine in literary envy (*Los prólogos* 139). The linking of female and envy and the emphasis on negative feminine stereotypes in the prologue to a work by a woman writer introduces traditional misogynistic discourse into the text and works to undermine the authority of the female speaker. Given the cultural horizon of expectations at the time, most readers undoubtedly retrieve the code words "envy" and "weaker sex" and apply them not merely to those male writers who oppose Pardo Bazán, but also to Pardo Bazán herself.

A letter to Pardo Bazán from the Marquis of Premio Real also combines expressed admiration for women writers and an underlying unease, in this case regarding morality and, by implication, sexuality. The speaker declares himself a product of the nineteenth century and consequently, a supporter of educational opportunities for women. He then turns to the question of naturalism and focuses immediately on the subject of morality. In response to *La cuestión palpitante*, he defends the English novel and, in particular, English women writers, arguing that they have none of Zola's immorality. Although he concedes that it is useful and even profitable to depict social vices, he feels that certain vices should be presented "cubiertos con la blanca losa de la decencia" ("Epístola a la autora"). The speaker evidently strives to reinstate the English novel and English women writers as appropriate models for Spain and Spanish women and to proscribe access to Zola, particularly for women writers and readers. In a response to the Marquis of Premio Real, published two weeks after the appearance of his letter, Pardo Bazán reiterates her distaste for the English novelists and their narrowly moralistic literature and repeats that the value of a work of art is in no way dependent on its appropriateness for family reading. The subject is not closed, however, and will resurface in a subsequent polemic with Luis Alfonso.

Somewhat later in 1883, Cánovas del Castillo publishes a two volume study of the "costumbrista", Estébanez Calderón. One of the few texts on the subject that does not appear to have been inspired by Pardo Bazán's study of naturalism, it is of interest not only because of the political significance of the author but because of the political ramifications of his literary evaluation. Chapter 5 of *"El Solitario" y su tiempo* studies the question of realism and attempts to distinguish between the "naturalism" of those writers devoted to the description of local customs and manners and that of Zola and his followers. The text speaker attacks the pessimism of contemporary naturalists and their emphasis on animal instinct (*"El Solitario"* 167), on a total lack of reason, free will, belief in higher ideals or anything that would serve to curb human behavior (172). In response to those, like Pardo Bazán, who suggest that knowledge of evil is a necessary step towards overcoming it, the speaker argues that the theoretical knowledge of evil provided by the naturalists is not new, not useful, and leads to the imitation rather than the avoidance of sin (173). The most vulnerable readers are clearly the lower classes and it is in this aspect that Estébanez Calderón offers an alternative model. His scenes show men and women influenced by instinct but never totally controlled by it (167) and are "bañados en hermosa luz de mediodía, atenuante y hasta redentora de las corrupciones y fealdades de la realidad" (166). The text mentions with some frequency the consoling intervention of the ideal in Estébanez Calderón (175; 200–01), which contrasts with the immoral, atheistic, hopeless portraits of the naturalists. A perceptible fear of an uncontrolled and uncontrollable lower class surfaces throughout the chapter on naturalism and is accompanied by nostalgia for earlier periods, when relations between the classes were less conflictive. The speaker's exaltation of the historical novel and desire to reestablish it as a valid literary model (170) reflects acute discomfort with the present. Notwithstanding Cánovas's stature as a leading Conservative and as head of the government from 1873–1881, the text largely sidesteps a direct consideration of political issues in keeping with the anti-political "sociolect" and with the tact principle. In this respect, it is worth noting that Cánovas's study is written and published shortly after Sagasta and the Liberals come to power in a burst of enthusiasm and hope for change[1]. Consequently,

---

[1] See Ruíz Martínez for an indication of the public liberal perception of the implications of the changes in government.

Cánovas cannot rely on the solidarity factor and must address his readership accordingly.

The year 1884 brings a series of polemics regarding naturalism. Towards the end of 1883 Pereda's *Pedro Sánchez* and Emilia Pardo Bazán's *La Tribuna* had appeared and both provoked reviews and comment as to their connections with Zola and his school. To a degree that has not been previously noted, the discussion reveals that the issues of political reform and the role of women – in particular, of female sexuality – are increasingly central to the debate, although their importance is routinely muted and allusions to them are frequently indirect. Luis Alfonso continues to combat naturalism in his review of *Pedro Sánchez*, praising the novel precisely because it is not naturalistic. Although the text speaker views the work as realistic, he contends that it avoids excessive descriptions of immoral actions and here, Alfonso specifically cites the indirect depiction of Pedro's return home and his discovery of his wife with a lover. As another example of the appropriate means to present such topics, the reviewer cites the *Quijote*, in which Dorotea very discreetly and indirectly describes the loss of her virginity. Alfonso's main criticism of the novel addresses the dénouement, in which nine characters die within a space of five pages. He is less concerned with the extent of the annihilation than with the fact that both the evil and the virtuous characters succumb. The residues of literary idealism are obvious, as he argues that a happy ending, with Pedro remarried to the virtuous Carmen and resettled in the provinces, would have been more appropriate ("Pedro Sánchez").

In the same month of January, J. Ixart publishes a long and intriguing review of Pardo Bazán's *La Tribuna*. While Ixart is much more open to naturalism than Alfonso and many other writers of the period, he is clearly uncomfortable with certain naturalistic practices in *La Tribuna*. The review opens with a discussion of the novelistic genre in general and repeats the now commonplace view that what was once a frivolous pastime for idle young men and women has become a true study of the contemporary individual and his/her interactions with the social milieu. Echoing Clarín and others, the speaker asserts that the novel is a more appropriate mechanism for teaching the general reader than history or philosophy. The initial remarks on Pardo Bazán classify her as a full-fledged member of the naturalistic school. Ixart, who writes as a young liberal, associated with *Artes y Letras* and other writers seeking to foster the introduction of naturalism in Spain (Pattison 92), strives to appropriate Pardo Bazán for the cause and to this end employs religious terminology to underscore the distance between her previously declared Catholicism or neo-Catholicism and her current practice of naturalism. He refers to her as having joined the "sect" with heart and soul, first as a preacher and then as a celebrant. In spite of his enthusiasm and in contrast to his desire to appropriate Pardo Bazán to the liberal cause, the text speaker swerves away from an open endorsement of her naturalism, specifically with regard to the portrayal of the lower classes. Although he praises her use of dialect and popular language, he emphasizes his own and his readers' distance from the lower classes, commenting that those not used to hearing lower-class people talk – and he uses the first person plural to include himself in this group – will be surprised to find how little the dialect has changed since Cervantes or the Celestina. A distinctly paternalistic tone echoes through the text, as when the speaker refers to Pardo Bazán's compassion for her characters:

> Discurre por ellas (entre líneas) como fluido invisible, el ardor generoso que despierta en los corazones sanos el espectáculo que ofrecen las clases menos cultas, con su espontaneidad y vigor, y esta secreta simpatía, esta fruición inefable se comunican al lector, embelesado y un sí es no es, enternecido con la ignorancia y bondades de aquella pobre gente. ("La Tribuna")

The expressed distance from the lower classes and the apparent discomfort with them echo the fears of revolution that dominate the middle classes on the heels of the Revolution of 1868, the First Republic and cantonalism. In that *La Tribuna* is the first novel to return to the topic and to specifically address the intervention of the lower classes in the political events, the echo is more distinct and more audible. The speaker criticizes the novelist for treating the political events too cavalierly:

> . . . habla de los sucesos de la Revolución de 68 con cierto desenfado burlón y la serena superioridad de Quien no ve o no quiere ver en ellos en aquel instante sino una serie de desaciertos y locuras sin antecedentes lógicos, ni muy hondas consecuencias. ("La Tribuna")

The speaker's condemnation of the protagonist continues the anti-revolutionary discourse, citing her stupid credulity that leads her to confuse the recently proclaimed political equality with social equality, which would enable her to marry her middle class seducer. The review closes ambiguously, with the text speaker lamenting the fact that *La Tribuna* did not provide a more complete study of the Revolution. While the appropriate and desired depiction of the Revolution is not entirely clear from the closing sentences, the preceding treatment of the lower classes, the comments on the protagonist, and the last sentence clarify the ambiguity. The review ends with a reference to Pardo Bazán's prologue to *La Tribuna* and states that the novel deceives the hopes that certain sentences in the prologue raise in the reader. Turning to Pardo Bazán's prologue, several key passages enter into the play of dialogue and echo with Ixart's review. The speaker of the prologue confesses to the presence of a moral or lesson in the novel and proceeds to clarify the anti-revolutionary nature of this moral:

> Porque no necesité agrupar sucesos, ni violentar sus consecuencias, ni desviarme de la realidad concreta y positiva para tropezar con pruebas de que es absurdo el que un pueblo cifre sus esperanzas de redención y ventura en formas de gobierno que desconoce, y a las cuales por lo mismo atribuye prodigiosas virtudes y maravillosos efectos. Como la raza latina practica mucho este género de culto fetichista e idolátrico, opino que, si escritores de más talento que yo lo combatiesen, presentarían señalados servicios a la patria. (2: 103)

It is this specific message that Ixart finds lacking in Pardo Bazán's *La Tribuna* and this absence brakes his move towards endorsing naturalism and her specific application of naturalism. While he accepts naturalism as a vehicle for change and the only alternative for the modernization of the Spanish novel and of Spanish culture, the echoes of earlier social turmoil and the fear of radical social change necessitate a swerve towards a moderated endorsement. *La Tribuna* is a pivotal text in the discussion of naturalism because it conjoins the political question with the issue of women's place in society and of female sexuality. The protagonist is an active political participant in the revolutionary events described in the novel and is also the victim of the local don Juan, who leaves her pregnant. The confluence of these two plots in a novel written by a woman novelist shifts the debate even more markedly towards the question of morality, female sexuality, and the desirability or lack of desirability of social change. Many of the texts published in 1884 deal directly or obliquely with these same issues.

During the early months of 1884, Luis Alfonso and José Ortega Munilla engage in a public debate on the merits of naturalism[2]. The discussion touches on a number of points but focuses primarily on the question of the morality of the movement. In several of the later essays, the text speakers repeatedly compare Alexandre Dumas's *La Dame aux Camélias* to Zola's *Nana*. Ortega Munilla defends Zola and argues that the degenerate figure of the prostitute at the end of *Nana* provides a much stronger moral lesson than the sanctified Camille of Dumas, who appears heroic and even purified in the end. The speaker accuses Alfonso of fostering a narrative that only entertains, while he proposes a novel that teaches, that corrects, and that elevates the common people both intellectually and morally. In "Novelas al uso", Alfonso responds and insists that whereas Dumas's heroine repents and tries to make amends, providing in the end a positive model for female behavior, Nana is shown to be a success. Her life only teaches that it's not such a bad way to make a living. In reviewing specific classical literary texts that include nudity or sexuality, the speaker comments that the Greeks, Italians, Dutch and Flemish presented the body as an example of harmony and perfect form, whereas naturalists focus solely on the prurient senses. Furthermore, even though Ovid and others are actually worse than Zola, they were not available to the general public, whereas Zola circulates widely.

The accessibility of the novel to readers of all classes and of both sexes clearly concerns the opponents of naturalism, who cling to an idealistic aesthetic and shrink from the penetrating examination of contemporary society advocated by the naturalists. However, as I have stressed repeatedly, the proponents of naturalism also shy away from the political and social implications of Zola's theory and Ortega Munilla provides yet one more example. In "Para terminar una polémica", he complains that too much emphasis has been placed on Zola and too many writers define morality only in terms of sexuality. He decries the fact that so little attention has been paid to the "tendencia moralizadora, evangélica de su campaña". Any reader who has studied Zola's writings recognizes an echo but a limited and very muted echo of his theoretical texts. While Zola does portray himself as an

[2] The polemic unfolds over the course of several months in the following articles: Alfonso's review of *Pedro Sánchez*, 4 Jan. 1884; Ortega Munilla's "Carta a D. Luis Alfonso", 11 Feb. 1884; Alfonso's "Novelas al uso", 18 Feb. 1884; Ortega Munilla's "Goliat y sus enemigos", 25 Feb. 1884; Alfonso's "Novelas al uso", 10 Mar. 1884; Ortega Munilla's "Para terminar una polémica", 14 Apr. 1884.

experimental moralist, he immediately moves on to describe the social, political and economic transformations that he hopes to inspire. In Spain, the silencing of political discourse muffles this segment of his discourse and focuses on the moral transformation of society to the exclusion of the political.

A second polemic that takes place in 1884 involves Eduardo Calcaño, Emilia Pardo Bazán, Luis Alfonso, and Víctor Balaguer. It opens with a letter to Víctor Balaguer, of the Spanish Royal Academy, from Eduardo Calcaño, then the Venezuelan envoy to Spain. Calcaño denounces naturalism as vile materialism and in an impassioned plea, calls for a new Lepanto to save the soul of humanity ("Carta literaria" 134). Among those aspects of Hispanic culture that Calcaño sees as threatened, religious faith and the role and position of women are paramount. Early in the text, the speaker points to the growth of atheism and laments the loss of respect for women:

> ¡Qué tontos éramos, antes, D. Víctor ¿No es cierto? Hasta a la mujer la creíamos digna del respeto humano. Como madre, era divinidad en nuestro hogar. ¡Qué dulce nos parecía reposar en sus rodillas y sentir su mano de seda jugueteando en nuestros cabellos! . . . Como esposa, la llamábamos ángel del hogar, y llegamos hasta a creer (¡lo que es la ignorancia!) que ser madre de nuestros hijos la hacía santa, que ser el báculo de nuestra vida la hacía adorable, y que amar mucho y padecer mucho le daban derecho a mucho perdón. (134)

The speaker is clearly responding to growing calls for a change in the perception of women, which he seeks to discredit by associating them with French naturalists. The tactic is not lost on Emilia Pardo Bazán, who responds to Calcaño in a letter also addressed to Balaguer and published in *La Epoca*. In her boldest defense of naturalism to date, she opens with an immediate allusion to the question of women's rights, addressing Balaguer as her illustrious friend and reminding her readers of the exclusion of women from the Royal Academy by clarifying that Balaguer will never be her colleague, at least not in the Academy. She accuses Calcaño of Latin American exaggeration and jokingly asks if realism is America's version of the bogeyman. As in her other texts, the speaker seeks to disassociate the political and the social from the literary and strongly denies that naturalism has contributed to a loss of respect for women. On the contrary, she argues that contemporary literature tends to rehabilitate the family and to proscribe adultery. In response to Calcaño's description of naturalists as a band of pirates that is invading the Spanish mainland, she openly confesses that she is happy to hoist the black flag and be counted among the pirates.

Pardo Bazán's letter provokes a number of replies from those who see her not only as voicing a desire for but also exemplifying change. In the first of several articles in *La Epoca*, Luis Alfonso strives to control Pardo Bazán's increasingly feminist voice and, failing that, to undermine her authority. "Cartas son cartas" opens with a commentary on the strange new custom of answering letters that were addressed to others, as when Pardo Bazán responded to Calcaño's letter to Balaguer. While confessing that he is now answering Pardo Bazán's letter to Balaguer, Alfonso seeks to maximize the sense of her audacity by pointing out that he first asked Calcaño's permission to intervene. The text speaker immediately follows with expressions of surprise and dismay at the tone adopted by Pardo Bazán, and at her lack of respect for a Minister and a member of the Academy. In a combined effort to control and discredit her voice, he suggests that she was unaware of Calcaño's stature, since a woman of her education would never knowingly have attacked him, and then emphasizes that many readers, including proponents of naturalism, commented to him on the inappropriateness of her letter. In a double attack, he denies that the institution of the family is so strong as to withstand the corrupting influences of naturalism and subtly weaves the subtextual question of female sexuality into the textual discussion of naturalism, of Emilia Pardo Bazán's novelistic practice and her personal conduct:

> Seguro estoy, amigo D. Eduardo, de que V. se habrá dicho allá para sus adentros que muy cerca debe de andar el contagio, y muy cargada ya la atmósfera de miasmas morbosas cuando una mujer, una dama como la Sra. Pardo Bazán – criada en aristocráticos pañales, educada con exquisito esmero, nutrida en sanas máximas, de tan exagerado espíritu religioso que es fama se significó como ferviente amiga del absolutismo, y a mayor abundamiento esposa y madre, reina en el salón y en el hogar; – cuando una señora en fin, de tales prendas, se burla de los que muestran celo exquisito en pro de la fe y la virtud, usa de la mayor desenvoltura retórica para juzgar, lo mismo a V. que a los que se han conquistado nombre eterno al cantar en su lira los más nobles ideales; se complace en salpicar sus escritos literarios de palabras de baja estafa y en exponer (sin duda como ofrenda a su penate Zola) algunos pormenores de un tratado de obstetricia al final de su novela más reciente. ("Cartas son cartas")

The allusion to the birth scene of the lower-class heroine described in *La Tribuna* in conjunction with the emphasis on Pardo Bazán's eminently orthodox education points to a profound fear of the dissolution of female class barriers and the spread of lower-class sexuality to the middle classes, a fear which is all the more apparent in the following passage:

> Si mujer tan discreta y noble prevarica de tal suerte, infringiendo en literatura las leyes a que hasta ahora las almas femeninas delicadas, escritoras o no han obedecido, ¿Cuánto no es de temer que las mujeres vulgares, indoctas y arrebatadas, vayan más allá y lleguen a la pornografía en literatura y al amor libre en las costumbres? ("Cartas son cartas")

Pardo Bazán's response to Alfonso appears two weeks later in *La Epoca* and directly addresses the issue of control of the female voice. The speaker accuses Alfonso of trying to keep women from talking and then proceeds to distance herself from the suggestions of radicalism by reiterating her Catholicism. Once more, the confession of Catholicism is qualified, so that it is not taken as fanatical or puritanical. Rather, the speaker links her naturalism with that of the "cristianos viejos", who wrote realistically during Spain's Golden Age. In answer to Alfonso's comments on the birth scene, she remarks that it is much less detailed than typical conversations on the topic between upper-class women.

Only one week later Alfonso replies with an even stronger attempt to reclaim Pardo Bazán and the feminine voice for idealism and for traditional female literature. Once more he claims to have received many letters supporting his position and here stresses the overwhelming agreement of his women readers. Both in the early passages of the article and towards the end, he warns her of the potential loss of her women readers and the advantage of a loyal female readership in literature as well as in other matters. With increasing indications of a male fear of the effects of naturalism on women readers, the speaker insists on the need for a strong ideal in men and, even more so, in women and then attempts to link naturalism and free love by rhetorically asking what moral Pardo Bazán and her school defend if it is not that of free love and the Romantic dogma of George Sand. In a final attempt to effect Pardo Bazán's return to her earlier works and away from both naturalist and feminist discourse, he evokes her poem to her son and her study of St. Francis of Assisi:

> No comprendo, amiga mía, que V., la autora tierna y dulce de los versos a su hijo Jaime, V. la piadosa narradora de la vida ejemplarísima de Francisco de Asís, V. que por ser mujer y mujer de privilegiada inteligencia tanto ha de comprender y estimar las delicadezas del sentimiento, crea V. que ese linaje de literatura no ha de ejercer dañina influencia en esta nerviosa existencia que lleva el mundo. ("Carta-Pacio")

The strategic linking of powerful anti-feminist authoritative discourse with Pardo Bazán's defense of naturalism evokes a strong response in her next article, "Carta-magna", which appears in *La Epoca* on May 6, 1884. Once more, she insists that the polemic is not political and expresses her surprise that it has provoked so much interest, even when it is a purely literary matter. She also seeks to dissociate the issue of women's rights by affirming that there are no men and women in literature, only writers, although she simultaneously justifies the inclusion of the birth scene as a key event in the exploration of the female experience. Echoing her own previous texts and those of other liberal proponents of naturalism, she attempts to distance herself from Zola, first in stating that she is not a fanatical follower and second in reiterating her opposition to *arte docente*. In a final swerve away from Zola and away from the radical charges voiced by Alfonso, she draws a distinction between philosophical naturalism, which has been condemned by the Church and by Leo XIII's recent Encyclical, and literary naturalism. Without retracting her previous endorsement, the article represents a clear attempt to return to the rhetoric of the middle in response to Alfonso's efforts to undermine her authority through continued allusions and echoes of anti-female and anti-feminist discourse.

Alfonso's next article appears on May 26, 1884 and with it, he proposes to terminate the polemic. To this end, he exploits and exaggerates all of the strategies previously analyzed. In keeping with patriarchal society and the persistent fear of women's appropriation of the word, he attempts to silence the female speaker, or at the very least, to reappropriate her voice and rechannel it in line with the traditional horizon of expectations. Alfonso's essay is structured as a mock interview between Alfonso and Pardo Bazán during a gathering at his house. The very fact that he meets her on his own territory places her in a position of inferiority. Textually, Pardo Bazán's authority is diminished in the early sections, in that the speaker describes how Alfonso wishes to visit with the other guests and consequently leaves her to chat with his wife. The wife, an obvious symbol of Pardo Bazán's disaffected female reader, is described as bored with contemporary novels. A second female visitor, with whom Alfonso speaks while his wife and Pardo Bazán converse, had previously written Alfonso in defense of his position and now encourages him to increase his opposition to naturalism and to Pardo Bazán's narrative practice and theory. In the face of these attacks, Alfonso now feigns to defend Pardo Bazán, suggesting at the same time the inferiority of her recent work: ". . . únicamente un poquillo desvanecida por el amor propio de figurar, no ya como la mejor por sus dotes literarios, sino como única en sus doctrinas y procedimientos" ("Cartilla").

At this point in the text, Alfonso approaches Pardo Bazán and laments that she and his wife have not been able to get along. He now turns his full attention to a critique of her recent and previous writings on naturalism, with a clear desire to coerce her back to idealism. He argues that morals are more refined in the nineteenth century than in the Golden Age and that certain topics are no longer acceptable. He complains of the insistent treatment of the lower classes and suggests that she devote her attention to those who are well educated and well born, and quotes Cervantes to illustrate his point that art only surpasses nature by perfecting it. Throughout the debate, Alfonso has relied on an anti-female discourse to reintegrate Pardo Bazán into an accepted feminine literary and political tradition or failing that, to mute her influence on female readers and writers. The repeated allusions to female readers and the fictionalized gathering with female guests who declare their opposition to Pardo Bazán and their inability to interact with her on a social level serve as echoes and reinforcements of a localized authoritative and patriarchal discourse. Other aspects of the question of naturalism recede in Alfonso's articles and the sexual identity of its primary proponent and the potential effects of her theory, practice, and person take precedence. Both envy and fear motivate the debate and the interweaving of the personal, the literary, and the sexual reveal the breadth and depth of the concerns. The fundamental importance of Pardo Bazán, the woman, to the entire discussion is such that Alfonso cannot begin to comprehend her desire to be considered as a writer rather than as a woman. The biological woman, stripped of the semantic category of feminine as defined in late nineteenth-century Spain, can only produce a monster, as he implies with sarcasm towards the end of his article. If she doesn't want her sex to be recognized in her writing, he will comply. "Pues convenido, y V. con su pan se lo coma, y no toco más este punto, no sea que, sin quererlo, se me quiebre de puro sutil" ("Cartilla").

Víctor Balaguer, the addressee of Calcaño's original letter and the pretext for the polemic, finally intervenes in the debate in the June 22 issue of *La Ilustración Española y Americana*. Balaguer's "Carta literaria" represents the Academy's continued endorsement of literary idealism. Drawing on patriotic and anti-revolutionary authoritative discourse, the speaker depicts naturalists as a band of mutineers, if not an army of revolutionaries, and insists that as a French movement, naturalism has no roots in Spain and will shortly disappear. The accusation of revolutionary ties, with all its implications, provokes a denial from Eduardo López Bago in "Naturalistas e idealistas". Echoing nationalistic voices from the previous debates, he argues that naturalism is not only not revolutionary, but rather, it is a reactionary literary movement, with roots in the past and in particular in the Spanish literary tradition of Cervantes.

Two remaining studies of naturalism published in 1884 are "Novelas españolas del año literario" by "Orlando" and Menéndez Pelayo's prologue to Pereda's *Obras completas*. "Orlando", writing in *Revista de España*, exemplifies a growing acceptance of naturalism as an appropriate literary response to the scientific age. He applauds naturalism for widening the literary horizon and reinserting "man" in his true surroundings (608). He is little concerned with the question of pessimism, which he views as being a reflection of reality. Nevertheless, echoes of literary idealism and an impulse to moderate French naturalism persist. Like Alas and others before him, Orlando insists that art is always more than mere imitation of life (602–03) and warns against excessive analysis and too much detail (606). In the discussion of the relationship between literature and the non-literary, the text speaker constructs a middle path between the moralistic novel advocated by Alarcón and Fernán Caballero and the socially committed narrative proposed by Zola. He specifically distances himself from Zola's political and social goals and denies that the novel contributes or should contribute in any way to a nation's progress (606). He likewise condemns *arte docente* and the manipulation of the plot and characters for ideological purposes. Nevertheless, he avoids a regression to the art for art's sake of the idealists and like other liberal proponents of naturalism in Spain, salvages the social and political implications of naturalism by reinserting the literary, ever so cautiously, into the social:

> No queda tras su [la novela naturalista] lectura, es verdad, el consuelo de la indignación contra el criminal, ni la esperanza de premio para la víctima, por la seguridad con que la conciencia afirma que, dadas tales circunstancias y tales personas, tenían que sucederse necesariamente aquellos hechos y no otros; pero sí nace, y ya es bastante, una protesta, aunque muda, tan grande como terrible es la ley que la motiva. (607)

Just as many contemporary critics sought to appropriate Emilia Pardo Bazán for their school of thought, whether conservative or liberal, pro-naturalist or anti-naturalist, proponents and opponents of naturalism fought vigorously over Pereda and his literary affiliation. Galdós, Pardo Bazán, and others (Pattison 63–83) claim Pereda for their cause, thereby downplaying the association of naturalism with liberal and leftist political ideology[3]. Menéndez Pelayo vigorously denies any association of Pereda and naturalism in his introduction to Pereda's *Obras completas* and takes every opportunity to refute Pardo Bazán's description of the movement. Notwithstanding his opposition to naturalism, the discourse of Menéndez Pelayo's introduction reveals a growing incorporation of liberal voices and discourses that enter into play with echoes of neo-Catholicism. While admitting that he is more inclined to idealism than realism, the speaker defends realism and

---

[3] Pardo Bazán specifies her desire to reclaim Pereda in Chapter 19 of *La cuestión palpitante*: "Para el realismo, poseer a Pereda es poseer un tesoro, no sólo por lo que vale, sino por las ideas religiosas y políticas que profesa. Pereda es argumento vivo y palpable demostración de que el realismo no fue introducido en España como mercancía francesa de contrabando, sino que los que aman juntamente la tradición literaria y las demás tradiciones, lo resucitan."

argues that all idealists are in some sense realists in that they seek to represent what is true and real (Prologue to Pereda, x). Although he attacks the demagogic tendency of the naturalists (xiv) as well as the emphasis on sex and crime (xxv) and the belief in determinism (xxvi), he largely avoids a confrontational approach and seeks instead to reconcile idealism with realism. He openly admits that Pereda uses naturalistic techniques and praises his uses of detail and of lower-class speech, but he insists that Pereda has arrived at his literary aesthetic individually and has no connections with the French school. In a direct response to *La cuestión palpitante* and the depiction of the naturalists as a diverse and varied group of writers, the text speaker contends that only Zola is a naturalist and the remaining writers associated with the school are really Romantics and idealists. According to this view, Flaubert, the Goncourt brothers, and Daudet combine realism and idealism and must be distinguished from Zola and his naturalism.

The success of the new literature and the growing authority of realism, tolerance, modernity, in contrast to the diminished persuasiveness of neo-Catholic rhetoric, require new textual strategies. The focus shifts from adamant opposition to moderate acceptance and a desire to control, moderate, or appropriate. Zola's naturalism becomes the target while other "naturalists" are redesignated "realists" and their ties to idealism and tradition are emphasized. Zola is attacked as boring and for confusing science and art. He is chastised for sacrificing art to utilitarian ends and for a theory that is contradictory and superficial. In a complete rejection of Alarcón and Fernán Caballero's moralizing art, the speaker incorporates liberal artistic discourse in his defense of truth and condemnation of moralistic sermons. At the same time, he strives to anchor this liberal discourse in national tradition by evoking the image of Velázquez: "Si realismo quiere decir guerra al convencionalismo, a la falsa retórica y al arte docente y sermoneador, y todo esto en nombre y provecho de la verdad humana, bien venido sea. Así pintaba Velázquez" (Prologue to Pereda's *Obras completas*, xlvi–xlvii). The conjoining of liberal and traditional discourse is also evident in the discussion of women, the family, and sexuality. The speaker makes only one specific reference to Pardo Bazán, characterizing her as "una ingeniosísima escritora gallega, mujer de muy brioso entendimiento y de varia y sólida cienca" (xviii). Later in the text, without naming Pardo Bazán, he evokes the negative feminine stereotype of the woman who constantly seeks center stage, and suggests that this desire for attention motivates the interest in naturalism. The lexical repetition of "ingenio", which echoes the previously cited adjective "ingeniosísima" as well as the allusion to Spaniards who are worthy of professing other higher, presumably religious, doctrines point to Pardo Bazán as the referent for the passage:

> ¿Quién sabe si en las apologías que han hecho de tan pobre doctrina ingenios españoles muy dignos de profesar otra más elevada, no ha entrado por mucho el anhelo de la singularidad, el odio a los lugares comunes y a las opiniones recibidas? (xxxi)

The faint echoes of anti-female discourse and of a desire to control the feminine resonate throughout the passage and in the text as a whole as it implicitly but continually refutes *La cuestión palpitante*. The issue surfaces with the greatest clarity in the discussion of Pereda's *El buey suelto*, a thesis novel in defense of marriage and the Christian family. Here the text speaker wavers between two discourses, signalling the tensions through metacommentary that makes reference to the anti-didactic liberal discourse, specifically enunciated by Emilia Pardo Bazán in *La cuestión palpitante*, at the same time that it justifies a return to *arte docente* as a means to fortify the family and control sexuality:

> Yo bien sé que los libros son la expresión de la sociedad, y que la sociedad sólo a medias es discípula de los libros; pero ¿quién negará que cada uno de ellos es leña echada en el fuego de la concupiscencia, incentivo del general descreimiento, piedra en que tropiezan las voluntades mal inclinadas, ocasión nueva de desaliento para las voluntades marchitas? Por eso es obligación ineludible en el escritor cristiano y de bien ordenado entendimiento, aplicar su ingenio a la reparacion del edificio social, lidiando por la familia, que es su primera y necesaria base. (lv)

Menéndez Pelayo's introduction to Pereda's *Obras completas* marks an important shift in Catholic and traditional opposition to naturalism. Although remnants of neo-Catholic discourse persist in the defense of the thesis novel, the traditional Catholic voice can no longer lay claim to authoritative stature and it now enters much more fully into dialogic interaction with liberal discourse. The liberal code words of tolerance and reconciliation and the rhetoric of the middle take hold in conservative texts as a result of a changing readership and a transformed authoritative discourse. Conservative opponents to naturalism will continue to speak out, but the claim to authority and to control of the readership is clearly diminished and necessitates new textual strategies.

The liberal response to naturalism continues to move gradually towards a greater acceptance of Zola and his theories. In 1885 Pedro Muñoz Peña publishes a long study of the contemporary novel in *Revista Contemporánea*. The text speaker applauds the renaissance of the novel in Spain and France and echoes other previous writers who characterize the narrative as the genre most appropriate for the new scientific age (260). In line with the rhetoric of the middle, the speaker calls for a harmonic balance of imitation and fantasy and condemns all forms of exaggeration. He specifically objects to the freedom of customs portrayed in the French novels but expresses his confidence that this aspect of naturalism will not pass to Spain. He also attacks Zola's determinism, in that it precludes progress (264), and calls for a novel that is not didactic but that indirectly educates the reader. Muñoz Peña carries forward the liberal voices of Revilla, Alas, Gómez Ortiz and others who seek to salvage the Krausist/Institutionist belief in progress at the same time that they repudiate revolutionary extremes. Significantly, the text speaker continues to view the religious problem as the single most important issue in Spain and his liberal convictions regarding religious tolerance condition all of his literary judgments. He praises Galdós and Valera for their treatment of the religious question but criticizes Alarcón as too "partial" and Pardo Bazán as somewhat retrograde (410–21). The confusion as to Pardo Bazán's philosophical and political affiliation, already evident in the 1882 articles of Alas, Vidart, and Pereira, persists in Muñoz Peña's study and in *La novela moderna* by Juan Pastor Aicart.

Pastor Aicart's study appears in 1886 and is a somewhat belated response to Pardo Bazán's *La cuestión palpitante* and to Juan Barcía Caballero's study by the same title, which appeared in part in *Revista Ibérica* in 1883 and then in book form in 1884 (Pattison 118). However, in that Barcía Caballero retracts his defense of naturalism in an epilogue published in Pastor Aicart's *La novela moderna*, the bulk of Pastor Aicart's comments are addressed to Pardo Bazán, as the most formidable and most dangerous of the proponents of naturalism. As in Luis Alfonso's articles, *La novela moderna* focuses on the question of morality and seeks to reincorporate Pardo Bazán into idealism and traditional feminine literary traditions. The text enters into a continuous dialogue with *La cuestión palpitante*, with frequent quotations of Pardo Bazán's text. Unlike the standard essayistic practice of quoting an authority as a means of accrediting the speaker, here the speaker seeks to redefine and control the quotation, thus silencing the female voice and reducing its authority. In direct opposition to Pardo Bazán's cautious definition of naturalism, the text speaker offers a definition that immediately introduces the subjects of immorality and utilitarianism: ". . . es una evolución oportunista del realismo, pesimista e inmoral en el fondo, antiestética en la forma y tendenciosa en sus fines" (17).

In the initial pages of the text, the speaker intermixes liberal and conservative discourse, calling on such liberal code words as "objectivity" and "reasoned analysis" and echoing the Krausist doctrine of literary evolution, but also injecting emotional commentary on the immorality, atheism, and fatalism of the naturalists. As the text advances and the focus centers on the subject of morality, the authorial "I" becomes more and more evident and it appropriates Pardo Bazán's word only to negate it. An early quotation from *La cuestión palpitante* is accompanied by gentlemanly praise for the writer and followed by firm but depersonalized condemnation of the negative effects of naturalism on public morals:

> **Si es pueril imputar al arte la perversión de las costumbres, cuando con mayor motivo pueden achacarse a la sociedad los extravíos del arte** (qtd. from Pardo Bazán 3: 35), como asegura con harto buen sentido, la distinguida escritora cuyo nombre honra tanto estas cartas, no se nos alcanza la fuerza lógica de las razones que aduce la crítica para poner en tela de juicio los motivos a que obedece la evolución francamente naturalista de la novela moderna. Dénsele al novelador, moldes cristianos, castos colores y más regocijadas escenas, y esperemos confiadamente la reacción. (54)

In the following pages the text speaker continually refers to the issue of naturalism as *la cuestión palpitante*, thus evoking the presence of Emilia Pardo Bazán without naming her. The tact principle, here reinforced by a gallant deference to women, precludes a direct attack on Pardo Bazán and her writings, but various textual strategies work to marginalize and discredit her. The chivalrous treatment evokes authoritative intersexual discourse and accredits the male speaker at the same time that it reenforces in the reader's mind the traditional image of women as delicate, passive, needful of protection – in sum, the antithesis of the polemic-loving Pardo Bazán. The text speaker avoids a direct, and ungentlemanly, confrontation with Pardo Bazán by addressing his remarks on the subject of morality to Barcía Caballero. In his *La cuestión palpitante*, Barcía Caballero had echoed Pardo Bazán in the defense of naturalism as a school that tries to correct the immorality of the present century by describing it in all of its horror (69). Pastor Aicort vigorously refutes this idea and insists that naturalism only gives classes in perversion. In that Barcía Caballero has already retracted his statements on the subject, the real but silenced target of Pastor Aicort's attack is Pardo Bazán and once more, it becomes apparent that the real threat is not so much immorality as female immorality and sexuality. Gradually, the focus shifts from Barcía Caballero to Pardo Bazán as the text speaker refutes her statement that it is laughable to ask the novelist to reward and castigate as a prelude to divine justice (Pardo Bazán 3: 152). Once more, he appropriates her voice and her words, but here the gallant deference gives way to the imposition of his authority and to the arrogation of masculine control over the female voice and the female body. The silencing of the female voice is effected in various ways in the following passage: in the opening sentences, Pardo Bazán's words are paraphrased or quoted verbatim but she is not cited as the author nor are her words set off by quotation marks (I have emphasized her words and indicated the source); in the following sentences, quotation marks are used to identify her voice which is then refuted and ridiculed; and finally, a collective male voice, introduced by the first person plural ("No eduquemos"), totally displaces the female voice and calls for a reimposition of traditional control:

> ¡Y se quiere que estos libros tan groseramente procaces sirvan de alimento intelectual pretendiendo desautorizar *el gravísimo cargo* que se les hace de no *poder andar en manos de mujeres* ¡Y se duda y se discute si es *más conveniente vivir en paradisíaca inocencia o conocer* todos los resortes y misterios del vicio! . . . (Emphasized passages from *La cuestión palpitante*). Pásmame verdaderamente a propósito de esto, que la Sra. Pardo Bazán confiese estar harta ya de "leer los elogios de ciertos libros, alabados tan solo porque nada contienen que a una señorita ruborice". Hartura es esa, que en Dios y en mi ánima juro, ni me explico ni comprendo. . . . No eduquemos a las mujeres literatas por solo tal vez el vano regocijo de aplaudirlas; bueno es que antes de serlo, si su vocación les llama decididamente a ingresar en el gremio, sepan ser buenas hijas, mejores esposas y cristianísimas madres. Y si dejamos en sus manos alguna novela u otros libros de amena literatura, tengamos siempre la seguridad de que pueden hojearlos sin ruborizarse y sin sentir el deseo de arrojarlos con desprecio y asco, como fruto mal sazonado o podrido, siquiera literariamente sea hermosa y seductora su corteza. ¡No se tenga por cosa de juego arrojar más leña seca en la ardiente hoguera de nuestras concupiscencias! ¡No se tenga por asunto baladí, animar el rescoldo que yace oculto bajo las cenizas siempre tibias de las pasiones nacientes o vencidas. (Pastor Aicort 86–87)

In conjunction with a clear desire to undermine Pardo Bazán's authority and to marginalize her, *La novela moderna* works to reintegrate her into traditional female discourse and behavior. The negative comments on Zola and naturalism that appear in *La cuestión palpitante* are cited and exploited to suggest a fundamental agreement between the text speaker and Pardo Bazán. The anti-Christian aspect of the movement is emphasized, as is the danger of inflaming the lower classes, with an eye to emphasizing the natural distance between the Catholic, upperclass woman writer and naturalistic topics. The text speaker echoes Pardo Bazán's condemnation of the thesis novel and, in a curious ideological crossover, argues forcefully for art for art's sake. On this basis, he condemns Galdós's tendentious novels, which he contends have contributed to a decline in the novelist's popularity. Having mentioned the threat of a loss of readership, the speaker then moves on to consider Pardo Bazán's novelistic production and here the questions of morality, female sexuality, lower class violence and revolution, as well as literary idealism and art for art's sake are brought together in a final effort to coerce the novelist into a more traditional literary and personal posture. Her early writings on naturalism are given qualified approval in that she proceeded with caution and limited her admiration to her theoretical writings while her novelistic production followed a different pattern. The text speaker offers high praise for *Pascual López*, a novel which Pardo Bazán herself describes as an imitation of the traditional Spanish picaresque and which contains a great deal more fantasy and invention than observation. He is also positive in his comments on *Un viaje de novios*, but criticizes what he perceives as a growing tendency to preach a message. *La Tribuna* elicits strong condemnation, not only because of the presence of a message but because of the nature of the message. The conjoining of female sexuality and lower class political activism in the novel clearly disturbs the speaker, who responds with the strongest of language and an almost threatening tone. He refers to the novel as a literary sin and expresses his confidence that Pardo Bazán will not repeat this type of transgression. The accusation of reprehensible political and social agitation is muted but clearly audible:

> La reincidencia acusaría sin duda alguna, el premeditado propósito de ir removiendo poco a poco, pero con audacia que seguramente no entra en los propósitos de nuestros novelistas, las últimas legamosas capas sociales, y tan deliberado propósito no sería ya ciertamente ni excusable ni defendible. (331)

In a final recommendation and attempt to reintegrate Pardo Bazán into the female tradition from which she has distanced herself, the speaker calls on her to not dirty her feet like the lower classes and to produce poetic scenes that make virtue attractive (332).

Emilia Pardo Bazán's presence in the debates on naturalism evidently raises a number of issues that liberal proponents of the movement would prefer to silence and that conservative opponents exploit in their efforts to discredit Zola and his followers. Speaking as a woman in late nineteenth-century Spain, Pardo Bazán struggles to accredit herself but confronts a resisting male reader who projects his own expectations, prejudices, fears and envies onto her voice. Her lack of authority is recognized by her contemporary male respondents, who seek to appropriate, dilute, redefine, or silence her discourse. In some cases, male writers feel obliged to re-speak or re-write her text because the presence of a female speaker obstructs communication. There is some of this in Alas and Vidart, but it is even more evident in Rafael Altamira's "El realismo y la literatura", which was published in *La Ilustración Ibérica* from April 24 to October 23 of 1886. Although Altamira seeks to justify his series of articles by lamenting the lack of good studies on naturalism, his views on the subject are virtually identical to those expressed by

Emilia Pardo Bazán in *La cuestión palpitante* and other writings. While he expresses a difference with her regarding the issue of morality, the difference has less to do with Pardo Bazán's stated opinion than the perception of that opinion by contemporary readers. The primary motivation for "El realismo y la literatura" is not so much a desire to provide new arguments or greater detail as to restate the case through a speaker and a voice that are less controversial and less likely to awaken fears of social and sexual change.

The initial sections of Altamira's text invoke localized authoritative discourse through abjuration of fanaticism, insistence on openness and caution, and the invocation of progress. The speaker praises the novel as the most modern of genres and describes its purpose as the creation of beauty. He then seeks to establish that naturalism is not distinct from realism, that the philosophical implications should not in any way interfere with the discussion of the literary merits, and that Zola is not the creator nor sole representative of the school. All of these ideas have been previously stated by Pardo Bazán, as have the insistence on the personality of the artist and the denial of absolute determinism in Zola, which Altamira expresses in later sections of his text. Notwithstanding the overwhelming similarity of their views, Altamira struggles to distance himself from Pardo Bazán and to differentiate their respective positions. Not surprisingly, he is more critical of naturalism with respect to the issue of morality; without mentioning Pardo Bazán, he speaks of a need to avoid "esa extrema izquierda del Realismo", by which he refers to sexual immorality and crudeness (3 Jul. 430). Significantly, in the very next article the speaker makes specific reference to Pardo Bazán and *La cuestión palpitante*, which he characterizes as one of the best studies on the subject but which he criticizes as excessively eclectic and vague.

He expresses strong disagreement with her statement that imagination plays a role in literary creation. In this instance, he struggles against a conservative appropriation of Pardo Bazán's discourse and a possible return to literary idealism:

> Si se da entrada en la escuela realista a las concepciones puras de la imaginación – que en el sentir de la Sra. Pardo Bazán son reales pues que existen, – se falsea la doctrina a riesgo de volver segunda vez al idealismo que se combate. (10 Jul. 442)

In a footnote, the speaker goes on to clarify that Pardo Bazán herself does not fall into idealism but contends that some readers could deduce such a regression from her text. The implication is that her discourse will be misunderstood and therefore must be clarified or re-stated.

Towards the end of the series, the text speaker returns to the issue of morality and once more he seeks to establish a distance from Pardo Bazán. Although he echoes many of her own arguments – crudity is not immorality, vulgarity in literature is not new and is typical of many classical works, naturalism paints the horrors of vice to lead the reader to virtue (11 Sept. 1886) – he expresses his concern over the growing French influence in style and in subject matter. In this vein, he chides Pardo Bazán for her use of French terms and a certain French "feel" to her style. While he does not, for the moment, link her to the French proclivity for topics such as adultery and sexuality, in the Oct. 2 article, he speaks of a need for prudence in the selection and presentation of materials. Authors should be discreet and take care not to lead their readers to evil. Referring to Zola's *Nana*, he concedes its merits as a novel but is clearly uncomfortable with its subject matter: "Una *Nana* es obra que se acepta luego de escrita, pero cuya creación no se debe aconsejar." He immediately follows with a call for Spanish novelists to abandon the obsession with prostitutes, adulterers, fallen women and to break with the monotonous repetition of this theme, which he traces to Pardo Bazán's *La Tribuna* (635).

Notwithstanding an overwhelming coincidence with Pardo Bazán's writings on the subject of naturalism, Altamira's "El realismo y la literatura contemporánea" works to establish a difference regarding the issue of morality, or more precisely, to differentiate his own position from the readings and misreadings of Pardo Bazán's outlook, particularly in the years following the publication of *La Tribuna*. If Altamira's text seeks to silence or marginalize the question of morality, and the threatening issues of female sexuality and a changing role for women that it implies, it simultaneously endeavors to voice the political implications of naturalism, which had been largely silenced or muted in Pardo Bazán's *La cuestión palpitante*. More than any of his liberal predecessors, Altamira enunciates clearly and repeatedly an acceptance of naturalism as a vehicle for the preservation of the Krausist/Institutionist faith in progress and in individual responsibility for progress. Throughout the debates on naturalism, writers such as Revilla, Pardo Bazán, González Serrano and Alas have defended the idea of authorial personality and have combatted the idea of determinism but nowhere is the connection between authorial personality, human individuality, free will, and the belief in progress expressed as emphatically and clearly as in Altamira's study. In addition, Altamira's text is generally devoid of the disclaimers of radical action and the rhetoric of the middle that characterize the antecedent liberal texts. There are a number of possible explanations for the vocalization of a previously silenced or muted subtext: Altamira belongs to a younger generation (he was born in 1866) and has little or no personal memory of the Revolution of 1868 and its consequences; the Restoration has been in effect for some thirteen years and both official and self censorship are less and less frequent; neo-Catholicism has lost much of its claim to authoritative discourse and the danger of confusing a defense of free will with traditional Catholic discourse has disappeared. Furthermore, the intrusion of the female voice and the subsequent confusion of naturalism with fears of female sexuality and emancipation require clarification and correction.

The text speaker first introduces the theme of progress and change in refuting idealism. Arguing that art should depict people as they are, he stresses that realism shows the individual as opposed to the abstract and universal ideal man or woman portrayed in idealistic literature (17 Jul. 1886 462). In the following passage, the speaker states that when readers come to know the world as it really is, instead of dreaming of some future Utopia, they will work with patience to improve the world in which they live. For this reason, in the Aug. 14 article, he refers to realism as pedagogy and states that it will teach young people about the world in which they are to act. The emphasis on individualism resurfaces in the discussion of authorial personality, where the text speaker argues that although the artist's presence is much less evident in the naturalistic novel, his/her personality does not disappear

(28 Aug. 1886). The following article concentrates on the question of the influence of the environment on the individual. The speaker denies that naturalism implies the absolute control of the individual, arguing that human beings can reject or struggle with their environment or even leave it to find more propitious surroundings. The link between the repudiation of determinism and the belief in progress is explicitly stated in a footnote: "No es fatal y completamente insuperable el determinismo del medio. Si esto fuese llegaríamos al estacionamiento, a la uniformidad y, por lo tanto, a la carencia del progreso" (Sept. 1886 571). The speaker underscores that individuals can modify their surroundings, but never without great and constant effort. In the closing article of the series, he refers repeatedly to naturalism as a literary revolution and ties it to the political, social, religious, and moral struggles that are taking place in a period of crisis:

> Hoy la literatura viviendo en y de una época de crisis, de transición, en que luchan dos estados sociales (el tradicional y el nuevo) y riñen cruda lucha las más opuestas influencias filosóficas, – al fin clasificables en dos grupos, filosofías **racionalistas y teolólogicas** –, tiende forzosamente a reflejar esa misma duda, esa misma impaciencia de que es presa igualmente el artista, como hombre de época. . . . Y así hacen bien los que defienden a capa y espada nuestra literatura de hoy contra las ya infructuosas literaturas del ayer. . . . defendiéndola, defienden su época, sus ideas, el espíritu de lucha, lo que forma la atmósfera intelectual, mejor o peor de nuestro cuarto de siglo. (23 Oct. 1886)

"El realismo y la literatura contemporánea" is the last major study of naturalism by a proponent of the movement. It incorporates virtually all of the arguments previously presented by other defenders of Zola and his school and echoes Emilia Pardo Bazán in all but two areas, both of which were present in antecedent texts but had been largely silenced or muted. In Altamira's study, the previously silenced political subtext is given greater voice and naturalism's efficacy as a vehicle for social and political change is clearly enunciated. On the other hand, the other silenced subtext that I have traced throughout the debate – the fear of female sexuality and of a change in women's role in society and in the family – continues to be muffled in Altamira's text as he strives to distance naturalism from the female voice and from the fears awakened in contemporary readers by this voice. On the last page of Altamira's final installment, the speaker announces the appearance of yet another study on naturalism, authored by Juan Valera and appearing in *Revista de España*.

During the previous years, Valera had occupied various positions at the Spanish embassy in Portugal (1881–1884) and Washington, D.C. (1884–1886) and was presently in Paris. His articles are not a direct response to Altamira, whom he had apparently not read, but they address and seek to refute the calls for socio-political transformation that appear as a muted subtext in other liberal writers and surface in Altamira's text. In fact, Valera's argument with naturalism focuses much more on the political implications and possible repercussions of the movement than any of his predecessors. This occurs at least in part because he is writing from France and has followed the debate regarding the reception of naturalism in Spain in French texts. He confesses in the first paragraphs of his study that he had read Pardo

Bazán's *La cuestión palpitante* in the French translation and he obviously had access to the French texts that discuss the movement. In France, in contrast to Spain, Zola's radical politics are frequently mentioned and his opponents take every opportunity to decry the socialist and revolutionary nature of his writings. Ferdinand Brunetière's *Le Roman Naturaliste*, (1883) typifies French anti-naturalist discourse. At one point, the text expresses his fear that under his literary guise, Zola is nothing more than another Proudhon (111). As I will illustrate in the discussion of Valera's text, it echoes Brunetière and anti-naturalist French discourse on more than one occasion and in this manner, introduces a new voice into the Spanish debate. Valera's *Apuntes sobre el nuevo arte de escribir novelas* is not only an echo of Brunetière and other French texts; it is also a delayed answer to Pardo Bazán's *La cuestión palpitante* and represents yet one more attempt to silence the female voice or to reinstate it within traditional female discourse.

Valera's text opens with a statement of opposition to Pardo Bazán's study and proceeds to argue against Zola, naturalism, and the political and social ideologies that inform the movement. One of his primary concerns is the popularity of the novel as a genre, with the resulting spread of naturalism's message to the lower classes. In the first pages of his study, he comments that of all books, the novel is the most influential and the most read (2: 611) and in the closing paragraphs, he incorporates a long quotation from Gualtero Besant, which describes the wide circulation of the novel among the least educated classes and its influence on such diverse areas as public morality, philosophy, and religion. Notwithstanding Valera's persistent defense of art for art's sake, he admits to the influence of contemporary literature on contemporary society, and his study seeks to create a literature that exercises an influence more in keeping with his own ideology. The closing sentence of his study states this very clearly and even alludes to Zola's medical metaphor:

> Sin duda, que la poesía debe curar. Apolo era médico y poeta; pero la medicina de las novelas no es la que Zola quiere (OC 698).

The link between literature and socio-political activity is explicity enunciated on several occasions. In Chapter 1, the speaker states that aesthetic-naturalistic doctrines have a fatal transcendence and subsequently declares that he is opposing those precepts that if left unrefuted would lead to barbarism. A few sentences later, he refers to a gangrene that must be prevented from infecting the healthy sectors of society (2: 616). Later, in Chapter 7, he expresses the same idea with even greater clarity:

> Pero nada de esto se opone a que note yo con dolor que la civilización en su conjunto padece hoy enfermedad gravísima, la cual reina en Francia más que en parte alguna. Contra esta enfermedad, y a fin de que la remedie quien pueda, escribo estos artículos. Cierto es que no deben tratar sino de la novela; pero la novela es espejo de la vida y representación artística de la sociedad toda, y no ha de extrañarnos que, al tratar de ella, se eleve la mente a consideraciones más altas. (2: 659)

Later in the text, the speaker clarifies that the naturalistic novel is not just a mirror of society, but that it is capable of inspiring the reader to action:

En toda esta literatura espantosa se advierte, a no dudarlo, el reflejo de grandes extravíos que hay en la sociedad; pero también, a más de ser reflejo esta literatura, puede ser causa y puede dar ejemplo. Por lo pronto, excita a la extravagancia, convida a deleites absurdos y aguijonea la ira y el despecho de no conseguirlos. (2: 668)

Although the kinds of actions that the text speaker fears and the agents who will effect them are not explicitly clarified in this passage, they are alluded to with frequency in other parts of the text. Naturalistic writers are depicted as anti-bourgeois (2: 653), and even compared to Robespierre and other revolutionary leaders: "Como ahora la guillotina no anda lista, los Robespierre, los Saint-Just y los Marat tienen que limitarse a escribir cuentos y a poner en ellos a los aristócratas y a los burgueses como en la picota" (656). Later, the text speaker refers to the Commune and says that although it was defeated, its spirit lives on and inspires naturalism (2: 658). In discussing Baudelaire and the French novelist Luisa Michel, he refers to their adulation of the proletariat and their depiction of the bourgeoisie as demons (2: 668). His analysis of Zola's *Germinal* questions the purpose of the minute description of life in the mines and concludes that it can only be to incite hatred against the rich and happy of the world (2: 671). After reading the novel, the only possible remedy that occurs to the reader is the total destruction of the existing social order or of humanity in its entirety (2: 682). Several pages later he reiterates that the novel teaches the inefficacy of any "partial revolution".

The fear of revolution and in particular, of a violent proletarian uprising against the middle and upper classes, informs much of *Apuntes sobre el nuevo arte de escribir novelas* and explains the insistence on the doctrine of free will and on the cultivation of a literature that encourages resignation and hope rather than rebellion and despair. The emphasis on free will ties in with the liberal and Krausist/Institutionist discourse but in Valera's text, the focus is not on progress and change but on control and responsibility. In the first reference to the individual will, the speaker links freedom and moral responsibility: "en lo que yo no consiento, no ya la negación, pero ni la duda, es en que soy libre, en que soy responsable, en que llevo la ley moral grabada en el alma" (2: 637). A few sentences later, he specifically addresses the issue of free will among the lower classes, arguing that neither ignorance nor poverty deprive the individual of free choice (2: 637). The entire section echoes in both language and tone Brunetière's comments in "Le roman expérimental" that appeared in 1879. In that text, Brunetière insists that all individuals create their own destiny, their own happiness or misfortune (113). He also defends the value of culture and education, arguing that the degradation and passion depicted in *L'Assomoir* could exist, but only in the working class (126). Valera similarly criticizes Zola for denying the efficacy of education and cultural refinement in controlling the baser instincts (2: 637). If there is no freedom, if human beings are mere machines or animals, then there is no reason to believe in justice (2: 684) and the only possible solution is to blame the existing social organization or nature or God, if he exists (2: 680).

The view espoused in *Apuntes* portrays naturalism as a movement that depicts social injustice without providing solutions and exacerbates the problem by presenting individuals, especially lower-class individuals, as determined by their environment and thus, lacking any responsibility for their actions. Without a belief in religion, in divine justice, and in individual responsibility, naturalism provides no controls against violent individual and group upheaval. The text speaker remarks in chapter 7 that as a result of naturalism, men and women appear more desirous of pleasure and less patient, less resigned to suffering (2: 668). On another occasion, he condemns Zola's pessimism and his emphasis on the negative as contravening resignation:

> . . . también es vicio verlo todo negro y complacerse en pintarlo así y no resignarse ni conformarse con nada. Ahora la filosofía experimental, esto es, la negación de la religión y de la metafísica, ha quitado a muchos las esperanzas ultramundanas. (629)

The speaker clearly yearns for a return to a literature that fosters resignation, belief in otherworldly justice, or at least refrains from stirring up the masses. In Chapter 1, the text speaker laments the transformation of literature from a form of entertainment to one of serious study (2: 613–14). In contrast to Zola's aesthetic, *Apuntes* proposes a literature that evades reality and thus avoids the creation of any political and social turbulence. Repeatedly in the study, the text speaker contrasts the old literature, which he portrays in favorable terms as distracting the reader (2: 613) or providing solace (2: 640), with naturalistic novels, which disturb the reader's digestion and lead to a general discontent. Verisimilitude is important to the novel but if the novel is too similar to life, it fails in its mission, which is to "purificar las pasiones" (622). The desire to maintain a safe distance from reality motivates the speaker's treatment of obscenity and sexuality in classical literature. On various occasions in *Apuntes*, he argues that the crudities of certain classical texts are acceptable because, in contrast to naturalistic obscenities, their purpose is to entertain, to make the reader laugh. Syphilis, fights between women, or suicide are artistically admissible only if they are treated as comical or grotesque (624–25). The truth, if presented as the truth, only leads to despair and dissatisfaction; it is preferable to falsify reality:

> ¿Con qué fruto sazonado regala [Zola] nuestro paladar, y ya que no deleite, qué provecho nos trae el retratar la verdad, si la verdad es siempre inmunda? ¿No sería mejor mentir para consuelo y presentar a los hombres, a fin de que imiten y copien lo que puedan, dechados de perfección, aunque sean falsos? (2: 645)

The ability of the novel to reach a large and susceptible audience plays an important role in the determination of artistically appropriate and inappropriate subject matter or treatment. Blasphemy, pessimism, and obscenity are acceptable in lyric poetry because "en verso . . . no tiene la misma importancia que en prosa cualquier atrocidad que se diga" (2: 639). Furthermore, half of the readers don't understand poetry and so it neither scandalizes nor perverts (2: 646).

In contrast to naturalism with its dangerous invitation to pessimism and discontent, Valera proposes a Christian literature. He takes pains to differentiate between Christian resignation and neo-Catholic fatalism and the "vale of tears" view of life:

¿Cómo negar que a veces los escritores ascéticos han ponderado en demasía los males de este mundo, lugar de prueba, destierro de los espíritus, valle de lágrimas, en el cual gemimos y suspiramos por la patria celestial? Pero el Divino Maestro parece como que los contradice, al afirmar en el Sermón de la Montaña que en la patria celestial debemos poner la mira, pero que todo lo demás se nos dará también sin que lo pidamos. Busquemos el reino de Dios y su justicia, y las otras cosas que nos hagan falta vendrán por añadidura. (2: 662)

He also distances himself from neo-Catholic discourse in his tolerance for obscenity and his defense of Byron, Espronceda, and certain other heterodox writers. In *Apuntes*, Catholicism is less a theological position than a source of social control. Like the historical novel, fairy tales, or comic narratives, religious texts separate the reader from a reality that invites change and consequently, is better left out of literary consideration:

. . . pienso que me estará mejor, en vez de leer a Zola, leer algún libro devoto y ascético, que me inspire la paciencia, me induzca a la penitencia y me reverdezca las esperanzas del Cielo; o leer un cuento alegre que me haga reír; o leer algún cuento de hadas que me haga soñar. (2: 672)

It is evident that political considerations play a major role in *Apuntes sobre el nuevo arte de escribir novelas*. More than any other oppositional text, it continually links Zola to socialism and radical political movements, echoing Brunetière and French anti-naturalist discourse. Certain resonances of neo-Catholic discourse can be heard in its call for a return to a Christian literature and to literary idealism, but it also incorporates a more tolerant attitude towards religious heterodoxy and in general, subordinates theological considerations to social and political concerns.

The interplay with Emilia Pardo Bazán's texts and the feminine voice also reveals a preoccupation with halting threatened social transformation and with effecting a return to previous literary and social models. The speaker echoes previous texts in expressing his surprise and dismay that a woman of Pardo Bazán's stature would declare herself a naturalist (2: 613). He makes frequent references to the woman reader of novels (2: 614), communicating a concern that naturalism is particularly dangerous for the female audience. He often uses examples or metaphors that depict women as inferior or worthy of reprimand. He compares naturalism to a beautiful woman who deceives other women into using poisons and damaging ointments on the pretext that they will improve their beauty. On the same page, he criticizes literary fads and reminds the reader of Mme. Scuderi, whose novels were once popular but have long since been forgotten (2: 616). In that *Apuntes* is advertised as a response to Pardo Bazán's study of naturalism, the belittling remarks on women and women writers subtly undermine her authority. The mention of fads also serves to introduce the idea that as a woman, Pardo Bazán has to dress according to the latest style (2: 617). In general, the text speaker suggests that Pardo Bazán's adoption of naturalism is a passing whim or that she simply misunderstands the movement and erroneously declares herself a naturalist. Early in the text, the speaker declares that they have two completely different understandings of what constitutes naturalism (2: 618). Later he distinguishes between "real naturalism" and the naturalism imagined by Pardo Bazán (632). In the section defending the existence of free will, he writes that she is as much an idealist as he is, and not at all a naturalist (2: 635).

Apuntes also mounts a strong attack on the immorality of naturalism and works to discredit Pardo Bazán's defense of the movement in this area. The text speaker quotes from a Mexican woman writer to confront Pardo Bazán's female voice with a more traditional female voice. Concepción Jimeno condemns the naturalistic novel and while she does not name Pardo Bazán, she refutes the contention put forth in *La cuestión palpitante* and other texts that naturalistic novels contain a moral teaching. In Jimeno's view, "cuando la moral se oculta bajo el fango, es imposible que éste no salpique el rostro de quien la busca" (2: 646). Valera extends the metaphor to insist that what is hidden beneath the mud is the denial of any morality. As in previous texts, immorality is consistently associated with sexuality and in particular, female sexuality. In listing the crudities and vulgarities of naturalism, the first item is virtually always a reference to extramarital sex (2: 671, 2: 680–81). Further evidence of the identification of sin with female sexuality appears in an anecdote intercalated in *Apuntes* regarding an American woman whose only defect was an uncontrollable propensity to gossip. In the effort to cure her habit, the woman penned the following prayer: "Let me sin deeply that I may cast no stone." In commenting, the text speaker writes that her husband never really had cause to worry, revealing the generalized assumption that female sin is synonymous with sexuality (2: 661).

The association of sexuality, capricious stylistic change, and dangerous religious heterodoxy with Pardo Bazán are cleverly insinuated in the last chapter, in a final attempt to both undermine her authority and reclaim her for traditional, orthodox discourse. The text speaker opens with a general allusion to those who follow Zola: "Los que se someten, a veces lo hacen por moda y sin caer en la cuenta de lo que hacen, sin comprender a las claras lo que significa la bandera bajo la cual se alistan" (689). The mention of faddishness echoes Menéndez Pelayo and Valera's own previous accusation that Pardo Bazán is simply following the latest fashion while the reference to the flag harks back to the pirate flag of Pardo Bazán's "Bandera negra". Without naming her, she is the clear referent of the charge that some of Zola's followers don't really understand the movement nor the significance of their actions. The next sentence reenforces this reading by directly naming Pardo Bazán, although it swerves away from any specific identification of her as the subject of the previous sentence. More significantly, the text speaker leads into an analogy which simultaneously introduces the topics of female sexuality and religious unorthodoxy:

> No dude la señora doña Emilia Pardo Bazán de que los que se llaman hoy naturalistas en España, por amor a lo que priva en Paris, son como el *Escarmentado* de Voltaire, que repitió, sin darles importancia, ciertas palabras arábigas que le dijo su hermosa querida turca en momentos de deleite o de abandono, y al día siguiente se halló en casa con un imán que venía a tiro hecho para imponerle el signo de su religión, porque había renegado de la fe cristiana y convertídose al islamismo. (2: 689)

Against the backdrop of the entire debate on naturalism, the allusion to a seductive and treacherous woman who leads an unsuspecting male victim astray evokes a number of textual reminiscences that work to the detriment of Pardo Bazán and naturalism: female sexuality, female caprice, heresy, irresponsibility and a lack of understanding of the conversion and its consequences. In order to reenforce this image, the text speaker affixes another analogy and suggests that the conversion to naturalism may have its origins in the desire to annoy someone, as when a certain young man attempted to irritate his father by converting to Lutheranism. The Lutheran minister suspected his motives, and told him to go back to his church and to his father. After disparaging Pardo Bazán's knowledge and motives and stigmatizing her position by associating it with heresy and sexual licentiousness, the text speaker now proceeds to reclaim her for idealism, Catholicism, and the traditional feminine model. He compares the Lutheran minister to Zola, who dismissed Pardo Bazán's naturalism as purely literary in a prologue to the translation of Narciso Oller's *La mariposa*. He then insists that Spanish and French naturalism are two entirely different entities and refutes Pardo Bazán's inclusion of Pereda and other Spanish novelists within the movement. Finally, he categorically denies that Pardo Bazán, the Christian and pious author of the study of Saint Francis of Assisi, can be considered a naturalist (2: 689).

Two different discourses operate in the treatment of Pardo Bazán in Valera's *Apuntes*. The traditional chivalrous discourse that governs male-female communication appears throughout the text but more frequently in the initial chapters. Early references to her talent, her discretion, her excellent judgment abound. However, alongside this gentlemanly deference is an ironic, innuendo-filled discourse that works to undermine her authority and to discredit her voice. This second discourse, which exploits the readers' latent fears of female sexuality and emancipation, operates with increasing frequency in the latter part of the text. The transition from an early deference to later resentment and hostility toward Pardo Bazán and the female voice is characteristic of the entire debate on naturalism. The early respect expressed by such writers as Alas, Vidart, and Pereira gives way to increasingly strong attacks as she moves further away from the traditional feminine voice and traditional female literary codes. Veiled allusions to sexual incontinency and religious unorthodoxy that were initially introduced as textual strategies designed to undermine naturalism by casting a shadow on one of its principal proponents are displaced by a more personal condemnation. As naturalism yields to other *fin de siècle* movements, the need to refute or reappropriate Pardo Bazán's voice disappears but the disparaging comments increase. I commented earlier on Leopoldo Alas's criticism of the feminine subject matter and ambience of *Morriña* and his allusions to Pardo Bazán's sexual promiscuity in his review of *Insolación*. His review of *La prueba* in 1890 continues in the same line but curiously reverses his earlier position with regard to Pardo Bazán's naturalism. In the early and mid 1880s, when Clarín was encouraging the introduction of naturalism in Spain, he labored to disassociate Pardo Bazán from the movement. In 1890, when Clarín is turning to spiritualism and other late nineteenth-century trends, he labels her as naturalist in order to suggest her literary tardiness and her superficiality. Furthermore, he strongly implies that her Catholicism is a sham and that as a novelist and a person, she is incapable of spirituality and is only cognizant of the body:

Creía que iba a ver, si no una sincera, patética, natural confidencia de la misma dama, cristiana también que escribía, por lo menos algo que en reflejo me hablase de una vez, la primera de las cosas hondas e importantes de que jamás ha hablado Da. Emilia, a pesar de su catolicismo y su naturalismo. Puede un autor católico ser naturalista, sí, pero ha de vérsele lo católico lo mismo que lo naturalista. A Da. Emilia se le ve lo naturalista, pero no se le ve lo católico. A Zola se le ve lo naturalista y lo racionalista . . . y lo pesimista; a Da. Emilia se le ven muchas cosas, pero no se le ve la *cristiana* que dice tiene dentro. Porque ya comprenderá ella que tratándose de un artista no bastan manifiestos, como puede darlos Pidal, ni apologías de la fe. No es eso lo que se busca. Es . . . la *soul* cristiana. Y no parece. ("La Prueba" 3, 6).

The personal attacks on Pardo Bazán and the allusions to sexual promiscuity continue in several articles involving Luis Coloma's controversial novel *Peque-ñeces*. Pardo Bazán reviews *Pequeñeces* in her *Nuevo Teatro Crítico* and in her study, she classifies Coloma as a realist. Juan Mañé y Flaquer, long an opponent of realism and naturalism (Pattison 116–17), rejects this classification, remarking that Coloma is not to be compared to Pardo Bazán because in his novel, there is not a single kiss exchanged between members of the opposite sex while in Pardo Bazán's novels and in realism in general, sonorous kisses can be heard throughout. The gravity of the charge provokes an immediate and heated response from Pardo Bazán:

¿No comprende el Sr. Mañé que cierto género de aseveraciones envuelve una imputación *ofensiva* hasta podría decirse *calumniosa*, porque atribuye *sin fundamento* a mis libros un pronunciado carácter erótico que no tienen? ("Notas literarias" 92)

She subsequently goes on to rebuke him "porque ya sabe él que no es fácil quitarse de encima ciertas acusaciones" (94). Her concern is further evidenced by a second article, appearing in volume 12 of *Nuevo Teatro Crítico*, in which she reiterates her response to Mañé y Flaquer and insists that she has consciously been very sparing in her use of kisses.

Accusations of immorality and religious unorthodoxy also surface in Conrado Muiños Sáenz's article on Coloma and Pardo Bazán. Muiños Sáenz is an Augustinian priest who writes in the conservative religious publication *La Ciudad de Dios*. The article is one of the last important studies on naturalism and is of interest because it exemplifies certain shifts that have occurred in the discussion. Like many of the texts of the late 1880s and early 1890s it focuses primarily on Pardo Bazán and on the issue of female emancipation. The text speaker denies any desire to silence her voice or to send her where some liberals, perceived as more tolerant and cultured than Catholic clerics, have sent her. However, he is clearly uneasy with her feminist tendencies. He expresses his admiration but also his pain at the new and dangerous tendencies which he observes in her work. In particular, he alludes to her short story "No lo invento", which had appeared in volume 3 of *Nuevo Teatro Crítico* in 1891 and which is a chilling story of a necrophiliac grave digger who avenges the scorn of the local townspeople by "raping" all of the young female corpses prior to burying them. The story contains a strong feminist subtext which questions the Spanish honor code, the sexual treatment of women in Spain, and the victimization of women in general. In contrast to "No lo invento" and her other risqué writings, Muiños Sáenz recommends Coloma's *Pequeñeces* and novels that present a Catholic viewpoint. Like Alas, he remarks that in Pardo Bazán's novels there is no evidence of her Catholicism and warns that she is going to lose her Catholic readers if she is not more careful. All of these issues have surfaced in other texts of the period and similar opinions have been voiced by writers of both the right and the left. This very similarity is significant in that Muiños Sáenz represents a traditional Catholic point of view. However, his text is in no way comparable to the neo-Catholic texts and discourse prevalent in the 1870s and reveals the loss of authoritative stature accorded previously to Catholicism and neo-Catholicism. The Catholic speaker now competes for authority with other voices and discourses and enters into dialogic play with them in order to accredit him or herself. Muiños Sáenz echoes feminist discourse and seeks to establish his liberal credentials by pointing out the sexist bias of his "liberal" opponents. He distances himself from traditional neo-Catholic discourse by invoking the "liberal" Valera to condemn the crudities of the naturalistic novel. Although he clearly seeks to reintegrate Pardo Bazán into traditional Catholic female discourse, he neither threatens nor imposes his authority. Rather, he appeals to her to be kinder in her treatment of the Catholic press and of Catholic writers.

Muiños Sáenz's "La crítica de *Pequeñeces* and Pequeñeces de la Crítica" illustrates the changing nature of Spanish discourse as it developed during the last quarter of the nineteenth century in the debates over naturalism. Liberal discourse, which operated from a marginal, impotent position in the 1870s, gradually reasserts itself and comes to occupy a central location in the competition for authority. Muiños Sáenz recognizes this shift and incorporates the moderate voice of Valera and other aspects of liberal discourse to accredit his own more conservative voice. The defense of Catholicism here reveals a weakened position, brought on by the collective acceptance of religious tolerance, of freedom of conscience, and of openness to new ideas and to European liberalism, initially introduced by Krausists and subsequently promulgated by Institutionists and other liberals. Other texts of the late 1880s and early 1890s reveal the growing power of liberal discourse in the increased vocalization of political concerns that were largely silenced throughout the 1870s and the early 1880s. Notwithstanding the liberal and conservative fear and resentment of the female voice, Muiños Sáenz's text acknowledges its existence and also recognizes its power, although he attempts in his own way once again to silence or control it.

Emilia Pardo Bazán identifies 1891 as the end of naturalism (*La España Moderna* Mar. 1891 68–69) and after that year, no major studies of the movement appear. As I have attempted to show, even before that date, the emphasis had shifted from naturalism *per se* to Pardo Bazán's endorsement of the movement and the implications of this endorsement. The presence of a female speaker in the debate radically changed the nature of the discussion and as far back as 1881, with the prologue to *Un viaje de novios*, the question of women's right to discourse and male resistance to it was increasingly central to the debate. The issue of morality became intertwined with the subject of female sexuality and the fear of radical social transformation. The discussion of the political implication of naturalism was also affected by Pardo Bazán's entry into the debate, in part because of the perception of her conservatism and in part because of the fear that a woman's voice would be misread. Numerous texts devote considerable energy to repudiate, reappropriate, or restate Pardo Bazán's word.

The political as well as the anti-feminist and feminist issues have been largely ignored by previous studies of the critical reception of naturalism, which focus primarily on the questions of determinism, crudity, and literary issues such as authorial impersonality or the importance of observation. As the analysis of various pivotal texts has shown, all of these diverse aspects come together in the complex interweaving and dialogic interplay of discourses that is characteristic of the essay. Over time, certain discourses acquire greater authoritative status and others recede to the background. From 1879 to 1891, the liberal endorsement of literary idealism gradually gives way to the acceptance of naturalism while conservative writers generally continue to endorse idealism with some concessions to their opposition. The silenced political subtext also changes and towards the late 80s is voiced with increasing openness. As Pardo Bazán and other women writers achieve greater literary success, male resentment and hostility grow commensurately. Not all texts incorporate all of the various discourses that enter into the critical debates but every text reveals the confluence of multiple competing discourses and viewed as a whole, they reveal the gradual evolution of Spanish discourse from idealism to naturalism and all that this change implies.

CONCLUSION

Late nineteenth-century Spain consolidates the transition of Spanish culture from the classical to the modern age, as defined by Roland Barthes, Mikhail Bakhtin, and Michel Foucault. During this period, traditional centers of power are displaced or radically transformed. Authority becomes more diffuse and new voices compete with each other and with traditional forces for public recognition. The essay provides an ideal form for the expression of competing voices and discourses. It arises as a genre precisely at a moment when new social classes, new cultural forms and increased geographic mobility demand new discursive modes. Essayistic discourse is marked by opposition to the authoritative word and responds to the writer's desire to establish a new, personal authority, to stake out a claim in the confusion of multiple and clashing discourses. Essays are inherently dialogic, in that they represent an individual response to the ongoing conflicts and to previous essays or utterances. In responding to other discourses, the essay enters into dialogue with them and incorporates them into the text. The dialogic character of the essay is further enhanced by the peculiar nature of the relationship between essayistic text speaker and reader and text and context. The essay retains a close connection with the "real world" of the reader and the author. Consequently, essayistic discourse invests a tremendous amount of energy into constructing its own authority and develops a number of textual strategies to this end. The "I" of the text is a product and producer of these diverse textual strategies, and should not be confused with the I of the author.

The nineteenth-century debate on naturalism condenses many of the cultural conflicts that take place at that particular moment. The confluence of many voices and discourses that typifies both the essay and moments of historical conflict reveals itself in all of the texts involved in the critical reception of naturalism in Spain. The conversations of the 1860s and 70s involve such diverse components as nationalism, Catholicism, neo-Catholicism, Krausism and other forms of German idealism, all of which evolve over time and in relation to each other. The philosophical and theological debates regarding the nature of the universe, of human destiny, and the transformability of the individual and of society also inform the discussions of art and its role within culture. Conservative and liberal writings on art reveal an extraordinarily complex shifting of positions over time. In the decades of the 70s and 80s there is a move away from idealism among liberal and leftist writers and at certain moments, they adopt positions which are identical to those advocated previously by writers who are their ideological antagonists.

The situation is further complicated by the political events of the late 60s and early 70s and also, by the growing presence of women in all aspects of Spanish culture and by their calls for social change. The Revolution of 1868, the First Spanish Republic, and chiefly, the cantonalist movement lead to the political disillusionment of the intellectuals of the period. Liberals and progressive who oppose violence find themselves caught between the newly empowered radical left (anarchism and socialism) and their old antagonists, the Carlists and neo-Catholics. Throughout the 1870s and well into the 1880s, liberal and progressive writers seek to disassociate themselves from violence and revolution by silencing all but the most oblique references to political events and issues. The fear of radicalism and violence also brakes the liberal evolution towards the acceptance of naturalism. Zola provides a theory and a practice that enable a progressively inspired narrative; however, the image of the cantons and the social disorder of the early 1870s prevent Spanish liberal writers from endorsing Zola and his political program. On the other hand, the right wing condemnation of positivism and naturalism, the liberal desire to salvage some program for change, and their own disillusionment with literary and philosophical idealism compel liberal writers to move cautiously but steadily towards the acceptance of naturalism and Zola. The silencing of political discourse, the echoes of calls for radical social change and the fear which they provoke combine with the various discourses and echoes of discourses already studied to further enrich the confluence of voices and discourses that constitutes the critical reception of naturalism.

A final and little studied factor in the polemic over naturalism is the appearance of Emilia Pardo Bazán as an important voice in the discussion. The presence of a woman impacts both the left and the right and changes the nature of the debate. The underlying anxiety at the entry of a female speaker and the causes for this anxiety are largely silenced but leave traces in the subtexts and echoes that they produce. With the appearance of Pardo Bazán's prologue to *Un viaje de novios* and especially after the publication of *La cuestión palpitante*, the discussion shifts in large part to women's access to public speech and to questions of female sexuality. Traditionalist hysteria that women's emancipation will lead to sexual liberation and free love is echoed in liberal writings and writers of all ideological persuasions work to silence, refute, dilute, or reappropriate Pardo Bazán's word. Each essayist works to accredit the textual speaker and in dialogue with Pardo Bazán, male essayists actively seek to discredit her textual ''I'', in order to validate patriarchal discourse and values.[1] The texts of the late 1880s and early 1890s reveal the shift in

[1] It is interesting to note that the discourses and voices that were silenced in the nineteenth century continue to be silenced in contemporary critical works that deal with the period, its authors, and its texts. Early in this study I pointed out that the sidestepping of the political ramifications of naturalism continues in contemporary studies that stress the exclusively literary character of Spanish naturalism. Numerous essays in Lissorgues's collection of studies on realism and naturalism reassert this view. The silencing and devaluing of the feminine voice persists in some quite recent studies. The confidence with which critics rank Pardo Bazán behind Galdós and Clarín, or as secondary to Valera and Pereda, as if such value judgements were objective and undebatable is one example. A particularly egregious instance can be found in Guillermo de Torre's essay, ''Emilia Pardo Bazán y la cuestión del naturalismo''. De Torre describes Pardo Bazán's *La cuestión palpitante* as ambiguous, perplexing (245), full of excuses, excessive caution, and circumlocution (250), with no recognition that the same can be said for any number of essays written by male authors on the

focus that occurs with the intervention of the female voice and display the confluence of voices, silences, and echoes that constitute the critical reception of naturalism in Spain. The overlapping and interweaving of the various voices, discourses, and echoes in the individual texts produces a larger text – the critical reception of naturalism in Spain – that is multilayered, contradictory, and symptomatic of the tensions, collisions, and paradoxes that exist in late nineteenth-century Spanish culture.

Nationalism, Catholicism and neo-Catholicism, Krausism, Institutionism, literary and philosophical idealism, liberalism, anti-feminism and feminism, naturalism, positivism, to name the principle discourses that I have traced in this study, come together in dialogic interplay and mutually influence and transfigure each other. The various discourses change in relation to each other in a single synchronic slice of time and also diachronically, as historical and cultural events and their own dialogic interplay combine to create new relationships and new meanings. The idealism that Pattison identifies as displacing naturalism in the 1890s (166) is not the same idealism that operated in the 1860s and 70s, although it carries forward echoes and voices of that period. The dynamic of the discourse is very different in the 1890s. Neo-Catholic discourse is no longer sovereign, liberal discourse lays greater claim to authority but is increasingly challenged by the proletariat and by the radical political groups that it has feared for so long. Women are no longer confined to traditional religious discourse and add another oppositional voice to the collective conversation. In addition, changing historical and social circumstances necessarily transform the language and the discourse.

An examination of the Spanish discourse of the 1890s would require another in-depth study, but it is important to point out that it incorporates in the form of voices, silences, and echoes the Spanish discourse of the 1880s that I have analyzed here. As Dreyfus observes, language is a dense web with its own history, and any study of literary or non-literary texts must explore both their density and their history. In the preceding chapters, I have identified the multiple strands that make up the web constituting the discussion of naturalism and I have traced the development of these strands and their changing relationship over time. Many studies seek to define naturalism or other literary movements as a list of characteristics. This both ignores the diachronic development of specific traits over time and fails to account for the complex overlapping, multilayering, and mutually transforming voices and discourses that constitute a literary movement. In contrast to previous studies of naturalism and in keeping with contemporary theories of language and literature, I have avoided a purely literary approach. Building on the work of Lukacs, Adorno, Pratt, Bakhtin and other theorists, I have developed a theory of the essay and added essayistic discourse as yet another strand in the web. After examining the argumentative-expository character of the essay and its essentially dialogic nature, I have traced the diverse voices and discourses that come together in the critical

---

same topic. In the final analysis, de Torre observes, the most interesting, and by extension important, contribution of Pardo Bazán's *La cuestión palpitante* is found not in her text but in the reply which it provoked from Juan Valera! The devaluation of this important text and the attempt to silence the female speaker are lamentably apparent.

reception of naturalism. Naturalism is the product of these diverse strands, which work in dialogic interaction with each other.

As Bakhtin has taught us, the dialogic nature of language is such that each word carries with it remnants of its contacts with other words and each discourse contains traces of neighboring discourses. Neither the discussion of naturalism nor any other literary polemic can be isolated from the non-literary world in which it is inserted. Conversely, the non-literary world does not exist independently and may work out its tensions or conflicts through literary theory or practice, as occurs with the critical reception of naturalism in Spain. In the theoretical discussion of naturalism, Spaniards found a vehicle to express and move tentatively towards resolving many of the social, political, religious, and artistic tensions that characterize late nineteenth-century society. With the breakdown of traditional authoritative voices and the intense competition for control of discourse, the potential for social fragmentation and a total breakdown of communication was ever-present. The events of 1868, the Carlist Wars and the cantonalist movement were persuasive evidence of the threat to national unity. Official and self-censorship in the early years of the Restoration sought to control discourse and thus, avoid the expression of the existing discord. Through the complicated play of affirmation and response, silences and echoes produced in essayistic discourse and expressed in the context of literary naturalism, Spanish writers of opposing ideologies succeeded in voicing otherwise unspeakable concerns and sustaining a national dialogue.

WORKS CITED

ABEL, Elizabeth, ed. *Writing and Sexual Difference*. Chicago: U of Chicago Press, 1982.

ADORNO, T. W. "The Essay as Form." Trans. Bob Hullot-Kentor. *New German Critique*. Spring–Summer 1984: 151–75.

ALARCÓN, PEDRO DE. "La moral en el arte." *Revista Europea* 25 Feb. 1877: 225–37.

ALAS, LEOPOLDO. *B. Pérez Galdós: Estudio crítico biográfico*. Madrid: Fernando Fe, 1889.

———. *Folletos literarios*. 7 vols. Madrid: Fernando Fe, 1888–1890.

———. Rev. of *Gloria*, by Benito Pérez Galdós. *Revista Europea* 18 Feb. 1877: 207–12.

———. Rev. of *Los pazos de Ulloa* by Emilia Pardo Bazán. *La Ilustración Ibérica* 29 Jan. 70–71 and 5 Feb. 1887: 86–87.

———. *Mezclilla*. Madrid: Fernando Fe, 1889.

———. Rev. of *Morriña*, by Emilia Pardo Bazán. *Madrid Cómico* 9 and 23 Nov. 1889.

———. *Nueva campaña (1885–1886)*. Madrid: Fernando Fe, 1887.

———. "Palique." *Madrid Cómico*. 5 June, 1897.

———. *Los Prólogos de Leopoldo Alas*. Ed. David Torres. Madrid: Playor, 1984.

———. Rev. of *La Prueba* by Emilia Pardo Bazán. *Madrid Cómico* 20 Sept. 1890.

———. *Solos*. Madrid: Alfredo de Carlos Hierro, 1881.

———. *Teoría y crítica de la novela española*. Ed. Sergio Beser. Barcelona: Laia, 1972.

ALCÁZAR HERNÁNDEZ, JOSÉ. "Del naturalismo en la novela contemporánea." *Revista de España* 84 (1882): 106–16.

ALFONSO, LUIS. "Carta-Pacio de Luis Alfonso a Emilia Pardo Bazán." *La Epoca* 21 Apr. 1884.

———. "Cartas son cartas." *La Epoca* 31 May 1884.

———. "Cartilla." *La Epoca* 26 May 1884.

———. "Novelas al uso." *Los Lunes de El Imparcial*. 18 Feb. 1884; 10 Mar. 1884.

———. Rev. of *La papallona* by Narciso Oller. *La Epoca*. 2 Feb. 1882.

———. Rev. of *Pedro Sánchez* by José María de Pereda. *La Epoca*. 4 Jan. 1884.

———. Rev. of *La Tribuna* by Emilia Pardo Bazán. *La Epoca*. 7 Jan. 1884.

ALONSO MARTÍNEZ, MANUEL. "Exposición y crítica del sistema krausista." *Memorias de la Real Academia de Ciencias Morales* Vol 4. Madrid: Gutenberg, 1883.

ALTAMIRA, RAFAEL. "El realismo y la literatura contemporánea." *La Ilustración Ibérica* 24 Apr. 1886: 262–66, 1 May 1886: 278–79, 15 May 1886: 311–15, 5 Jun. 1886: 359–63, 19 Jun. 1886: 399, 26 Jun. 1886: 414, 3 Jul. 1886: 427–30, 10 Jul. 1886: 442–46, 17 Jul. 1886: 459–62, 24 Jul, 1886: 467, 31 Jul. 1886: 483, 14 Aug. 1886, 515, 28 Aug. 1886: 550–55, 4 Sept. 1886: 567–74, 11 Sept. 1886: 586–90, 18 Sept. 1886: 603–06, 25 Sept. 1886: 615–19, 2 Oct. 1886: 634–38, 9 Oct. 1886: 647–54, 16 Oct. 1886: 663–70, 23 Oct. 1886: 678–82.

ANDERSON, CHRIS, ed. *Literary Non-Fiction*. Carbondale and Edwardsville: Southern Illinois UP, 1989.

ARANGUREN, JOSÉ LUIS. *Moral y sociedad*. Madrid: Cuadernos para el Diálogo, 1966.

ARPA Y LÓPEZ, SALVADOR. *Compendio de retórica y poética*. Cadiz: Federico Joly, 1879.

———. *Historia de literatura española*. Madrid: Sucesores de Rivadeneyra, 1889.

——. *Principios de literatura general o Teoría del arte literario*. Cadiz: Revista Médica, 1874.

AULLÓN DE HARO, PEDRO. *El ensayo en los siglos XIX y XX*. Madrid: Playor, 1984.

AZCÁRATE, GUMERSINDO. *Estudios filosóficos y políticos*. Madrid: M. M. de los Ríos, 1877.

——. *Minuta de un testamento*. Preface Elías Díaz. 1876. Barcelona: Cultura Popular, 1967.

——. "El pesimismo." *Revista Europea* 4 Mar. 1877: 257–65.

AZCÁRATE, PABLO DE. *Gumersindo de Azcárate: Estudio biográfico documental, Semblanza, Epistolario, Escritos*. Madrid: Tecnos, 1969.

BAKHTIN, MIKHAIL. *The Dialogic Imagination*. Trans. Caryl Emerson and Michael Holquist. Austin: Texas UP, 1981.

——. *Problems of Dostoevsky's Poetics*. Trans. Caryl Emerson. Minneapolis: Minnesota UP, 1984.

——. *Speech Genres and Other Late Essays*. Trans. Vern W. McGee. Austin, Texas UP, 1986.

BALAGUER, VICTOR. "Carta literaria a Eduardo Calcaño." *La Ilustración Española y Americana*. 22 June, 1884.

BALMES, JAIME. *Obras completas*. Vols. 1–8. Madrid: Biblioteca de Autores Cristianos, 1949.

BARCÍA CABALLERO, JUAN. "Misión docente y misión social de la mujer." *Conferencia en la Escuela Normal de Maestros de La Coruña*. Santiago: Eco de Santiago, 1914.

BARRANTES, VICENTE. "Las deformidades literarias de la filosofía de Krause." *Revista Europea* 2 Apr. 1876: 193–98.

BARTHES, ROLAND. *Writing Degree Zero/Elements of Semiology*. Trans. Annette Lavers and Colin Smith. Boston: Beacon Press, 1970.

BÉCQUER, GUSTAVO ADOLFO. *Obras*. Barcelona: Vergara, 1962.

BIOY CÁSARES, ADOLFO. *Ensayistas ingleses*. Barcelona: Editorial Exito, 1968.

BLANCO AGUINAGA, CARLOS. *El Unamuno contemplativo*. México: El Colegio de México, 1959.

BLANCO ASENJO, RICARDO. "Del Realismo y del idealismo en literatura." *Revista de la Universidad de Madrid* (1873): 386–93.

BLEZNICK, DONALD W. *El ensayo español del siglo XVI al XX*. México: Colección Studium, 1964.

BÖHL DE FABER, CECILIA. "Respuesta al Sr. D. Vicente Barrante." In Iris Zavala. *Ideología y política en la novela española del siglo XIX*. Salamanca, 1971.

BONY, ALAIN. "L'espace du texte: Spatialité de l'éssai périodique addisonien." *Espaces et représentations dans le monde angloamericain aux XVIIe et XVIIIe siécles*. Paris: Université de Paris-Sorbonne, 1981.

BOOTH, WAYNE. *Rhetoric of Fiction*. Chicago: U of Chicago Press, 1961.

BRETZ, MARY LEE. "Emilia Pardo Bazán on John Stuart Mill: Towards a Redefinition of the Essay." *Hispanic Journal* 9 (1988): 81–88.

BROOKS, CLEANTH. *The Well Wrought Urn*. New York: Harcourt Brace, 1947.

BROWN, DONALD FOWLER. *The Catholic Naturalism of Pardo Bazán*. Chapel Hill: U of North Carolina Press, 1957.

BROWNMILLER, SUSAN. *Against Our Will: Men, Women and Rape*. New York: Simon and Schuster, 1975.

BRUNETIÈRE, FERDINAND. *Le Roman Naturaliste*. Paris: Calmann Lévy, 1883.

CACHO VIU, VICENTE. *La Institución Libre de Enseñanza*. Madrid: Rialp, 1962.

CADALSO, JOSÉ. *Cartas marruecas: Noches lúgubres*. Madrid: Cátedra, 1978.

CALCAÑO, EDUARDO. "Carta literaria al Excelentísimo Señor Don Victor Balaguer de la Academia Española." *La Ilustración Española y Americana*. 29 Feb. 1884.

CAMPOAMOR, RAMÓN DE. "A la lenteja." *Revista Europea* 65 (1875): 441–44.

——. "Dudas y tristezas." *Revista Europea* 62 (1875): 321–26.
CANALEJAS, FRANCISCO DE PAULA. *Curso de literatura general. Parte primera.* N.P.: La Reforma, 1868.
——. *Curso de literatura general. Segunda parte.* Madrid: Manuel Minuesa, 1869.
——. "La educación literaria de la mujer." *Tercera conferencia dominical.* 7 Mar. 1869. Madrid: Rivadeneyra, 1869.
——. *Estudios críticos de filosofía, política y literatura.* Madrid: Bailly-Bailliere, 1872.
——. "El panentismo." *Revista Europea* 63 (1875): 361–64; 67 (1875): 526–32.
——. *La poesía moderna.* Madrid: Revista de legislación, 1875.
CÁNOVAS DEL CASTILLO, A. *"El Solitario" y su tiempo.* Madrid: A. Pérez Dubrull, 1883. Vol. 1.
CARR, RAYMOND. *Spain (1808–1939).* Oxford: Oxford UP, 1966.
CHAMPIGNY, ROBERT. *Pour un esthétique de l'essai.* Paris: Minard, 1967.
CLAVIJO Y FAJARDO, JOSÉ. *El pensador.* Vols. 1–5. Madrid: 1762–67.
CLEMESSY, NELLY. *Emilia Pardo Bazán como novelista.* Trans. Irene Gambia. Madrid: Fundación Universitaria Española, 1981. 2 vols.
CONCEJO, PILAR. "El origen del ensayo hispánico y el género epistolar." *Cuadernos Hispanoamericanos* 373 (1981): 158–64.
CRANE, R.S. *The Language of Criticism and the Structure of Poetry.* Toronto: U. of Toronto Press, 1953.
CROCE, BENEDETTO. *Aesthetic as Science of Expression and General Linguistics.* Trans. Douglas Ainslie. London: MacMillan, 1922.
CULLER, JONATHAN. *On Deconstruction.* Ithaca: Cornell UP, 1982.
——. *Structuralist Poetics.* Ithaca: Cornell UP, 1975.
DAVIS, GIFFORD. "The Spanish Debate over Idealism and Realism Before the Impact of Zola's Naturalism." *PMLA* 84 (1969): 1649–56.
——. "The 'Coletilla' to Pardo Bazán's *Cuestión palpitante.*" *Hispanic Review* 24 (1956): 50–63.
——. "The Critical Reception of Naturalism in Spain Before *La cuestión palpitante.*" *Hispanic Review* 22.2 (1954): 97–108.
DEL ALAMO, NICOLÁS. "El positivismo." *Revista de España* 114 (1887): 208–19.
DERRIDA, JACQUES. *Dissemination.* Trans. Barbara Johnson. Chicago: U of Chicago Press, 1981.
——. *Of Grammatology.* Trans. Gayatri Spivak. Baltimore: Johns Hopkins UP, 1976.
——. "The Law of Genre." *Glyph: Johns Hopkins Textual Studies.* Baltimore: Johns Hopkins UP, 1980. Vol 7.
——. *Writing and Difference.* Trans. Alan Bass. Chicago: U of Chicago Press, 1978.
DIDION, JOAN. "Why I Write." *The New York Times* 5 Dec. 1986, sec. 7: 2, 98–99.
DILLON, GEORGE. *Constructing Texts: Elements of a Theory of Composition and Style.* Bloomington, Indiana UP, 1981.
DIXON, PETER. *Rhetoric.* London: Methuen, 1971.
DONOSO CORTÉS. *Obras completas.* Madrid: Biblioteca de Autores Cristianos, 1970. 2 vols.
——. *Obras completas.* Madrid: Editorial Católica, 1946. 2 vols.
DREYFUS, HUBERT L. and PAUL RABINOW. *Michel Foucault: Beyond Structuralism and Hermeneutics.* Chicago: U of Chicago Press, 1982.
EAGLETON, TERRY. *Literary Theory.* Minneapolis: U of Minnesota, 1983.
EISENSTEIN, HESTER. *Contemporary Feminist Thought.* Boston: G. K. Hall, 1983.
El ensayo: Reunión de Málaga de 1977. Málaga: Diputación Provincial de Málaga, 1980.
ELBANZ, ROBERT. "Autobiography, Ideology, and Genre Theory." *Orbis Litterarium* 38.3 (1983): 187–204.
Enciclopedia Universal Ilustrada. Espasa-Calpe, 1930. Vol. 37.
EPSTEIN, JOSEPH. "Writing Essays." *The New Criterion* June (1984): 26–34.

ETREROS, MERCEDES, MARÍA ISABEL MOTESINOS, AND LEONARDO ROMERO. *Estudios sobre la novela española del siglo 19*. Madrid: Consejo Superior de Investigaciones Científicas, 1977.

Etudes litteraires. Special edition on the Essay. 5.1 (1972).

FEIJOO, BENITO JERÓNIMO. *Obras escogidas*. Madrid: Rivadeneyra, 1863. Vol. 56 of *Biblioteca de Autores Españoles*; Madrid: Artes Gráficas, 1961. Vols. 141–143 of *Biblioteca de Autores Españoles*.

FERNÁNDEZ ALMAGRO, MELCHOR. *Historia política de la España contemporánea*. Madrid: Alianza, 1968.

FISH, STANLEY. *Self-Consuming Artifacts: The Experience of Seventeenth-Century Literature*. Berkeley: U of California Press, 1972.

FORNER, JUAN PABLO. *Exequias de la lengua española*. Madrid: La Lectura, 1925.

——. *Oración apologética por la España y su mérito literario*. Badajoz: Diputación de Badajoz, 1945.

FOSTER, DAVID WILLIAM. *Para una lectura semiótica del ensayo latinoamericano*. Madrid: Porrúa Turanzas, 1983.

FOWLER, ROGER. *Literature as Social Discourse: The Practice of Linguistic Criticism*. Bloomington, Indiana UP, 1981.

FOUCAULT, MICHEL. *The Order of Things*. New York: Vintage Books, 1973.

FRAME, DONALD M. *Montaigne: A Biography*. New York: Harcourt Brace, 1965.

——. *Montaigne's Discovery of Man*. New York: Columbia UP, 1967.

FRYE, NORTHRUP. *Anatomy of Criticism*. Princeton, Princeton UP, 1973.

GASCÓN PELEGRI, VICENTE. *El cantonalismo en la ciudad y reino de Valencia*. Valencia: Mari Montañana, 1974.

GASS, WILLIAM. "Emerson and the Essay." *Habitations of the World*. New York: Simon and Schuster, 1985. 9–49.

GIL CREMADES, JUAN JOSÉ. *Krausistas y liberales*. Madrid: Dossat, 1981.

GILBERT, SANDRA M. AND SUSAN GUBAR. *The Madwomen and the Attic*. New Haven: Yale UP, 1979.

——. "Tradition and the Female Talent." *The Poetics of Gender*. Ed. Nancy K. Miller. New York: Columbia UP, 1986. 183–207.

GINER DE LOS RÍOS, FRANCISCO. "El arte y los artes." *Revista Mensual de Filosofía, Literatura y Ciencias*. III (1871): 193–202.

——. *Ensayos*. Ed. Juan López-Morillas. Madrid: Alianza, 1969.

——. *Ensayos y cartas*. México: Fondo de cultura económica, 1965.

——. *Estudios filosóficos y religiosos*. Madrid: Francisco Góngora, 1876.

——. *Estudios literarios*. Madrid: R. Labajes, 1866.

——. *Estudios de literatura y arte*. Madrid: Victoriano Suárez, 1876.

——. *Obras completas*. Vols. 3, 15. Madrid: La Lectura, 1926.

GINER DE LOS RÍOS, HERMENEGILDO. "Acerca de lo armónico y lo inarmónico en el arte." *Filosofía y arte*. Madrid: M. Minuesa, 1878.

GINER DE LOS RÍOS, HERMENEGILDO AND JUAN GARCÍA AL DEGUER. *Curso de literatura española*. Madrid: M. Minuesa, 1889.

GLENDINNING, NIGEL. *A Literary History of Spain: The Eighteenth Century*. London: Ernest Benn, 1972.

GEROULD, KATHERINE FULLERTON. "An Essay on Essays." *The North American Review* Dec. 1935: 409–18.

GÓMEZ MARÍN, JOSÉ ANTONIO. *Aproximaciones al realismo español*. Madrid: Ediciones Castilla, 1975.

GÓMEZ-MARTÍNEZ, JOSÉ LUIS. *Teoría del ensayo*. Salamanca, Universidad de Salamanca, 1981.

GÓMEZ-MOLLEDA, MARÍA DOLORES. *Los reformadores de la España contemporánea*. Madrid: C.S.I.C., 1966.

GÓMEZ ORTIZ, E. *El naturalismo: Naturalismo en el arte, política y literatura*. Madrid: M. P. Montoya, 1882.

GONZÁLEZ SERRANO, URBANO. *Cuestiones contemporáneas*. Madrid: Fernando Fe, 1883.

——. *Ensayos de crítica y de filosofía*. Madrid: Aurelio J. Alaria, 1881.

——. "Estudios sobre el positivismo." *Revista de Filosofía* 5 (1873): 216–30; 270–80.

GROSS, JOHN J. AND RICHARD C. CARPENTER, eds. *The Examined Life: Four Centuries of the Essay*. Cleveland: World Publishing Co., 1967.

GUILLÉN, CLAUDIO. *Literature as System*. Princeton: Princeton UP, 1971.

HALL, MICHAEL. "Searching and Not Finding: The Experience of Donne's Essays in Divinity." *Genre*. 14.4 (1981): 423–40.

HALLIE, PHILIP P. *The Scar of Montaigne*. Middleton, Connecticut: Wesleyan University, 1966.

HARARI, JOSUÉ V. ed. *Textual Strategies: Perspectives in Post Structuralist Criticism*. Ithaca, Cornell UP, 1979.

HAVERKATE, HENK. *Speech Acts, Speakers and Hearers: Reference and Referential Strategies in Spanish*. Amsterdam: John Benjamin, 1984.

HENNESSY, C.A.M. *The Federal Republic in Spain: Pi y Margall and the Federal Republican Movement*. Oxford: Oxford UP, 1962.

HERRNSTEIN SMITH, BARBARA. *On the Margins of Discourse*. Chicago: U of Chicago Press, 1978.

HOLLAND, NORMAN. *The Dynamics of Literary Response*. New York: Oxford UP, 1968.

HOEY, MICHAEL. *On the Surface of Discourse*. London: George Allen and Unwin, 1983.

HOY, DAVID COUZENS. *The Critical Circle*. Berkeley: U of California Press, 1982.

"El ideal del arte." *Revista Europea* 25 Apr. 1875: 318–20; 23 May 1875: 475–79.

ISER, WOLFGANG. *The Act of Reading*. Baltimore: Johns Hopkins UP 1978.

——. *The Implied Reader*. Baltimore: Johns Hopkins UP, 1974.

IXART, J. Rev. of *La Tribuna* by Emilia Pardo Bazán. *La Epoca*. 7 Jan. 1884.

JACOBUS, MARY. "The Difference of View." *Women Writing and Writing about Women*. ed. Mary Jacobus. New York: Barnes and Noble, 1979. 10–21.

JAUSS, HANS ROBERT. *Toward an Aesthetic of Reception*. Trans. Timothy Bahti. Minneapolis: U of Minnesota Press, 1982.

JIMÉNEZ-LANDI, ANTONIO. *La Institución Libre de Enseñanza*. Madrid: Taurus, 1973.

JONES, ANN ROSALIND. "Surprising Fame: Renaissance Gender Ideologies and Women's Lyric." *The Poetics of Gender*. Ed. Nancy K. Miller. New York: Columbia UP, 1986. 74–95.

JOVER ZAMORA, JOSÉ MARÍA. "La imagen de la primera república en la España de la Restauración." Inaugural Address. Real Academia de la Historia. Madrid: Espasa Calpe, 1982.

JOVELLANOS, GASPAR MELCHOR DE. *Obras*. Madrid: 1845. 5 vols.

JUTGLAR, ANTONIO. *Ideología y clases en la España contemporánea*. Madrid: Edicusa, 1968.

LARRA, MARIANO JOSÉ DE. *Obras*. Madrid: Gráficas Orbe, 1960. *Biblioteca de Autores Españoles*. Vols. 127–29.

LEECH, GEOFFREY. *Explorations in Semantics and Pragmatics*. Amsterdam: John Benjamin, 1988.

LISSORGUES, YVAN, ed. *Realismo y naturalismo en España en la segunda mitad del siglo XIX*. Barcelona: Anthropos, 1988.

LÓPEZ, MARIANO. "Los escritores de la Restauración y las polémicas literarias del siglo XIX en España." *Bulletin Hispanique*. 81 (1979): 51–74.

LÓPEZ-BAGO, EDUARDO. "Naturalistas e idealistas." *La Ilustración Militar*. 20 Jul. 1884: 456–57.

LÓPEZ-CORDÓN, MARÍA VICTORIA. "Federalismo y cantonalismo." *Cuadernos Historia 16*. 170 (1985).

LÓPEZ-JIMÉNEZ, LUIS. *El naturalismo y España: Valera frente a Zola*. Madrid: Alhambra, 1977.

LÓPEZ-MORILLAS, JUAN. *El krausismo español*. 1956. México: Fondo de Cultura Económica, 1980.

LÓPEZ-SANZ, MARIANO. *Naturalismo y espiritualismo en la novelística de Galdós y Pardo Bazán*. Madrid: Pliegos, 1985.

LUKACS, GEORG. *Soul and Form*. Cambridge: MIT Press, 1974.

MACHEREY, PIERRE. *A Theory of Literary Production*. Trans. Geoffrey Wall. New York: Routledge and Kegan Paul, 1986.

MARICHAL, JUAN. *Teoría e historia del ensayismo hispánico*. Madrid; Alianza, 1984.

Marqués de Premio Real. "Epístola a la autora de la Cuestión palpitante." *La Epoca* 8 Apr. 1883.

MARTÍN GAITE, CARMEN. *Usos amorosos de la postguerra española*. Barcelona: Anagram, 1987.

MARTÍN MATEOS, NICOMEDES. "El catolicismo y la filosofía alemana." *Revista de España* 15 (1879): 541–56.

MARTÍNEZ, JOSÉ LUIS. *El ensayo mexicano moderno*. Vol I. México: Fondo de cultura económica, 1971.

MARTÍNEZ RUIZ, JOSÉ. *Obras completas*. Madrid: Caro Raggio, 1919. Vol 12.

MEDINA, JEREMY. *Spanish Realism: The Theory and Practice of a Çoncept in the Nineteenth Century*. Madrid: Porrúa Turanzas, 1979.

MEDIONI, MARÍA-ALICE. *El cantón de Cartagena*. Madrid: Siglo XXI, 1979.

MENÉNDEZ PELAYO, MARCELINO. "De Re Bibliográfica." *Revista Europea*. 16 Jul. 1876: 65–73.

——. *Epistolario de Valera y Menéndez Pelayo (1877–1905)*. Madrid: Espasa-Calpe, 1946.

——. *Historia de los heterodoxos españoles*. Madrid: Librería Católica de San José, 1881. Vol. 7.

——. "Mr. Masson redimuerto." *Revista Europea*. 24 Sept. 1876.

——. "Noticias de algunos trabajos relativos a heterodoxos españoles." *Revista Europea*. 8 Oct. 1876: 459–66.

——. *La novela española vista por Menéndez Pelayo*. Ed. Mariano Baquero Goyanes. Madrid: Editora Nacional, 1956.

——. Prologue to *Obras completas* by José María de Pereda. Madrid: Viuda e Hijos de Manuel Tello, 1909.

MESONERO ROMANOS, RAMÓN DE. *Obras*. Vol 1–3. Madrid: Renacimiento, 1925.

MIGNOLO, WALTER. D. "Discurso ensayístico y tipología textual." *Textos, modelos y metáforas*. Veracruz, México: Universidad de Veracruz, 1984.

——. *Teoría del texto e interpretación de textos*. México: Universidad Autónoma, 1986.

MITCHELL, JULIET. *Women's Estate*. New York: Vintage Books, 1953.

MOI, TORIL. *Sexual/Textual Politics: Feminist Literary Theory*. New York: Methuen, 1985.

MUIÑOS SÁENZ, FR. CONRADO. "La Crítica de *Pequeñeces* y Pequeñeces de la crítica." *La Ciudad de Dios*. 24 (1891): 571–89.

MUÑOZ PEÑA, PEDRO. "La novela contemporánea." *Revista Contemporánea*. 57 (1885): 257–76; 404–22.

NIETO, EMILIO. "El realismo en el arte contemporáneo." *Revista Europea* 49 (1875): 425–29; 50 (1875): 465–68: 51 (1875): 493–501; 52 (1875): 528–35.

NOCEDAL, CÁNDIDO. "Discurso inaugural". *Discursos leídos en las recepciones públicas que ha celebrado desde 1847 la Real Academia Española*. Vol 2. Madrid: Nacional, 1860.

NUÑEZ DE ARCE, GASPAR. Preface. *Gritos de combate*. Madrid: Fernando Fe, 1891.

NÚÑEZ RUIZ, DIEGO. *La mentalidad positiva en España: Desarrollo y crisis*. Madrid: Tucar, 1975.

O'LEARY, R. D. *The Essay*. New York: Thomas Y. Crowell, 1928.

"Orlando". "Novelas españolas del año literario." *Revista de España*. 99 (1884): 600–23.

ORTEGA MUNILLA, JOSÉ. "Carta a D. Luis Alfonso." *Los Lunes de El Imparcial* 11 Feb. 1884.

——. "Goliat y sus enemigos." *Los Lunes de El Imparcial* 25 Feb. 1884.

——. "Madrid". *Los Lunes de El Imparcial* 20 Feb. 1882.

——. "Para terminar una polémica." *Los Lunes de El Imparcial* 14 Apr. 1884.

ORTEGA Y GASSET, JOSÉ. *Obras completas*. Madrid: Revista de Occidente, 1957. Vol 3.

ORTÍ Y LARA, JUAN MANUEL. *Lecciones sobre el sistema de filosofía panteística del alemán Krause*. Madrid: Tejado, 1865.

OSSORIO, ANGEL. *Diccionario político español*. Buenos Aires: Mundo Atlántico, 1945.

PALACIO VALDÉS, ARMANDO. "Don Benito Pérez Galdós." *Revista Europea* 212 (1878): 335–39.

——. "Fernán Caballero." *Revista Europea* 209 (1878): 241–46.

——. "Don Manuel de la Revilla." *Revista Europea* 198 (1877): 766–68.

——. "Don Manuel de la Revilla." *Revista Europea* 299 (1879): 633–38.

PALACIO VALDÉS, ARMANDO AND LEOPOLDO ALAS. *La literatura en 1881*. Madrid: Alfredo de Carlos Hierro, 1882.

PARDO BAZÁN, EMILIA. "Bandera negra. Carta a Victor Balaguer." *La Epoca*. 17 Mar. 1884.

——. "Carta de Emilia Pardo Bazán a Sr. D. Luis Alfonso." *La Epoca*. 14 Apr. 1884.

——. "Carta-magna a Luis Alfonso de Emilia Pardo Bazán." *La Epoca*. 6 May, 1884.

——. *La mujer española y otros artículos feministas*. Ed. Leda Schiavo. Madrid: Editora Nacional, 1976.

——. "Notas literarias." *Nuevo Teatro Crítico*. 10 (1891): 85–94; 12 (1891): 80–92.

——. *Obras completas*. Madrid: Aguilar, 1973. Vols. 2–3.

——. "Respuesta a la epístola del Señor Marqués de Premio Real." *La Epoca*. 23 Apr. 1883.

PARRILLA ORTIZ, PEDRO. *El cantonalismo gaditano*. Cadiz: Caja de Ahorros de Cadiz, 1983.

PASTOR AICART, JUAN B. *La novela moderna*. Alcoy: Francisco Compañy, 1886.

PATTISON, WALTER T. *El naturalismo español*. Madrid: Gredos, 1969.

PEREIRA, AURELIANO. "Dos cartas acerca del naturalismo en el arte literario." *Revista de España* 88 (1882): 509–523.

PÉREZ DE AYALA, RAMÓN. *Obras completas*. Madrid: Aguilar, 1965–66. Vols. 1–3.

PÉREZ FIRMAT, GUSTAVO. "The Novel as Genres." *Genre* 12 (1979) 269–92.

PÉREZ GALDÓS, BENITO. "Observaciones sobre la novela contemporánea de España." *Revista de España* XV (1870): 162–72.

——. *Obras completas*. Madrid: Aguilar, 1962. Vol. 4.

PI Y MARGALL, FRANCISCO. "Del arte y su decadencia en nuestros días." *Revista de España* 36 (1874): 441–49.

PRATT, MARY LOUISE. *Toward a Speech Act Theory of Discourse*. Bloomington: Indiana UP, 1977.

PUIG CAMPILLO, ANTONIO. *El cantón murciano*. Cartagena: Vda. de M. Carreño, 1932.

"El realismo en el arte dramático." *Revista Europea* 56 (1875): 115–19; 58 (1875): 194–99; 60 (1875): 273–74; 61 (1875): 313–15.

REVILLA, MANUEL DE LA. Rev. of *El arte y los artistas contemporáneos de la península* by Francisco M. Tubino. *Revista de España* 23 (1871): 625–32.

——. "Carta al Sr. D. Ramón de Campoamor." *Revista Europea* 67 (1875): 533–35.

——. *Críticas*. 1st Series. Burgos: Timoteo Arnaiz, 1884; 2nd Series. Burgos: Timoteo Arnaiz, 1885.

——. "Don Benito Pérez Galdós." *Revista Contemporánea* 14 (1878): 117–24.

——. "La emancipación de la mujer." *Revista Contemporánea* 18 (1878): 447–63: 19 (1878): 162–81.

——. Rev. of *La familia de León Roch* by Benito Pérez Galdós. *Revista Contemporánea* 19 (1879): 500–10.

——. "El naturalismo en el arte." *Revista de España* 68 (1879): 164–84.

——. "Revista crítica." *Revista Contemporánea* 3 (1876): 375–83; 505–09.

——. "Revista crítica." *Revista Contemporánea* 4 (1876): 122–25.

——. "Revista crítica." *Revista Contemporánea* 6 (1876): 114; 475–78.

——. "Revista crítica." *Revista Contemporánea* 12 (1877): 499–507.

——. "Revista crítica." *Revista Contemporánea* 13 (1878): 372–73.

——. "Revista crítica." *Revista Contemporánea* 14 (1878): 505–09.

ROSMARIN, ADENA. *The Power of Genre*. Minneapolis: U of Minnesota Press, 1985.

RUBIO, CARLOS. *Historia de la revolución española*. Vol 1. Madrid: 1869, 2 vols.

RUIZ DE QUEVEDO, MANUEL. "La instrucción de la mujer." *Revista Europea* 254 (1879): 9–13.

RUIZ MARTÍNEZ, L.A. "Crónica política del interior." *Revista de España* 9 (1884): 437–58.

RUTE, LUIS DE. "Breves indicaciones sobre la filosofía a los matemáticos." *Revista de España*. 9 (1869): 41–68.

SALMERÓN, NICOLÁS. Prologue. *Filosofía y Arte*. By Hermenegildo Giner de los Ríos. Madrid: M. Minuesa, 1878.

SANROMÁ, JOAQUÍN MARÍA. "Primera Conferencia sobre la Educación Social de la Mujer." 21 Feb. 1869. Madrid: Rivadeneyra, 1869.

SANZ DEL RÍO, JULIÁN. "Cartas inéditas de don Julián Sanz del Río." *Revista Europea*. 1 (1874): 66–68.

——. *Ideal de la humanidad*. Madrid: Martínez García, 1871.

SAPIR, EDWARD. Abstract of "Conceptual Categories in Primitive Languages." (paper presented to the National Academy of Sciences). *Science* 74 (1931): 578.

SCANLON, GERALDINE M. *La polémica feminista en la España contemporánea*. Madrid: Siglo veintiuno, 1976.

SCHOLES, ROBERT. *Elements of Literature*. New York: Oxford UP, 1978.

SHAW, DONALD L. *El siglo XIX. Historia de la literatura española*. Barcelona: Ariel, 1980.

SOEMAKER, WILLIAM H. *Las cartas desconocidas de Galdós en La Prensa de Buenos Aires*. Madrid: Cultura Hispánica, 1973.

SOLER, HIPÓLITO ESTEBAN. *El realismo en la novela*. Madrid: Cincel, 1981.

SPIRES, ROBERT. *Beyond the Metafictional Mode*. Lexington: University of Kentucky Press, 1984.

TAPARELLI, LUIS. "Las causas de lo bello según los principios de Santo Tomás." *Revista Contemporánea* 18 (1878): 30–54; 19 (1879): 24–43; 19 (1879): 300–22; 19 (1879): 422–28; 19 (1879): 138–61.

TIBERGHIEN, GUILLERMO. "Estudios sobre la religión." *Revista de Filosofía* 4 (1872): 567–72.

TIRKKONEN-CONDIT, SONJA. *Argumentative Text Structure and Translation*. Jyvskyl, University of Jyvskyl, 1985.

TORRE, GUILLERMO DE. *Del 98 al barroco*. Madrid; Gredos, 1969.

UNAMUNO, MIGUEL DE. *Obras completas*. Madrid: Afrodisio Aguado, 1958. Vols. 1,3.

——. *Obras completas*. Madrid: Escelicer, 1967. Vol 7.

VALERA, JUAN, *Obras completas*. Madrid: Aguilar, 1942. Vol 2.

VARELA, JOSÉ LUIS. "Raiz y función del ensayo español de hoy." *El ensayo: Reunión de Málaga de 1977*. Málaga: Diputación Provincial de Málaga, 1980.

VEESER, H. ARAM, Ed. *The New Historicism*. New York: Routledge, Chapman and Hall, 1989.

VERGÉS MUNDÓ, ORIOL. *La I Internacional en las Cortes de 1871*. Barcelona: Cátedra de Historia General de España, 1964.

VIDART, LUIS. "El arte por la belleza, a José Navarrete." *El Globo* 25 Apr. 1877.

——. "El naturalismo en el arte literario y la novela de costumbres." *Revista de España* 85 (1882): 181–97.

——. "Una teoría y un ejemplo: *La cuestión palpitante de Emilia Pardo Bazán.*" *Revista de España* 100 (1884): 18–46.

WAUGH, PATRICIA. *Metafiction*. London: Methuen, 1984.

WHORF, BENJAMIN. *Language, Thought, and Reality. Selected Writings of Benjamin Lee Whorf*. Ed. J. B. Carroll. Cambridge: MIT Press, 1956.

WIMSATT, W. K. AND MONROE BEARDSLEY. "The Intentional Fallacy" and "The Affective Fallacy" in *The Verbal Icon*. Lexington: U of Kentucky Press, 1954.

ZAVALA, IRIS. *Ideología y política en la novela española del siglo XIX*. Salamanca: 1971.

ZOLA, EMILE. *Les Oeuvres Complètes*. Paris: François Bernourd, 1928. Vol 46.